THE STORY OF ROME

Verginius left his beautiful young daughter Verginia in the care of her nurse.

THE
STORY OF ROME

FROM THE EARLIEST TIMES
TO THE DEATH OF AUGUSTUS

BY MARY MACGREGOR

YESTERDAY'S CLASSICS
CHAPEL HILL, NORTH CAROLINA

Cover and arrangement © 2006 Yesterday's Classics.

This edition, first published in 2006 by Yesterday's Classics, is an unabridged republication of the work originally published by Frederick A. Stokes Company, in 1912. The color illustrations by Paul Woodroffe, W. Rainey, and Dudley Heath in that volume are rendered in black and white in this edition. For a listing of books published by Yesterday's Classics, please visit www.yesterdaysclassics.com. Yesterday's Classics is the publishing arm of the Baldwin Project which presents the complete text of dozens of classic books for children at www.mainlesson.com under the editorship of Lisa M. Ripperton and T. A. Roth.

ISBN-10: 1-59915-034-4

ISBN-13: 978-1-59915-034-5

Yesterday's Classics
PO Box 3418
Chapel Hill, NC 27515

TO

IAN AND WILLIE TAYLOR

Dear Ian and Willie,—The Story of Rome has been written, as you know, in your beautiful, quiet old garden.

And as the story grew, the short cold days of winter passed and the long warm days of summer were here.

In the garden a miracle had been wrought. It had become alive.

After slow, persistent struggle with storm and frost, the delicate bare branches were no longer bare, but clothed in living green. The hard black earth too had stirred, and shoots and blades appeared, until at length the garden was ablaze with gold, purple, crimson.

Sometimes I dreamed that, in its own different way, the Story of Rome too was a miracle, wrought out of the tears and throes of a brave and ambitious people.

For the story tells of the birth of a city and of its growth through storm and struggle, until it became a great world empire.

The city which Romulus founded was built upon a single hill; soon seven hills were not great enough to contain her. And when Augustus, the first Emperor of Rome, began to reign, part of Europe,

Asia Minor, Egypt, Syria, and a large portion of Africa formed his kingdom.

Although the story was written in the quiet of your garden, little of its peace has stolen into the tale, and for that you boys may care for it the more.

As you read, fierce battle-cries will ring in your ears, and the clash of arms will startle you. You will hear the tramp of armies marching to new lands to conquer them and their treasures for Rome, the city of their love.

Sometimes you will catch your breath in horror as you read of terrible and cruel deeds, for the Romans were often pitiless, showing little mercy to those they conquered.

But at other times your breath will come quick with wonder as you read of the dauntless courage, the rare endurance of these mighty men of old.

And if there are many things which you do not admire in the people of Rome, yet they possess one virtue which you and every British boy and girl may not only admire, but gladly imitate.

What that virtue is I will leave you to find out for yourselves as you read *The Story of Rome*.—Yours affectionately,

MARY MACGREGOR.

CONTENTS

		Page
I.	THE LADY ROMA	1
II.	THE SHE-WOLF	5
III.	THE TWIN BOYS	9
IV.	NUMITOR RECOGNISES HIS GRANDSONS	12
V.	THE SACRED BIRDS	15
VI.	THE FOUNDING OF ROME	18
VII.	THE SABINE MAIDENS	21
VIII.	THE TARPEIAN ROCK	25
IX.	THE MYSTERIOUS GATE	28
X.	THE KING DISAPPEARS	32
XI.	THE PEACE-LOVING KING	35
XII.	HORATIUS SLAYS HIS SISTER	40
XIII.	THE PRIDE OF TULLUS HOSTILIUS	46
XIV.	THE KING WHO FOUGHT AND PRAYED	48
XV.	THE FAITHLESS FRIEND	50
XVI.	A SLAVE BECOMES A KING	55
XVII.	THE CRUEL DEED OF TULLIA	58
XVIII.	THE FATE OF THE TOWN OF GABII	63
XIX.	THE BOOKS OF THE SIBYL	67
XX.	THE INDUSTRY OF LUCRETIA	71
XXI.	THE DEATH OF LUCRETIA	74
XXII.	THE SONS OF BRUTUS	77

CONTENTS

XXIII.	Horatius Cocles, or the One-Eyed	82
XXIV.	Gaius Mucius Burns his Right Hand	89
XXV.	The Divine Twins	93
XXVI.	The Tribunes	97
XXVII.	Coriolanus and his Mother Veturia	100
XXVIII.	The Roman Army in a Trap	108
XXIX.	The Hated Decemvirs	113
XXX.	The Death of Verginia	117
XXXI.	The Friend of the People	123
XXXII.	Camillus Captures the City of Veii	127
XXXIII.	The Statue of the Goddess	132
XXXIV.	The Schoolmaster who Proved a Traitor	135
XXXV.	The Battle of Allia	140
XXXVI.	The Sacred Geese	143
XXXVII.	The City is Rebuilt	152
XXXVIII.	Camillus Sets the Camp of the Volscians on Fire	157
XXXIX.	The Battle on the Banks of the Anio	160
XL.	The Curtian Lake	167
XLI.	The Dream of the Two Consuls	172
XLII.	The Caudine Forks	179
XLIII.	The Disgrace of the Caudine Forks Avenged	185
XLIV.	Fabius among the Ciminian Hills	187

CONTENTS

XLV.	THE BATTLE OF SENTINUM	192
XLVI.	THE SON OF FABIUS LOSES A BATTLE	196
XLVII.	PYRRHUS, KING OF THE EPIROTS	200
XLVIII.	THE ELEPHANTS AT THE BATTLE OF HERACLEA	205
XLIX.	PYRRHUS TRIES TO FRIGHTEN FABRICIUS	211
L.	PYRRHUS IS DEFEATED	217
LI.	THE ROMANS BUILD A FLEET	220
LII.	THE BATTLE OF ECNOMUS	225
LIII.	THE ROMAN LEGIONS IN AFRICA	227
LIV.	REGULUS IS TAKEN PRISONER	231
LV.	THE ROMANS CONQUER THE GAULS	236
LVI.	THE BOY HANNIBAL	241
LVII.	HANNIBAL PREPARES TO INVADE ITALY	247
LVIII.	HANNIBAL CROSSES THE ALPS	250
LIX.	THE BATTLE OF TREBIA	257
LX.	THE BATTLE OF LAKE TRASIMENUS	262
LXI.	HANNIBAL OUTWITS FABIUS	269
LXII.	FABIUS WINS TWO VICTORIES	275
LXIII.	THE BATTLE OF CANNÆ	279
LXIV.	THE DESPAIR OF ROME	283
LXV.	THE DEFEAT OF HASDRUBAL	289
LXVI.	LIVIUS AND CLAUDIUS ENJOY A TRIUMPH	295
LXVII.	THE CAPTURE OF NEW CARTHAGE	299
LXVIII.	SCIPIO SAILS TO AFRICA	306

CONTENTS

LXIX.	THE ROMANS SET FIRE TO THE CAMP OF THE NUMIDIANS	311
LXX.	HANNIBAL LEAVES ITALY	315
LXXI.	THE BATTLE OF ZAMA	319
LXXII.	SCIPIO RECEIVES A TRIUMPH	322
LXXIII.	FLAMININUS IS COVERED WITH GARLANDS	326
LXXIV.	THE DEATH OF HANNIBAL	333
LXXV.	THE HATRED OF CATO FOR CARTHAGE	340
LXXVI.	THE STERN DECREE	344
LXXVII.	THE CARTHAGINIANS DEFEND THEIR CITY	348
LXXVIII.	THE DESTRUCTION OF CARTHAGE	353
LXXIX.	CORNELIA, THE MOTHER OF THE GRACCHI	361
LXXX.	TIBERIUS AND HIS FRIEND OCTAVIUS	366
LXXXI.	THE DEATH OF TIBERIUS GRACCHUS	372
LXXXII.	THE DEATH OF GAIUS GRACCHUS	376
LXXXIII.	THE GOLD OF JUGURTHA	389
LXXXIV.	GAIUS MARIUS WINS THE NOTICE OF SCIPIO AFRICANUS	393
LXXXV.	GAIUS MARIUS BECOMES COMMANDER OF THE ARMY	396
LXXXVI.	THE CAPTURE OF JUGURTHA'S TREASURE TOWNS	402
LXXXVII.	THE CAPTURE OF JUGURTHA	406
LXXXVIII.	JUGURTHA IS BROUGHT TO ROME IN CHAINS	412
LXXXIX.	MARIUS CONQUERS THE TEUTONES	416

CONTENTS

XC.	Marius Mocks the Ambassadors of the Cimbri	424
XCI.	Metellus is Driven from Rome	430
XCII.	Sulla Enters Rome with his Troops	435
XCIII.	The Flight of Marius	441
XCIV.	The Gaul Dares Not Kill Gaius Marius	446
XCV.	Marius Returns to Rome	450
XCVI.	The Orator Aristion	456
XCVII.	Sulla Besieges Athens	460
XCVIII.	Sulla Saves Rome from the Samnites	464
XCIX.	The Proscriptions of Sulla	467
C.	The Gladiators' Revolt	472
CI.	The Pirates	477
CII.	Pompey Goes to War with Mithridates	482
CIII.	Cicero Discovers the Catilinarian Conspiracy	489
CIV.	The Death of the Conspirators	494
CV.	Julius Cæsar is Captured by Pirates	498
CVI.	Cæsar Gives up his Triumph	503
CVII.	Cæsar Praises his Tenth Legion	506
CVIII.	Cæsar Wins a Great Victory over the Nervii	511
CIX.	Cæsar Invades Britain	516
CX.	Cæsar Crosses the Rubicon	522
CXI.	Cæsar and the Pilot	528

CONTENTS

CXII.	THE FLIGHT OF POMPEY	532
CXIII.	CATO DIES RATHER THAN YIELD TO CÆSAR	538
CXIV.	CÆSAR IS LOADED WITH HONOURS	542
CXV.	THE NOBLES PLOT AGAINST CÆSAR	546
CXVI.	THE ASSASSINATION OF CÆSAR	551
CXVII.	BRUTUS SPEAKS TO THE CITIZENS	556
CXVIII.	MARK ANTONY SPEAKS TO THE CITIZENS	560
CXIX.	THE SECOND TRIUMVIRATE	564
CXX.	THE BATTLE OF PHILIPPI	567
CXXI.	THE DEATH OF BRUTUS	571
CXXII.	ANTONY AND CLEOPATRA	575
CXXIII.	THE BATTLE OF ACTIUM	581
CXXIV.	ANTONY AND CLEOPATRA DIE	585
CXXV.	THE EMPEROR AUGUSTUS	591

CHAPTER I

THE LADY ROMA

LONG, long years ago, Troy, one of the great cities in Asia Minor, was taken by the Greeks.

Many mighty Trojans had defended their city well, and among them all none had fought more bravely than the prince Æneas.

But when Æneas saw that the Greeks had set fire to the city, he fled, carrying, it is said, his father on his shoulders, and grasping by the hand his son Ascanius.

Moreover, so precious to him was the sacred image of the goddess Pallas, that he saved it from the burning city.

The gods, pleased with his reverence, helped him in his flight by building a ship. So when Æneas reached the sea he at once embarked in it, with his followers and their wives, and sailed away to seek for a new land in which to build a new city.

As the Trojans sailed they saw a bright star shining above them. Day and night the star was

THE STORY OF ROME

always to be seen, showing the seafarers the direction in which to steer.

At length the Trojans reached the western shore of Italy, and here, at a town called Latium, they disembarked.

The women were weary of the sea, and no sooner had they landed than they began to wonder how they could persuade their husbands to journey no farther, but to settle in the pleasant country which they had reached.

Among these women was a lady of noble birth, who was wise as she was good.

Roma, for that was the lady's name, proposed that they should burn the ship in which they had sailed. Then it would be impossible for their husbands to go any farther in search of a new home.

The other women agreed to Roma's daring plan, and with mingled hope and fear the ship was set on fire.

When the men saw the flames devouring the vessel they were troubled, but when they found out how it had been set on fire, they were angry.

Yet, as anger could not give them back their ship, and as Italy was a pleasant land, the men did as the women wished. They settled near a hill called Mount Palatine, and there they built a city.

Some old stories tell that the city was called Rome after Roma, the noble lady who had first thought of setting the ship on fire.

But other stories say that the country in which Æneas landed belonged to a king named Latinus, who welcomed the Trojan, and gave him ground on which to build. Æneas married Lavinia, the daughter of the king, and called the city which he built after her Lavinium.

Soon after this, King Latinus was killed in battle, and then for three years Æneas ruled well and wisely not only over his own Trojan followers, but also over the subjects of his royal father-in-law. His people he now called Latins, in memory of King Latinus.

When the three years were passed, war broke out against the Etruscans, who were at that time the most powerful tribe in Italy.

One day a terrible storm overtook the armies on the battlefield; so dark grew the clouds that the soldiers could not see each other.

When at length the sky cleared Æneas had disappeared, and was seen no more on earth.

"The gods have taken him away," said the Latins. So they built an altar, and henceforth worshipped their king as the god Jupiter.

Ascanius, who had escaped from Troy with his father, now ruled in Lavinium. But he soon found that the city was not large enough for all his people; so, leaving Lavinium, he built a new city, and called it Alba Longa, or the Long White City.

THE STORY OF ROME

Alba Longa stood in the midst of the Alban hills, not far from the site on which Rome itself was soon to be built.

CHAPTER II

THE SHE-WOLF

AFTER the death of Ascanius nearly three hundred years passed away, and then a king named Proca died, leaving behind him two sons. The name of the elder was Numitor, the name of the younger Amulius.

The crown belonged by right to Numitor, the elder son, but Amulius, who was ambitious, was not willing that his brother should reign. So he said to Numitor, "One of us shall wear the crown, and to the other shall belong the gold and treasures left by our father Proca."

The story does not tell if Numitor was indignant with his brother, and said that the crown belonged to him; it only tells that Numitor chose to reign, as was indeed his right.

Amulius then seized the gold and treasure, and bribed his followers to drive Numitor from the throne and to make him king.

This, in their greed, they were soon persuaded to do.

Ere long Numitor was banished from the city, and Amulius, to his great content, began to reign.

But the king was soon surprised to find that the crown rested uneasily upon his head.

It might be that the children of Numitor would some day wrench the crown from him, even as he had wrenched it from their father.

That this might never be, Amulius, thinking to get rid of fear, ordered Numitor's son to be slain, while his daughter Silvia was kept, by the command of the king, in a temple sacred to the goddess Vesta. Here the maiden tended the altar fire, which was never allowed to die.

But the god Mars, angry, it might well be, with the cruelty of Amulius, took pity upon the maiden and sent twin sons to cheer her in her loneliness. Such strong beautiful babes had never before been seen.

As for the king, when he heard of the birth of these little boys he was both angry and afraid, lest they should grow into strong men and wrest his kingdom from him.

In his fear Amulius ordered Silvia to be shut up in a prison for the rest of her life, and her beautiful boys he commanded to be thrown into the river Tiber.

Heavy rains had fallen of late, and as the king knew, the river had overflowed its banks, but of this he recked not at all, although, indeed, the flood was to be his undoing.

THE SHE-WOLF

A she-wolf, coming to the edge of the river to drink, heard their cries.

Two servants, obeying the cruel order of Amulius, placed the baby boys in a basket, and going to the Tiber, flung their burden into the river.

Like a boat the basket floated hither and thither on the water, until at length, carried onward by the flood, it was washed ashore at the foot of a hill called Mount Palatine.

Here, under the shade of a wild fig-tree, the basket was overturned, and the babes lay safe and sound upon the dry ground, while the river stole softly backward into its accustomed channel.

Before long the babes awoke hungry and began to cry. A she-wolf coming to the edge of the river to drink heard their cries, and carried them away to her cave, where she fed them with her milk, just as she would have fed her lost cubs. She washed them, too, as she was used to wash her own children, by licking them with her tongue.

CHAPTER III

THE TWIN BOYS

THE twin boys, it was said, were guarded by the god Mars. So it was not strange that, as they grew older, the god should send his sacred birds, the woodpeckers, to feed the children. In and out of the cave the birds flew each day, bringing with them food for the little boys.

But neither the wolf nor the birds could do all that was needful, so before long, the god who watched over the children sent Faustulus to their aid.

Faustulus was one of the herdsmen of King Amulius. He had often seen the wolf going in and out of the cave, and had noticed, too, how the woodpeckers came and went each day. So when the wolf went off to prowl in the woods, Faustulus ventured into the cave, where to his amazement he found two beautiful and well-fed children. He took them in his arms and carried them home to his wife. She gladly welcomed the little strangers, and, naming them Romulus and Remus, brought them up as though they had been her own sons.

THE STORY OF ROME

As the years passed the boys grew ever more beautiful. Stronger and braver, too, they became, until the rough herdsmen among whom they dwelt called them princes.

The lads soon showed that they were fitted to lead the herdsmen. If wild beasts attacked the flocks, or if robbers tried to steal them, Romulus and Remus were ever the first to attack, and to drive away either the robbers or the wild beasts.

Faustulus lived on Mount Palatine, near to the spot where the boys had been washed ashore when they were babes.

This hill belonged to the cruel king Amulius, and it was his sheep and cattle that the princes, unwitting of the evil the king had done to them, defended from danger.

Not far from Mount Palatine was another hill, named Mount Aventine, and here also were herdsmen guarding flocks, but these herdsmen belonged to the dethroned King Numitor. Numitor was living quietly in the city of Alba.

Now it chanced that the herdsmen of Amulius began to quarrel with the herdsmen of Numitor. One evening, forgetting all about their enemies, the shepherds on Mount Palatine were merrymaking at a festival in honour of the god Pan.

Then the herdsmen on Mount Aventine said one to the other, "See, here is our chance. We will lay an ambush for these unwary merrymakers."

THE TWIN BOYS

As the gods willed, they captured none other than Remus, and well pleased with their prize, they carried the prince a prisoner to their master Numitor.

CHAPTER IV

NUMITOR RECOGNISES HIS GRANDSONS

The young prisoner was brought before Numitor in the city of Alba. No sooner had the old man's eyes fallen on the lad than he threw up his hands in amaze, and gazed more keenly at the prisoner.

"No herdsman this," muttered the old king to himself, "rather does he bear himself as a prince."

Scanning the face before him even more closely, it seemed to Numitor that the features were not unknown to him. Dreams of his lost daughter Silvia gladdened his heart.

Gently the old man tried to win the confidence of the lad, asking him who he was, and whence he came.

Remus was touched by the kindness of Numitor, and answered: "I will hide nothing from you, sire, for you seem of a princely temper, in that you give a hearing and examine before you punish."

Then he told the old man the story that Faustulus had often told to him and Romulus, of how the

NUMITOR RECOGNISES HIS GRANDSONS

wolf had found them as babes on the banks of the river Tiber, and had carried them to her cave and fed them with her milk.

Long before Remus had ended his story, Numitor knew that it was his grandson, his daughter Silvia's child, who stood before him, and his old heart beat quick with joy. Here at length was one who would take his side against the cruel King Amulius.

At this moment Romulus, leading a rough band of herdsmen, approached the city gate, determined to rescue his brother from the hands of Numitor.

In the city were many folk who groaned under the tyranny of Amulius. These, hearing that Romulus was without the city gate, stole noiselessly away to join the prince, believing he had come to punish the king.

Meantime Romulus had divided his followers into companies of a hundred men. At the head of each company was a captain, carrying a small bundle of grass and shrubs tied to a pole.

These rough standards were called "manipuli," and it was because they carried these manipuli that captains in the Roman army came to be called Manipulares.

When Amulius heard that Numitor had recognised in the prisoner one of his long lost grandsons he was afraid. Then, hearing the shouts and blows of Romulus and his men as they attacked the city gate, he rushed to defend it, determined that the second prince should not enter the city.

But Romulus captured the gate, slew the king, and entered the city in triumph.

Here he found Remus, no longer a prisoner as he had feared, but the acknowledged grandson of Numitor.

The old king welcomed Romulus as joyfully as he had welcomed his brother, and the two princes, eager to please the gentle old man, placed him upon the throne from which he had so long ago been driven.

They then sped to the prison where their mother Silvia had lain since the princes had been born. Swiftly they set her free, and cheered her by their love and care as good sons ever will.

CHAPTER V

THE SACRED BIRDS

THE grandsons of Numitor could no longer live as shepherds on Mount Palatine, which they had learned to love. Nor could they dwell quietly in Alba, for all their lives they had been used to live free among the mountains, nor had they been subject to any king.

So the princes made up their minds to leave Alba, and to build a city for themselves on the hills they loved.

But the brothers could not agree on which hill to build their city, Romulus choosing the Palatine, Remus the Aventine.

Not knowing how to settle their dispute, they asked Numitor to help them. He bade them, as the custom was, to appeal to augury—that is, to watch for a sign or omen from the gods. These signs were given in many different forms, sometimes by the flight of birds, as happened now.

The princes determined to follow their grandfather's advice. Romulus went to Mount Palatine,

Remus to Mount Aventine, and patient through one long day they watched for a sign.

But no sign appeared. The slow hours passed, and night drew on apace, yet still the brothers never stirred.

Then, as darkness faded before the dawn, Remus saw, far off, dark, moving shapes. Were the gods going to be gracious, the prince wondered, and after so many hours send a sign?

Nearer and nearer drew the dark shapes.

"Ah!" Remus cried sharply, "it is a good omen." For now he could see that the moving forms were six vultures winging their way toward the west. These birds were sacred to the gods, and did no harm to corn, fruit, or cattle, nor would they, indeed, wound any living thing.

Swiftly Remus bade a messenger to go tell his brother of the good omen vouchsafed to him. But even as his messenger sped to do his will, Remus was crestfallen. For before him stood one of the servants of Romulus to tell him that his brother, too, had seen a flight of vultures, but while Remus had seen six birds, Romulus had seen twelve.

What was to be done? It seemed now that the brothers were not thinking on which hill the city should stand, but of which of them should build the city. Remus believed that the augury proclaimed him as the founder of the new city. Romulus was sure that it was he who was intended by the gods to build

THE SACRED BIRDS

it; for had not he seen twelve vultures while his brother had seen but six?

The princes turned to their followers, demanding who should be their king. Then loud and lusty was the answering shout: "Romulus, Romulus, he shall be our king!"

CHAPTER VI

THE FOUNDING OF ROME

It was in the year 753 B.C. that Romulus was chosen king. He at once began to make preparations to build a city on the Palatine hill. The foundation he wished to lay on the twenty-first of the glad month of April, for, as Romulus knew, this was a feast-day among the shepherds.

Often he, with his brother, had joined the herdsmen on that day, to offer cakes to the goddess Pales, to beseech her blessing on themselves and on their flocks. And when the prayers and sacrifices were over, how gladly he had joined in the shepherds' games and jollity! No better day could be found on which to lay the foundation of the new city.

When the feast-day arrived, a hole was first dug on the spot where the city was to stand.

Into this hole the king flung the first fruits of the earth, corn and fruit.

Each of his followers then took a handful of earth which he had carried with him from his own, perhaps distant, home, and flung it also into the hole, which was then filled to the top.

Here, too, an altar was built, on which the people laid offerings to the gods. From henceforth the spot, where the temple had been erected, was to be the hearth or centre of the new city.

Romulus then throwing his toga, or as we would say, his mantle, around him, with one end covering his head, took a white bull and a cow and yoked them to a sacred plough, the share of which was made of brass.

With this ploughshare the king then made a furrow to mark the boundary of the city, bidding his followers watch that the upturned earth fell inward to the hearth of the city. Not a clod must be allowed to lie without the furrow. When the plough reached the different spots at which the gates of the city were to stand, it was carefully lifted over the spaces.

As he guided the plough, Romulus cried to his gods that his city might become strong and endure, and ever grow more powerful in the great world.

Out of a clear sky thunder crashed, lightning flashed over the hills as Romulus uttered his petitions, and the people believed that the storm was the answer of the god Jupiter to the prayers of their king.

When these sacred rites were ended, Romulus bade his men begin at once to build the wall which was to surround his city.

The wall itself was sacred. None might enter the city, save by the gates. So the king bade one of his followers, named Celer, to guard the sacred furrow, and to see that no one dared to scale the wall or jump across it, as it was being built.

Remus, who was still angry that he had not been chosen king, had been standing near to Romulus as he laid the foundation of the city. Then, as the wall began to rise before him, a swift rage sprang up in his heart, and he leaped across it, crying: "Shall such defences as these guard your city?"

Celer, the watchman, seeing that Remus had scorned the order of the king, raised his spade in sudden fury and struck the young prince dead to the ground.

Then, fearing lest Romulus should punish him for his hasty deed, he fled. Fear lent him wings, and his name from that day became a byword to betoken great speed.

Our own word, "celerity," comes from Celer, the swift-footed servant of Romulus.

When Romulus was told that his brother had been slain, he showed neither grief nor anger. "Thus perish every one who may attempt to cross these walls," were his stern words to those who brought the sad tidings.

Celer, it was plain, had fled in needless haste.

CHAPTER VII

THE SABINE MAIDENS

WHEN Romulus had built his city and surrounded it with a wall, he began to fortify the hill on which it was built. This was necessary because hostile tribes held the neighbouring hills, and might at any moment attack the new city.

The king ordered his followers to scrape the steep slopes of the Palatine until they were smooth. Then great slabs of stones, fitted into each other without mortar, were built into the sides of the hill, from the base to the summit.

Romulus was pleased when he saw this great fortification finished, for he knew that it was almost impossible that an enemy should scale the smooth surface of the hill and lay siege to the city.

Not far from the foot of the Palatine flowed the river Tiber, a safe highway to the sea. So the king as he gazed, first at his well-fortified city and then down to the swift flowing river, felt that he had indeed chosen his site with wisdom.

The Palatine was only one of seven hills, and each of the other six was added to the city during the

THE STORY OF ROME

reign of the six kings who ruled after Romulus. Five of these hills were called montes or mountains, while the other two, being only spurs that jutted out from the tableland, were called colles or hills.

But I have not yet told you the name of the city! Amid the shouts of his people the king named it Rome, after its founder Romulus.

Rome was built and fortified, yet the king was dissatisfied, for now he found that he had not enough people to dwell in the city.

The king must by this time have taken possession of the Capitoline hill, which was close to the Palatine, for here he resolved to build a city of refuge, that those who fled to it might gradually be removed to Rome.

Asylum, which is the Greek word for refuge, was the name of this city, and it was open to all those who had been forced by crime or misfortune to flee from their own homes.

To this Asylum hastened robbers, exiles, slaves who had fled from their masters, as well as those who had stained their hands with blood.

The city of refuge was soon crowded, and many of these rough and criminal folk were then sent to Rome, until Romulus had as many subjects as he wished.

But there were no women among those who fled to the king for protection, and Romulus saw that he would have to find wives for his new subjects.

THE SABINE MAIDENS

So he begged the neighbouring tribes, among which was a tribe called the Sabines, to allow their daughters to marry his new subjects. But the king's request was refused. Give their daughters to robbers and murderers, to men who had been outlawed! The tribes did not hesitate to mock at Romulus for thinking that such a thing could be.

Romulus was not a king to be lightly thwarted. He was determined at any cost to gain wives for his subjects.

So, as his neighbours had proved churlish and refused his request, he made up his mind to capture their daughters by guile, or by a trick, as we would say. Nor did he take long to lay his plans. He invited his neighbours, among whom were the Sabines, to a feast and games which he wished to celebrate in honour of the god Consus.

They, eager to enjoy the feast and the great spectacle of the games, came flocking into Rome on the appointed day, bringing with them their wives and daughters.

Fearlessly they came, and were greeted with great hospitality by the king, who knew that he must hide his anger until his plot had been successful.

The feast began with solemn rites, sacrifices being offered to the gods, and especially to Consus, in whose name the festival was held.

When the sacrifices were ended, the guests mingled carelessly with the Romans, thinking only of the games and races.

THE STORY OF ROME

The king, seeing that the moment had come, gave the signal for which his people were waiting.

A band of armed men at once rushed in among the guests, and in spite of their screams and struggles, carried away the Sabine maidens.

The parents of the maidens hastened to leave the city where the laws of hospitality had been so cruelly transgressed. As they went, they called down the anger of the gods upon Romulus and his people.

CHAPTER VIII

THE TARPEIAN ROCK

THE tribes who had been at the feast of Consus were so angry with the king that many of them went to fight against him, without waiting to gather together a large army. Thus Romulus soon defeated and scattered his foes.

Moreover, having slain one of the kings with his own hand, he stripped him of his armour, and tying it to a pole, carried it back to Rome, where he offered it to Jupiter. This was the earliest Triumph celebrated at Rome. In days to come the Triumphs of the Roman generals became famous. They were held when the soldiers returned victorious from a great battle. The general at the head of his army rode into the city in a chariot drawn by beautiful horses. Other chariots followed, filled with the treasures and spoils of war, while the most noble prisoners, often loaded with chains, were dragged along behind the chariots. The day on which a Triumph was celebrated was always held as a holiday by the citizens of Rome.

Now, among the tribes which Romulus had robbed, none had suffered so heavily as the Sabines.

But they, more wary than the king's other foes, did not attempt to avenge their wrongs until they had had time to collect a large and powerful army. Nearly two years had passed before this army was led by Tatius, the King of the Sabines, against the Romans.

The fortress on the Capitoline hill Romulus had entrusted to the care of a chief named Tarpeius. Now Tarpeius had a daughter named Tarpeia, and she loved ornaments and jewels of gold and silver.

As the Sabines, led by Tatius, drew near to attack the fortress, Tarpeia looked out of a spy-hole and saw that the enemy was adorned with beautiful golden bracelets. The longer she looked, the greater became her desire to possess these dazzling ornaments. What would she not do to wear such splendid jewels? She would—yes, she would even betray the fortress into the hands of the Sabines, if only she might hear the tinkle of the golden bracelets on her arms.

So, leaving the spy-hole, Tarpeia slipped secretly out of the fortress and spoke to the Sabines, offering to show them how to take the citadel if they would give her in reward "what they wore on their left arms."

The Sabines agreed to do as Tarpeia wished, but in their hearts they despised the maiden for her treachery.

But she, heedless of all save the ornaments that would soon be hers, hastened back to the fortress.

Then, when it grew dark, she stealthily opened the gate, outside of which stood the waiting foe.

As the Sabines marched into the fortress, Tarpeia cried to them to remember their promise and give her her reward.

Then Tatius bade his men not to refuse "the least part of what they wore on their left arms," and himself taking off his bracelet, threw it to her, together with his shield, which he also bore on his left arm.

His men did as their king had done, so that Tarpeia soon fell to the ground and was killed by the weight of the shields that covered her.

The traitress was buried on the hill which she had betrayed. From that day traitors were punished by being thrown over the steepest rock on the Capitoline hill, which was named after the maiden who betrayed her city, "The Tarpeian Rock."

CHAPTER IX

THE MYSTERIOUS GATE

THE fortress on the Capitoline hill was now in the hands of the Sabines, but they had still to fight with the Romans who dwelt on the Palatine hill.

Romulus was, indeed, already to be seen leading his men into the valley that lay between the two mountains.

The battle was long and fierce, and disaster well-nigh overtook the Sabines.

In the valley was a swamp, and in this swamp the whole of the enemy's army would have been engulfed, had not Curtius, one of their most gallant soldiers, warned them of danger.

He himself had been carried by his horse into the mire. Nobly he tried to free his steed, but his efforts were all in vain. The more the animal struggled, the deeper it sank into the swamp, until at length Curtius was forced to leave his horse that he might save himself. This swamp was ever after known as the Curtian Lake.

THE MYSTERIOUS GATE

Hour after hour the battle raged, until at last Romulus and his followers were driven backward. In their dismay the Roman army rushed through one of the gates into their city, hastily shutting it behind them, that the foe might not also enter.

But lo! so says the legend, the gate would not remain shut, but opened, as it seemed, of its own accord.

Twice again the terrified Romans tried to close it, and twice it opened as mysteriously as before.

The Sabines reached the gate as it opened for the last time.

In through the open gate pushed the triumphant enemy, when suddenly a great flood of water gushed forth from the temple of the god Janus, which stood near to the gate.

Overwhelmed by the force of the water, the Sabines were swept, not only out of the gate, but far away from the city, and Rome was saved.

But although the Sabines had been forced to flee, they had not been conquered. Again and again they marched against Romulus, for they could not forgive him for the loss of their daughters.

In one of these battles Romulus was wounded by a stone and fell to the ground. His followers, seeing that their king was wounded, lost courage and began to retreat.

But the king was soon on his feet, calling to his men to stand and fight. But it seemed as though they dared not turn to face the foe.

Then, in his great need the king stretched out his hands to heaven and besought Jupiter to come to his aid, promising that he would build a temple to his name, so only he would stay the flight of his army.

Even as he prayed the answer came. No voice from heaven commanded them to stand, yet the Romans were suddenly ashamed of their cowardice and turned once more to face the foe.

But as the battle was about to begin with redoubled fury the Sabine women rushed in between the two armies with loud cries, entreating now their fathers and brothers, now their husbands to end this cruel slaughter.

They even begged that they themselves might be slain, for, "Better it is that we perish," said the women, "than live as widows and orphans."

In their arms the women carried their little sons, and these babes stretched out their tiny arms toward their grandsires, as though they too would beg for peace. The lamentable cries of their daughters, the sight of their little grandchildren made the Sabines hesitate, and soon the warriors in either army let their weapons fall to the ground in mood no longer warlike. "Then fathers and sons-in-law clasped hands in friendship. The old men embraced their daughters, and carried their baby grandsons on their shields. Surely a sweeter way was that to use the shield."

Peace was then made, and the Romans and Sabines agreed to become one, while Romulus and Tatius ruled together over their united people.

Five years later Tatius was killed in a quarrel, and Romulus again ruled alone.

CHAPTER X

THE KING DISAPPEARS

As the years passed, the city of Rome became ever larger and more powerful. The king, too, grew haughty, and as his greatness increased, careless of the welfare of his people. His subjects, who had formerly loved Romulus, now began to hate him, so insolent seemed to them his behaviour.

Dressed in a scarlet robe, the king spent his days lying on a couch, while young lads, called Celeres, waited upon him. This name was bestowed upon them because of the swiftness with which they sped to do the king's behests.

Nor was this all, but when Romulus at times roused himself to walk through the streets of the city, the Celeres went before him, bearing staves. These they used, to thrust aside any of the common people who dared to disturb the king by their presence.

The staves angered the people, but even more did they resent the leather thongs which the Celeres wore, for these were used to bind and take prisoner whoever displeased the king.

THE KING DISAPPEARS

After he had reigned forty years a strange thing happened.

Romulus ordered the people to assemble on the Field of Mars, which reached from the city to the river Tiber, for here a festival was to be held. But when the king and his subjects met, a terrible storm arose. Dark and yet darker grew the sky, while fierce gusts of wind, blowing now in one direction, now in another, confused the terrified crowd. Flashes of lightning gleamed across the faces of the throng, then darkness, more dense, fell across the field, hiding each from the other. Thunder rolled until the earth seemed to shake at the sound.

In terror and distraught with fear, the crowd fled to their homes, lashed by a ceaseless torrent of rain.

And the king? When the storm was over the king was nowhere to be found. He had disappeared, and was seen no more on earth in human form.

"His enemies have slain him," said some among the people. But others thought that the god Mars had carried the king to heaven in a chariot.

Proculus, a friend of Romulus, told the people a story, which made them believe that their king had himself become a god.

One day, as Proculus was walking from Alba to Rome, Romulus stood before him, clad in shining armour.

His friend was afraid when he saw the king, so tall and comely had he become, and he cried: "Why,

O King, have you abandoned us, and left the whole city to bereavement and endless sorrow?"

Proculus did not seem to know that Romulus had lost the love of his people many years before.

The figure in shining armour answered his friend in these wise words:

"It pleased the gods, O Proculus, that we, who came from them, should remain so long a time amongst men as we did, and having built a city to be the greatest in the world for empire and glory, should again return to heaven.

"Farewell, and tell the Romans that by the exercise of temperance and fortitude they shall attain the height of human power. We will be to you from henceforth the god Quirinus."

The Romans listened eagerly to Proculus, and when his story ended, they determined to build a temple on the Quirinal hill in honour of their new god.

And each year, on the 17th February, the day that Romulus had been taken from their sight, the Romans held a festival in honour of Quirinus, calling it the Quirinalia.

CHAPTER XI

THE PEACE-LOVING KING

AFTER the disappearance of Romulus, the Romans and Sabines each wished to appoint a new king.

Romulus had been a Roman, so the Sabines said that now it was but just that a Sabine king should rule.

The dispute between the people lasted for a whole year, and then at length it was determined that the new king should be a Sabine, but that the Romans should be allowed to choose him.

Now among the Sabines dwelt a man named Numa Pompilius. He was honoured by the Romans as well as by his own people, for he was both good and wise. He had indeed been known for his wisdom since he was a boy. And if, when he was young, any one ventured to dispute his wisdom, his friends would point to his grey hair, believing there was no need to speak. For the hair of Numa Pomilius had been grey from the day of his birth, and that surely was a sign from the gods to show that he already was and ever would be wise.

Often he was to be seen, a solitary man, walking in the fields and groves which were consecrated to the gods. At other times he would spend long days and weeks alone in desert places.

It was to this strangely quiet, thoughtful man, who was now about forty years old, that the Romans sent ambassadors to beg him to become their king.

Numa Pompilius had no wish to rule. Moreover, he deemed that the people would desire a more warlike king than he was like to be. So he bade the messengers return to Rome, saying: "I should but be, methinks, a laughing-stock, while I should go about to inculcate the worship of the gods and give lessons in the love of justice and the abhorrence of violence and war to a city whose needs are rather for a captain than for a king."

In spite of these words, the ambassadors still urged Numa to return with them to Rome. "Your presence," said they, "will help to put an end to war and discord."

Then the wise man consulted the gods, and they sent a flight of sacred birds as a sign that he should reign in Rome.

So Numa Pompilius set out with the ambassadors, and when he reached the city he called together the people to ask them if they were willing to obey his commands.

They, greeting him as "a holy king, and one beloved of the gods," promised to obey him in all things. Thus, almost against his will, the wise man

THE PEACE-LOVING KING

became king. But being king, he was not the man to shirk the duties belonging to his royal state.

His first act was to dismiss the band of three hundred Celeres, which had formed the life-guard of Romulus, for this king trusted his subjects, and believed that they would safeguard him from danger.

To train the Romans in the love of truth he built on the Capitol a temple to the goddess Fides, or Faith, bidding them invoke this goddess above all others. At the same time he told them ever to remember as they went about their daily work that their promises were as sacred as their oaths.

In the temple no sacrifice of sheep, oxen, or bird was ever offered, for the good king would not have his gifts to the gods stained with blood. Fruits, cakes, corn, these were the offerings he bade the people bring to the temple.

Pompilius himself had loved to work and to walk in the fields, so now he encouraged the Romans to labour in the country, dividing among them a large part of the land which Romulus had conquered.

In these and other ways the king did all he could to curb the fierce passions of his subjects, who, when left to themselves, were swift to turn to war and bloodshed, rather than to peace.

Many of the people reverenced their peace-loving king, but others mocked at his gentle ways.

Even the feasts of the king were more simple than some of the Romans liked, and these discontented ones grumbled at the plain fare of which they were invited to partake.

One day, so the legend runs, the king ordered, as was his custom, a simple meal to be prepared, and to this meal he invited many of his friends.

They came, for the king had asked them, but, as they expected, the food was plain, the plates were of earthenware, and water was served in bottles of stone.

But no sooner had the guests seated themselves at the table than behold! as if by magic, the plain food was changed into the choicest viands, the water became the richest wine, while the earthenware dishes disappeared, and in their place stood plates of silver and of gold.

The guests were startled, yet it pleased them well that the gods should show such favour to their king, for they never doubted that it was thus the gods treated those who honoured them.

Henceforth the people grumbled less, and were more ready to obey their sovereign.

Numa Pompilius ruled for forty-three years, caring, during his long reign, for the welfare of his people.

Even the enemies of Rome did not venture to disturb this good and gentle king. So, while he ruled, the weapons of war were laid aside. The gates of the temple of Janus, too, which were only opened in time of war, remained closed during the reign of Numa Pompilius.

THE PEACE-LOVING KING

It seemed that the gods did indeed show goodwill to this pious king, for neither sickness nor famine troubled the country as long as he sat upon the throne, and the Romans prospered in all that they undertook.

When he was eighty years of age Numa Pompilius passed away in a death as peaceful as his life.

The Romans mourned his loss, for he had been to them father as well as king.

Quietly they laid his body to rest, beyond the Tiber, on the hill Janiculum which looks toward the west.

CHAPTER XII

HORATIUS SLAYS HIS SISTER

Tullus Hostilius, the king who succeeded Numa Pompilius in 672 B.C., loved war as much as Pompilius had loved peace.

He feared lest already the Romans had lost the renown that had been theirs on the battlefield when Romulus was king. So he determined to find a pretext for war as soon as possible, that his soldiers might show that courage was still theirs, and that their fame might spread as of old to the neighbouring tribes.

Such was the warlike character of Tullus Hostilius, that it was soon found necessary to throw wide the gates of the temple Janus.

It chanced that shortly after the new king came to the throne some Roman and Alban countrymen quarrelled, each saying that he had been robbed by the other.

Tullus at once took the side of his own people, sending to the King of Alba to demand that the goods which had been stolen should be restored. The King of Alba at the same time sent messengers

HORATIUS SLAYS HIS SISTER

to Tullus, claiming that justice should be meted out to those who had robbed his subjects.

The King of Rome received the messengers from Alba so courteously and treated them so well, that they forgot the errand on which they had been sent, until startled by the return of the Roman ambassadors.

They, having been refused justice by the King of Alba, had, ere they left, declared that the Romans would avenge the wrong done to their countrymen.

Tullus was well pleased with the report of his ambassadors. He sent away the careless messengers of Alba, bidding them tell their king that it was he who had provoked the war.

The two kings speedily collected their armies and marched to the battlefield. But before the war began the King of Alba died. Then the Albans chose one of their number, named Mettius, to be Dictator.

He, standing between the two armies, begged that the victory might be decided by single combat, so that many lives might be spared.

To this Tullus agreed, sending forth as the Roman champions three brothers, called the Horatii, while the choice of Mettius fell upon three Alban brothers, named the Curiatii.

A great silence fell upon the two armies as the combatants stood forth, armed to the teeth, and the contest which was to settle the fate of Rome and Alba began.

Should the Horatii win, Rome would seize Alba as its prize. Should the Curiatii be the victors, Rome would be forfeit to the Albans.

Fierce and yet more fierce fell the blows of the champions, until at length, two of the Horatii lay slain on the ground, while the three Curiatii were wounded.

Then, to the dismay of the Roman army, Horatius, on whose courage the safety of Rome depended, turned and fled, pursued by the three wounded men.

But the Romans need not have feared that Horatius had turned coward. His flight, as they soon saw, was but a feint to separate his enemies.

As the swiftest of the Curiatii gained upon him, the Roman champion turned and smote him to the ground. Without a moment's pause Horatius then attacked the second brother, who had now reached his side, and he also fell before the fury of the Roman's stroke. The last of the Curiatii had been forced to follow more slowly, as his wounds had been severe. He, too, was now stricken down by the conqueror.

Rome was saved! At the thought great shouts rent the air, and Horatius was led in triumph toward the city.

As the glad procession drew near to the gate, the sister of Horatius came out to meet her brother. She was the promised bride of one of the Curiatii.

HORATIUS SLAYS HIS SISTER

When she saw Horatius wearing on his shoulders the cloak
of her betrothed, she broke into bitter sobs.

When she saw Horatius, wearing on his shoulders the cloak of her betrothed, which she herself had embroidered, she broke into bitter sobs and began to curse him for his cruel deed.

Then Horatius, in sudden passion, drew his sword and stabbed his sister, crying: "So perish the Roman maiden who shall weep for her country's enemy."

Great was the service Horatius had done for Rome that day, yet his rash act could not be allowed to pass unpunished. He was taken prisoner, and brought before two judges, who condemned him to death.

But Horatius refused to submit to his sentence, and appealed to the people of Rome to save him. And for the sake of his old father, who had already that day lost two sons, as well as because he himself had risked his life for his country, the people listened to his plea and set him free.

Yet, as a public penance, he was obliged to pass beneath a yoke and offer sacrifices to the spirit of the sister he had slain.

The yoke under which Horatius had to pass was formed of two beams of wood which were thrust into the ground, and across the top of which a third beam was placed. Sometimes the yoke was made by using three swords in this way.

But it was a wooden yoke under which Horatius stooped, and one of the beams was treasured for many years, and named the "sister's beam."

HORATIUS SLAYS HIS SISTER

Yet it was not only the memory of his penance that was preserved. To recall his courage to the Romans who would follow him, the arms which Horatius had taken from the Curiatii were hung on a pillar in the market-place. And in days to come the citizens would point to this pillar, saying: "It is the pillar of Horatius."

CHAPTER XIII

THE PRIDE OF TULLUS HOSTILIUS

By the victory of Horatius, the Albans became subject to Rome, and were forced to help them in their wars.

Mettius, the Dictator, never ceased to hope that he would yet be able to throw off the yoke of Rome.

So when Tullus summoned him to bring an army to help the Romans in their battle against the Etruscans, Mettius brought an army as he was bidden, but when the battle was at its height, he secretly told his men to give no aid to the Romans.

In spite of the treachery of Mettius, Tullus was victorious.

The Dictator, hoping that the king knew naught of his deceit, boldly praised him for the victory he had won.

But Tullus knew that Mettius had done nothing to help him win the battle, and so angry was he with his treachery that he ordered him to be torn to

THE PRIDE OF TULLUS HOSTILIUS

pieces by horses. Then the king ordered the Albans to be disarmed, and after burning their city, he carried off the people to Rome.

The Roman nobles, or patricians as they were called, welcomed the Alban nobles to their city, while the countrymen of Alba soon became friends with the common people, or plebeians.

As in the reign of Romulus the Sabines and the Romans became one, so now the Albans and Romans were united. In this way the number of the citizens in Rome was nearly doubled.

Encouraged by his victories, Tullus spent the rest of his reign in wars with the Etruscans. His success, instead of making him humble, made him proud, and he grew careless of the service of the gods. Moreover, he neglected the wise and just laws made by the good King Pompilius.

Then, in sign of their displeasure, the gods sent a plague among the people, and the king himself was smitten with sickness. In his misery Tullus remembered the gods and prayed. But Jupiter was angry, and sent a shaft of lightning from the sky, which killed Tullus and destroyed his house.

Tullus Hostilius reigned for thirty-two years, and after his death, in 640 B.C., Ancus Marcius, a grandson of Pompilius, became King of Rome.

CHAPTER XIV

THE KING WHO FOUGHT AND PRAYED

LIKE his grandfather Numa Pompilius, Ancus Marcius loved peace.

His first act after he became king was to restore the service of the gods, which during the last reign had ofttimes been neglected. The sacred laws of Pompilius, too, he ordered to be written on tablets of wood and to be shown to the people.

Now among the enemies of Rome was a tribe named the Latins. The Latins, knowing that King Ancus spent his time in prayer and in offering sacrifices to the gods, began to plunder and destroy the country round about Rome, thinking to go unpunished. But they soon found that the king could fight as well as pray.

No sooner, indeed, had Ancus heard that the Latins were laying waste his dominions, than he commanded the priests to attend to the temple services. Then, placing himself at the head of his army, he marched against the enemy.

THE KING WHO FOUGHT AND PRAYED

The battle was fierce and long, but at length the Latins were beaten and their towns destroyed. His prisoners the king took back with him to Rome, bidding them make their home on the Aventine hill.

Ancus next determined to secure the command of the Tiber and to join the Janiculum hill to Rome by throwing a wooden bridge across the river, which was named the "Bridge of the Wooden Piles," for it was built entirely of wood. The beams were placed loosely, one alongside another, so that, should an enemy approach, it could be quickly taken to pieces.

Ancus loved peace, but he could not yet lay down his arms, for he saw that Rome ought to secure the land that lay between the city and the sea. So he led his army against the tribes to whom this land belonged, and, taking it from them, he built a town at the mouth of the Tiber, which he called Ostia. And here a busy harbour was soon to be seen, from which Roman ships set sail for the open sea.

For twenty-four years this good king reigned, and then, calm and content as his royal grandfather, he died. His name was ever held in honour by his people, for in time of peace he had been just, in time of war victorious.

The children of the king were still young when their father died, so they were left to the care of his friend, Lucius Tarquinius.

CHAPTER XV

THE FAITHLESS FRIEND

Lucius Tarquinius, to whom the king had entrusted the care of his children, was a Greek noble possessing great wealth. His real name was Lucumo, and being driven from his native town by a tyrant, he had taken refuge in the town of Tarquinii in Etruria. It was from this town that he took the name by which he was known in Rome.

But neither Lucumo nor his wife Tanaquil were content to spend their lives in such a sleepy little town as Tarquinii proved to be. So they determined to go to Rome, where, it was said, strangers were ever welcome.

One day, then, the husband and wife set out on their journey. As they drew near to the Janiculum hill, an eagle suddenly swooped down upon the travellers, and seized the cap which Lucumo was wearing. Then, uttering loud screams, the bird flew high in the air, only to return in a few moments to replace the cap on the head of its astonished owner.

Tanaquil seemed pleased with the strange behaviour of the eagle, and assured her husband that

THE FAITHLESS FRIEND

it was an augury or sign from the gods that he would rise to honour in the city to which they were going.

King Ancus heard of the wealth and the wisdom of the stranger who had come to Rome, and ere long he sent a messenger to Tarquinius, bidding him attend the king's councils. So wisely did Tarquinius behave that the king soon treated him as a friend.

When Ancus Marcius was dying, he did not fear the future for his children. They would be safe, he believed, in the care of Tarquinius. But he, alas! betrayed his trust that he might satisfy his own ambition.

After the death of the king, Tarquinius, pretending that he wished to make the sons of Ancus forget their grief, persuaded them to go away from the city to hunt.

In their absence the false friend appealed to the people to make him king, and this they did.

Tarquinius had gained his power by a treacherous deed, but by his courage on the battlefield he won the admiration of his subjects.

He fought against the Latins, and made many of their cities subject to Rome. And when the Sabines took up arms and marched almost to the gates of the city, Tarquinius, vowing that if Jupiter would come to his aid he would build a temple in his honour, rushed against the foe and drove it away.

Flushed with victory, he then went to war with the Etruscans, and forced them to acknowledge him as their king.

As a sign of their subjection the conquered tribe sent to Tarquinius royal gifts—a golden crown, a scepter, an ivory chair, an embroidered tunic, a purple toga, and twelve axes tied up in bundles of rods.

These gifts the king sent before him to Rome as a proof of his victory over the Etruscans.

Then, when peace was at length proclaimed, Tarquinius remembered the vow he had made to Jupiter, and began to build a temple on the Capitoline hill.

As the workmen were digging, in order to lay a good foundation, they found a human head. This was a sign, so said those who knew, that the spot on which the head had been buried should become the chief place of worship in Rome.

The temple, when it was finished, was named the Capitol, and in days to come it was indeed looked upon as the most sacred building in the city.

Although Tarquinius was but a usurper, yet he did all that he could to improve the kingdom over which he ruled.

He ordered great drains to be built, that the marshy valleys between the hills of Rome might become healthier. He also built a large circus and a racecourse, to encourage the games of the people,

THE FAITHLESS FRIEND

and in course of time the Roman games became famous.

In the valley between the Capitoline hill and the Palatine hill the king then began to build the Forum, or market-place. Round the Forum he set up booths, where the tradesfolk might carry on their business.

Meanwhile, the subjects of Rome had become so numerous, that the king wished to increase the three tribes into which Romulus had divided his people.

But a skilful augur, named Attius, forbade Tarquinius to alter what Romulus had consecrated with rites sacred to the gods.

The king could ill brook interference, and he mocked at the augur's words in the Forum, where the people had assembled.

Then, thinking to show that Attius was not really as wise as he was believed to be, he cried: "Tell me, O Attius, can the thing of which I am thinking at this moment come to pass?"

The augur, undisturbed by the mockery of the king, consulted the sacred birds. Yes, the omens were good. The thought in the mind of the king could be put into action.

Tarquinius pointed to a whetstone which lay before him, and said: "Can you then cut this whetstone in twain with a razor?"

Undismayed, Attius at once seized a razor, and with one stroke the stone was split in two.

Then the king was afraid, and dared not disregard the wisdom of the augur. So the number of tribes ordained by Romulus was left unchanged.

But Tarquinius doubled the nobles in each tribe, and also increased the companies of knights.

CHAPTER XVI

A SLAVE BECOMES A KING

Among the slaves of the king was a young boy named Servius Tullius. One day the lad fell fast asleep in the doorway of the palace.

As he slept, it chanced that Tanaquil, the queen, came out to walk in the palace grounds. When she saw Servius she would have roused him, save that a flame of fire was playing around his head, yet doing him no hurt.

But the attendants of the queen also saw this strange sight, and at once rushed off in search of water with which to put out the flame.

Tanaquil, however, called to them to return, saying: "Leave the lad to sleep. The flame will not injure him."

Then, hastening back to the palace, she told the king what she had seen, adding: "The gods have appointed Servius to great honour."

From that day the boy was no longer treated as a slave, but as the king's son, and when he was older he was married to the daughter of Tarquinius.

Little by little Servius Tullius was entrusted with the cares of State, while the Senate or elders of the people treated him as a prince.

Now the sons of Ancus, from whom Tarquinius had stolen the crown, were indignant when they saw the former slave treated with more honour than were they, and they grew afraid lest the king should appoint Servius to succeed him. That this might not be, they determined to kill Tarquinius.

Hiring two men, they bade them go kill the king, and they should be well rewarded for their deed.

So the men disguised themselves as shepherds, and begged to be admitted to the presence of Tarquinius, that he might settle their dispute, for, so they pretended, they had quarrelled with one another while they tended their flocks.

When they stood before the king one of the shepherds began to tell a piteous tale. While Tarquinius was listening, the other suddenly raised his axe, and with one great blow killed the king. The false shepherds then fled from the palace.

But the sons of Ancus had forgotten that Tanaquil was left to thwart their plans.

No sooner was the king slain, than she ordered the doors of the palace to be closed. Then, when the people heard it rumoured that the king was dead and rushed to the palace, Tanaquil opened an upper window and spoke to the crowds below.

"The king is but wounded," she told them, "he is not dead. He has commanded that you should obey Servius until he is again able to rule." But all the while Tarquinius lay in the palace, dead.

But the people, loyal, as they thought, to the wishes of their king, allowed Servius to rule. And the sons of Ancus knew that they had killed the king in vain.

A few days later it was known that the king was really dead; yet, although neither the Senate nor the people had chosen Servius to be king, he continued to sit upon the throne and to rule over Rome. Moreover, he was wise enough to try to win the hearts of the people by promising to give them land and to rule justly.

So well did he perform his royal duties, that when he called together an assembly of the people he was at once elected king.

CHAPTER XVII

THE CRUEL DEED OF TULLIA

Servius Tullius began to reign in 578 B.C. Like Pompilius and Ancus, he loved peace, and fought against none, save only the Etruscans.

With the Latins he made a treaty, after which the two tribes built a temple to Diana on the Aventine hill, and here every year sacrifices were offered for Rome and for Latium.

The city which Romulus had built on the Palatine had long ago become too small for the Romans. Little by little, cities had grown up on the neighbouring hills, and now Servius was able to enclose all the seven hills of Rome within the city, building around her a great wall of stone. This wall was called after the king the "Servian Wall," and so strongly was it built that it was still standing in the days of Augustus. Beyond the wall a deep moat was then dug, a hundred feet in breadth.

Having thus strengthened the city, Servius divided it into four regions, while the people were arranged in numerous tribes.

THE CRUEL DEED OF TULLIA

Should a citizen be wanted to appear before the king or the Senate, it was then an easy task to find the tribe to which he belonged and the region in which he dwelt.

Servius also made a law which pleased the Romans well, called an ordinance of the king.

This ordinance forbade the nobles to oppress the poor. It also decreed that, however lowly the birth of a Roman citizen, if he became rich he might hold positions of power in the State. This encouraged the poor man to be industrious, for if he could but gain wealth there was no ambition which he might not be able to satisfy.

But while the ordinance pleased the common people, it displeased the nobles, who had no wish to see the plebeians raised to positions which until now had been sacred to them and to their sons. They bore Servius no good will for passing this new law.

Trouble, too, was threatening the king through his two daughters, both of whom, as the Roman custom was, were named Tullia.

But although their names were the same, their natures were as different as summer is different from winter.

Tullia, the elder, was wicked and ambitious; Tullia, the younger, good and gentle.

Servius determined to marry his daughters to the sons of King Tarquinius, whose kindness had placed him on the throne.

The princes, as the princesses, were of strangely different natures. Lucius was proud, his temper violent; while Aruns was humble and good-natured.

Now the king thought that if the gentle Tullia married Lucius, he would become a better man; while he hoped that if his ambitious daughter married Aruns she would learn from him the grace of humility.

But Servius made a great mistake when he married his daughters. For before long Lucius hated his quiet wife, and killed both her and his brother Aruns, so that he and Tullia the elder might be free to marry each other.

No sooner had Lucius Tarquinius married Tullia, than, encouraged by her, he joined the discontented nobles, who hated Servius.

Day by day Lucius grew more bold, more rude to Servius, and at length he put on the royal robes and sat on the king's seat in the Senate house, unrebuked by the nobles.

Servius was now no longer young, but when he heard how Lucius had dared to behave he went at once to the door of the Senate house, and bade the prince come down from the throne, and lay aside the royal robes.

But Lucius paid no heed to the king's command. Then, as the king repeated his words, Lucius seized the old man and flung him down the stone steps of the Senate house.

Servius, bruised and dazed by his fall, yet struggled to his feet, and slowly turned away toward the palace.

Lucius dared not let the king live now that he had defied him. So, sending his servants after Servius, he bade them kill the old man.

It was easy to overtake him, and the fellows soon slew their king, leaving his body lying in the middle of the street.

When Tullia heard what her husband had done, she had no grief to spare for her father's cruel death. She ordered her chariot, and drove quickly to the Forum to greet her husband as king.

But Lucius did not wish the people to see the triumph of his wife, and he sternly bade her go home.

Tullia obeyed, heedless of his anger. She had room in her heart for only one thought. Lucius was king, and she, she was queen.

So full was her mind of the new honours that would now be hers, that her chariot had reached the street where the dead body of her father lay before she was aware. The driver drew up his horses sharply, seeing his murdered king lying across his path.

But Tullia angrily bade him drive on, and as he obeyed, her robe was stained with her father's blood. The street was ever after called the Via Scelerata, or the Way of Crime.

Lucius showed no shame for the murder of the king, and haughtily refused to allow his body to be buried with the usual rites.

And because of his pride the new king was named Tarquinius Superbus or Tarquin the Proud.

CHAPTER XVIII

THE FATE OF THE TOWN OF GABII

TARQUIN, having killed Servius, seized the throne, and began his reign by condemning to death the chief senators who had supported the old king. He also ordered the tablets, on which Servius had written many wise and good laws, to be destroyed. Refusing to summon the Senate, Tarquin then attempted to rule alone.

His cruelty was so great that he was soon hated both by rich and poor. Before many months had passed he was forced to surround himself with a bodyguard, lest he should be slain by those whom he had ruined. For, in order to grow rich, he imposed heavy fines on the wealthy, sometimes driving the nobles into exile that he might take possession of their goods. If they ventured to remonstrate, Tarquin did not hesitate to put them to death that he might seize their money.

As for the poor people, he forced them to work so hard that they were more like slaves than freemen. Often in despair they escaped from the king's cruelty by killing themselves.

After he had crushed the spirit of his subjects, Tarquin went to war with the Latins, conquering many of their cities, and even enrolling some of his prisoners in the Roman legions.

One ancient Latin town determined to resist the cruel king. Gabii, for this was the name of the brave little town, even opened its gates to the nobles who had been exiled from Rome.

In vain Tarquin sent legion after legion against the city. Its defenders still defied him, fighting with all their strength so as to protect their homes from the cruel hands of Tarquin the Proud.

Since he could not take the town by force, the king resolved to take it by treachery, and in this resolve he was aided by his son Sextus.

Sextus, pretending that he had been forced to leave Rome by his father's cruelty, fled to Gabii. Telling the citizens a piteous tale, he showed them his back, bare and bleeding from stripes, and begged to be taken into the town that his father might not capture him.

The citizens did not find it difficult to believe that the tyrant had ill-used his son, and they willingly opened their gates to the prince. And not only did they give him shelter, but, so great was their trust, that before long they gave him command of a company of soldiers.

THE FATE OF THE TOWN OF GABII

One day a Roman legion was seen marching toward the city. Sextus at once led his soldiers against it, and, instructed secretly by Tarquin, the Romans fled before the prince.

This made the men of Gabii still more sure that they could trust Sextus, so they foolishly gave him the chief command of the defences of the town.

Then Sextus sent in triumph to his father to know what he should do.

Tarquin the Proud was walking in his garden when his son's messenger arrived, and he listened in silence to his words. But he still walked up and down the garden paths, switching off with his stick the heads of the tallest poppies in the flower-beds. Then, still without a word, he sent the messenger back to Gabii.

But when Sextus heard of the fate of the poppies, he needed no words to explain his father's silence. He knew as well as if the king had spoken that as the tallest poppies had been beheaded, so he was to behead the leading nobles in Gabii.

The citizens knew nothing of what had happened in the king's flower garden, so they were startled and dismayed when, day after day, Sextus accused one and another of their nobles of crime or treason, and ordered them to be put to death. The prince then completed his treachery by delivering the town into the hands of the king.

Tarquin's next victory was over the Volscians, a powerful tribe which dwelt south of Latium. After plundering one of their richest towns, he determined with his new-found wealth to finish the great temple on the Capitoline hill, which had been begun by his father Lucius Tarquinius.

He adorned Rome with many other beautiful buildings, and ordered the great sewers, also begun by his father, to be finished. He then completed the Forum, or market-place. In the Forum the people bought and sold, and here also were held the great assemblies of the people.

CHAPTER XIX

THE BOOKS OF THE SIBYL

ONE day, when Tarquin the Proud was at the height of his power, a woman came to the city and demanded to see the king. She was a stranger, and carried in her arms nine books.

When she was brought before the king she asked him to buy the books, telling him that they were the sacred prophecies of the inspired Sibyl of Cumæ. Cumæ was in the Campania, and was the most ancient of the Greek towns in Italy. The prophecies were written on loose leaves, and in them, said the strange woman, the king would read the destiny of Rome, and how to fulfil it.

But the stranger asked so large a sum of money for the nine books that the king laughed and refused to buy.

Quietly, before the king's eyes the woman burned three of the nine books. Then, turning to him again, she offered the six books for the same price as she had before demanded for the nine.

She carried in her arms nine books.

THE BOOKS OF THE SIBYL

Tarquin laughed still more scornfully, and refused to buy the six as he had already refused to buy the nine books.

Quietly as before the woman burned three more books before the eyes of the king. Then turning to him she offered the three books that were left for the same sum.

Then the king laughed no more. He began to wonder if perhaps the gods had sent the books to Rome. So he consulted the augurs, and by their advice he now bought the three books for the sum which would have bought the nine.

The strange woman, having done her work, disappeared and was seen no more, while the books were put in a chest and kept in the Capitol, which was now complete.

Two Greeks were appointed to guard the Sibylline books, for they were written in the Greek language. And ever when death, pestilence, or war threatened the city, the books were consulted by the augurs, if perchance Rome might be saved from destruction.

Many years after the reign of Tarquin the Capitol was burned, and the sacred books were destroyed in the fire.

To the Romans the loss of the books was a greater blow than even the destruction of the Capitol.

The Senate sent ambassadors to Greece and to Asia Minor to beseech the sibyls there to find fresh oracles, that calamity might still be averted from Rome.

And the ambassadors were successful, for when they returned they brought with them new scrolls, which, when a new Capitol was built, were placed within its sacred precincts.

During the reign of Augustus, the oracles were removed to the temple of Apollo, which stood on Mount Palatine.

But long after the time of Augustus, in A.D. 400, they were burned in public by a famous Roman, for he was a Christian, and cared little for the ancient oracles, believing them to be but a useless relic of the old pagan days.

CHAPTER XX

THE INDUSTRY OF LUCRETIA

As the years passed, Tarquin was disturbed by terrible dreams. The evil deeds he had done came back to his memory, and haunted him by day and by night. Even in the temples of the gods he could find no rest from his fears.

One day, as sacrifices were being offered, the king saw a serpent stealing down a wooden pillar. Fascinated, he watched as it dropped slowly on to the altar and devoured the sacrifice. His fear told him that this was a bad omen, and, thoroughly alarmed, Tarquin determined to consult the Greek oracle at Delphi, for this oracle was famous not only in Greece, but throughout the world.

So he sent his two sons, Titus and Aruns, to Delphi. With them went the king's nephew, named Junius, but called Brutus because he was believed to be stupid. But Brutus only pretended to be stupid so that his uncle would not trouble to do him harm.

When the princes reached the dwelling of the priestess, the king's sons offered her valuable gifts, while Brutus gave to her only a simple staff. His cousins mocked at Brutus as they were used to do, for a priestess would not care for so poor a gift, they were sure. But Brutus was wiser than they deemed, for the staff had been made hollow, and then had been filled with gold.

As the king had bidden, the young princes asked the oracle the meaning of the serpent that had devoured the sacrifice on the altar.

It was indeed an evil omen. "The fall of Tarquin is at hand," was the sinister answer they received.

"Which of us shall reign after him?" demanded the king's sons with unseemly eagerness.

"He who shall first kiss his mother," responded the oracle.

Then the two princes cast lots to determine which of them should greet their mother first on their return.

But Brutus guessed that the words of the oracle had a deeper meaning.

As he left the Delphic temple, he pretended to slip, and falling to the ground, he secretly kissed the Earth, knowing that she was the mother of all men.

When the princes returned the king was at war, besieging Ardea, a town in Latium. It seemed that he had forgotten his fears, nor does the story tell what he thought of the answer of the oracle.

THE INDUSTRY OF LUCRETIA

Meanwhile the siege of Ardea dragged on month after month, so bravely did the inhabitants defend their town.

In the Roman camp, Prince Sextus and a noble named Collatinus one day whiled away the hours by wondering what their wives were doing. Each boasted that his wife was the more diligent and the more modest of the two women.

At length one of their friends idly suggested that Sextus and Collatinus should ride to their homes and find out how their wives were employed.

So the two officers, accompanied by their friends, ordered their horses, and rode first of all to Rome.

Here they found the wife of Sextus at a banquet, where she was dancing gaily, the merriest of all the merry throng.

It was late when they reached Collatia, where they found Lucretia, the wife of Collatinus, still busy with her maidens at the spinning-wheel.

The whole company agreed that of the two wives Lucretia deserved the greater praise. Then the frolic being over, the prince and his friends rode back to camp.

CHAPTER XXI

THE DEATH OF LUCRETIA

THE idle suggestion that had made Sextus and Collatinus ride from the camp to Rome and Collatia led to terrible disaster.

Sextus, having seen how wise and beautiful Lucretia was, wished to win her from her husband; and one day, leaving the camp, he again rode to Collatia, but this time he rode alone.

Lucretia, believing the prince was her husband's friend, received him with fitting hospitality when he arrived at her house, hot and tired after his ride. But when she found that he was not a true friend to Collatinus she was no longer kind. Then the prince grew angry, and treated Lucretia so cruelly that she knew she could never again be happy.

The next day she clad herself in black, and sent messengers to her father and her husband, bidding them come to Collatia with all possible speed.

When they arrived, she told them how Sextus had treated her, and making them swear to avenge her wrongs, she plunged a dagger into her heart and died.

THE DEATH OF LUCRETIA

Brutus, the king's nephew, had ridden from the camp with Collatinus, and he, too, swore to avenge Lucretia, and to see that never more should any of the race of Tarquin sit upon the throne of Rome.

This oath was also taken by the husband and father of Lucretia, as well as by two brave Romans named Publius Valerius and Spurius Lucretius.

The dead body of the Roman matron was carried to the market-place, and when the people were told what had happened, they broke out into loud cries, and mourned for her sad fate.

Brutus then hastened to Rome to tell the terrible tale. In the Forum, amid the assembled people, his voice rang out clear and fearless as he reminded them of the crimes of Tarquin the Proud, and denounced the king and his son Sextus.

"Will you suffer such a tyrant or any of his race to rule longer over you, O Romans?" demanded Brutus sternly. And the people in a storm of indignation shouted "No."

The Romans were in earnest. An army was at once enrolled, and, led by Brutus, set out to attack the king at Ardea.

Tullia, the queen, meanwhile, startled by the tumult in the Forum, fled from the palace. As her chariot drove along the streets the people muttered curses, calling down upon her the vengeance of her murdered father.

THE STORY OF ROME

Rumours had already reached the camp that Rome was in revolt, and Tarquin at once marched to the city with a division of his army to punish the rebels.

Brutus, on his way to Ardea, took care to avoid the king. He had determined to win over the army that was left before the besieged town.

When he reached the camp, he quickly roused the soldiers by the tale of Lucretia's wrongs.

They swore never again to own Tarquin or any of his race as king, and at once prepared to march to Rome.

Meanwhile, the king had reached the city only to find the gates closed, and the citizens, stern and resolute, manning the walls. No threats, no promises would make them open to the king whom they had determined to dethrone.

Tarquin, knowing that if he lingered he would have to face the army led by Brutus, turned away from the city and hastened to seek refuge in Etruria.

The Romans, having thus expelled their king, appointed a day to be celebrated as the Feast of Flight, or the Feast of the Expulsion of the Kings. This feast was held each year on the 24th February.

CHAPTER XXII

THE SONS OF BRUTUS

AFTER Tarquin the Proud had been driven away from Rome, the people determined that they would never again be ruled by kings.

They resolved to follow the wise laws of Servius, who had bidden them choose each year two men to rule, giving them equal power, the right to make laws, and to see that justice was done in the land.

The two men, chosen by the Senate and the people, were called Consuls.

In token of his office, each Consul had at his command six men, named lictors.

When a Consul went into the Forum or into the street, he was preceded by his lictors, who carried, as a sign of their master's power, rods to chastise and an axe to kill.

Rome had now become a Republic, and the first Consuls to be elected were Brutus and Collatinus.

THE STORY OF ROME

But if the Romans expected Tarquin to make no effort to recover his throne, they soon discovered their mistake.

Before long, the king sent messengers to Rome to ask that his own private possessions might be sent to him, and to this simple request the Senate and the people agreed.

As perhaps the Romans might have suspected, Tarquin had another reason for sending to Rome than the one his messengers carried to the Senate. He knew that among the younger patricians were many who wished to place him again upon the throne, and his messengers had come to talk secretly with these nobles. They even hoped to arrange the best time for the king's return.

But as the conspirators talked together, a slave chanced to overhear what they said, and he at once went to the Consuls and told them of the danger that threatened the city.

The conspirators were immediately seized and thrown into prison, while the slave was set free and made a citizen of Rome.

Among the prisoners were Titus and Tiberius, the sons of Brutus.

The brave Consul was dismayed to learn that his sons, whom he loved well, had been guilty of treason. How could he bear to pronounce judgment upon them as upon other traitors?

THE SONS OF BRUTUS

Yet soon he thrust aside his weakness. A true Roman must love his country better even than his own children.

So when the conspirators were brought before him he did not flinch. With stern, set face he condemned Titus and Tiberius to death along with the other traitors, nor did he stoop to ask the people to show mercy to his sons.

The young men were bound to the stake before his eyes, after which the lictors beat them with rods and then cut off their heads with the axe.

So angry were the Senate and the people with Tarquin for attempting to plot against the Republic, that they now refused to send to him his possessions. And not only so, but they divided his goods among the people, while the field between the city and the Tiber which Tarquin had sown with corn was destroyed, the corn cut down and thrown into the river. The angry citizens then dedicated the field to the god Mars, and henceforth it was known as the Field of Mars.

The Senate then made a law banishing for ever from Rome all who bore the hated name of Tarquin.

So Collatinus, whose other name was Tarquinius, resigned his Consulship and left the city in obedience to the law. And this he did, although he was the friend of Brutus, and hated the exiled king.

Valerius was then chosen Consul in his stead.

Meanwhile, Tarquin was full of wrath because he had not been able to enter Rome by craft, and he went to Etruria, and persuaded the Etruscans to help him to recover his throne.

But when the Etruscans proclaimed war against Rome, Brutus gathered together an army and led it against the enemy.

Close to a wood the battle raged. Aruns, one of Tarquin's sons, saw Brutus at the head of the Roman army, wearing the royal robes which he considered belonged to his house alone. In sudden fury he put spurs to his horse, and with his spear ready dashed toward his enemy.

Brutus saw Aruns drawing near, and he also spurred his horse forward and couched his spear.

Onward flew the two warriors until at length they met. Then each, pierced by the other's spear, fell from his horse and moved no more.

All day the battle raged, and still when night fell the victory was uncertain.

But, during the night, while both armies were encamped on the battlefield, a loud voice was heard coming from the direction of the wood.

It was Silvanus, the god of the wood, who was speaking. "The victory belongs to the Romans," said the god, "for they have slain one more than their enemy."

Obedient to the voice of Silvanus, the Etruscans on the following morning withdrew their army, while the Romans marched back to Rome.

THE SONS OF BRUTUS

In spite of their victory they were sad, for they carried with them the dead body of their leader.

Brutus was mourned by all the people. But the Roman matrons lamented more than others, setting aside a whole year in which to grieve for his death, because he had so bravely avenged the matron Lucretia.

CHAPTER XXIII

HORATIUS COCLES, OR THE ONE-EYED

AFTER the death of Brutus, Valerius ruled alone. But he soon displeased the people, for they thought that he behaved too much as though he were a king.

The Consul had indeed built himself a beautiful house, from the windows of which, had he wished, he could look down into the Forum.

When he walked from his house to the market-place, Valerius, it was true, was preceded by six lictors, bearing rods and axes, but this was a dignity accorded to the Consuls by the people themselves.

Valerius had in truth no wish to spy upon the people as they feared, nor did he try to use his authority unjustly.

Yet the people grumbled, and grew restless and suspicious, until at length the Consul heard that he had displeased them.

Valerius was not angry with the foolish citizens, but he resolved to make them ashamed of their groundless suspicions.

HORATIUS COCLES, OR THE ONE-EYED

So one evening, when it was dark, he sent for workmen and ordered them to pull his beautiful house to pieces.

When morning dawned, the people, gazing upward from the Forum to the Consul's house, were startled. What could have happened? There was no longer any house to be seen.

It was not for some time that they learned that it was their foolish suspicions that had caused the Consul to destroy his house.

Then, fickle as the Roman crowd always was, it changed its mind and hung its head, ashamed of the destruction it had caused.

But Valerius not only made the citizens ashamed of their suspicions, he made them love him for his humility.

When he came into the Forum, the Consul now ordered his lictors to carry the rods and axes in two separate bundles, while the axes were from this time always lowered when he entered the Senate-house, or stood before the assembly of the people.

Valerius also made a law that pleased the Romans well.

When a Roman was condemned to death by a magistrate, the Consul decreed that he should have the right to appeal to the people against the sentence. This, you remember, was what Horatius had done when he was condemned to death for slaying his sister.

THE STORY OF ROME

So completely had the Consul endeared himself to the Romans that they now called him Poplicola, or the Lover of the People.

Meanwhile, Tarquin the Proud had enlisted the aid of a powerful king, named Lars Porsenna.

This king now sent to Rome, bidding the people open their gates to Tarquin. When they refused, he at once marched against the city with a great army.

The Romans increased the guard and strengthened the forts on the Janiculum hill. At all costs the enemy must be prevented from crossing the Tiber by the wooden bridge that joined the hill to the city itself.

Slaves, cattle, goods—all were brought from the surrounding country, either within the walls of the city, or into forts without.

But in spite of all the Romans could do, Lars Porsenna reached the Janiculum, and storming the heights, drove the Roman soldiers down the hill toward the river. His men pursued the fugitives, who seemed to think of nothing save their own safety.

If the enemy was not to enter the city, the bridge must be defended until the Roman soldiers on the other side of the river had cut through the beams that supported it.

Then, as the enemy drew near and ever nearer to the bank of the river, a brave Roman, named Horatius Cocles, or Horatius the One-Eyed, whose country was dearer to him than life itself, cried to the Consul right manfully:—

> " 'Hew down the bridge, Sir Consul,
>   With all the speed ye may:
> I, with two more to help me,
>   Will hold the foe in play.
> In yon strait path a thousand
>   May well be stopped by three.
> Now, who will stand on either hand,
>   And keep the bridge with me?' "

There were not lacking Romans to answer the brave challenge:—

> " 'Lo, I will stand at thy right hand,
>   And keep the bridge with thee,' "

cried Spurius Lartius, one of Rome's strongest warriors, while the voice of another brave soldier, named Herminius, rang out clear above the noise of arms:—

> " 'I will abide on thy left side,
>   And keep the bridge with thee,'
> For Romans in Rome's quarrel
>   Spared neither land nor gold,
> Nor son, nor wife, nor limb, nor life,
>   In the brave days of old."

Fully armed, the three brave men sprang to the end of the bridge farthest from the city, and flung defiance at Lars Porsenna and his great army.

The king and his army, seeing but three stalwart warriors, laughed them to scorn, yet ere long their scorn gave way to amazement.

Before the missiles hurled upon them, before the fiercest sword-thrusts, Horatius and his comrades stood dauntless and unafraid, while at their feet rose a ghastly heap of those the brave Romans slew.

And while they held the bridge thus resolutely, behind them fell the blows of mighty axes, loosening the great beams that held the bridge secure.

Soon the axes had done their work. The bridge began to totter, to sway, and the Romans shouted to the noble three to come back ere the bridge gave way.

At the call, Lartius and Herminius turned and darted swiftly across the swaying planks.

But Horatius stayed behind. Not till the bridge fell into the river would he stir from his post.

Then, with a mighty crash the bridge gave way, and fell into the rushing torrent beneath.

Horatius, separated from his friends, stood alone, facing thirty thousand of the foe. Behind him tossed the broad surging river.

" 'Down with him,' cried false Sextus,
    With a smile on his pale face.
'Now yield thee,' cried Lars Porsena,
    'Now yield thee to our grace.'

"Round turned he, as not deigning
    Those craven ranks to see,
Nought spake he to Lars Porsena,
    To Sextus naught spake he;
But he saw on Palatinus
    The white porch of his home;
And he spake to the noble river
    That rolls by the towers of Rome.

" 'O Tiber! father Tiber!
    To whom the Romans pray,
A Roman's life, a Roman's arms,
    Take thou in charge this day!'
So he spake, and speaking sheathed
    The good sword by his side,
And with his harness on his back,
    Plunged headlong in the tide."

Not a sound was heard from either bank as Horatius, wounded and bleeding, disappeared in the flood.

Then the enemy, furious that it had allowed the great warrior to escape, hurled its spears after him.

But not one reached the bold swimmer, who, weighed down by his armour and weakened by his wounds, often sank, yet ever rose again and struggled onwards.

At length he reached the bank, where eager hands were waiting to draw him up into safety.

When the Romans saw that their hero was safe indeed, although exhausted with his efforts, a mighty shout of triumph rent the air.

Horatius was rewarded for his brave deed by the Senate, who gave him as much land as he could plough in a day, while in later days a monument was erected in memory of his prowess and placed in the Comitium. The Comitium was near to the Forum, and was sometimes counted as part of it.

CHAPTER XXIV

GAIUS MUCIUS BURNS HIS RIGHT HAND

Lars Porsenna had been repulsed, but he had not been defeated. He now besieged Rome so closely, that the people were soon suffering all the horrors of famine.

Then a youth, named Gaius Mucius, determined to save Rome by killing Lars Porsenna.

Gaining the consent of the Senate to his scheme, he disguised himself as a countryman, and found his way into the camp of the enemy. Beneath the folds of his simple dress, Mucius had concealed a dagger.

It had been easy to enter the camp, but now the lad was in a difficult position, for he did not know the king, nor did he dare to ask any one to point him out.

But seeing a courtier wearing a purple robe and distributing money to the soldiers, he believed he had found him. Drawing near, he stealthily drew his dagger and stabbed—not Lars Porsenna, but his treasurer.

Before he had time to escape, Mucius was seized and taken before the king.

The king threatened the young noble with torture, even with death, in order to make him reveal the condition of the Roman army. But Mucius thrust his right hand into a flame that was alight on an altar beside him, and held it there until it was burned to ashes. This he did without flinching, that Lars Porsenna might see that he feared no torture. As for death, when it came, he would bear it as a Roman should.

But the king, amazed at the courage of the youth, forgot his anger, and bade him return unharmed to Rome.

Then Mucius, touched by the kindness of the king, told him that three hundred Roman youths had sworn to take his life, and would not rest until one of them had succeeded in doing so.

Lars Porsenna was a wise king. He listened to the warning given to him by Mucius, and offered terms to the starving city, promising if they were accepted to withdraw with his army. But the terms were hard, for the king demanded that Tarquin's possessions should be sent to him, that the Romans should give up all their dominions on the right bank of the Tiber, that they should not use iron save to cultivate the ground, and that ten noble youths and maidens should be sent to him as hostages.

With starvation staring them in the face, the Romans were forced to agree to these terms, and the

GAIUS MUCIUS BURNS HIS RIGHT HAND

hostages that he had demanded were sent to the king as a pledge of good faith.

Among the hostages was a noble maiden named Clœlia. In the Etruscan camp she pined for the freedom of her own home, for the joy of seeing her own friends, and at length she determined to escape.

So one night, when it grew dark, she slipped out of the camp unnoticed, and found her way to the edge of the river.

Without hesitation she plunged into the water and swam across to the other side—to home, to freedom.

But a sad disappointment was in store for the maiden. The Romans refused to allow her to stay in Rome, for although they admired her courage, their treaty with Lars Porsenna must be kept.

So poor Clœlia was sent back to the king. But he, pleased that the Romans had behaved so honourably, set Clœlia free, and allowed her to take many of the other hostages back with her to Rome.

Soon after this, Lars Porsenna refused to help Tarquin the Proud any longer, and breaking up his camp on the Janiculum he went back to his own country. His tents, which were full of corn and provisions, he gave to the starving city.

So grateful were the Romans for the food that they rewarded Lars Porsenna with royal gifts—a throne and sceptre of ivory, a golden crown, and a purple robe.

And these gifts the king well deserved, for he had proved a generous foe.

CHAPTER XXV

THE DIVINE TWINS

TARQUIN THE PROUD was an old man now, but he was not yet ready to believe that he would never again reign in Rome.

Once more he prepared for battle, invoking the aid of the Latins, for he believed that the Romans would quail before this fierce and warlike people.

The Romans did not quail, but they knew that they would need brave men to lead their army. So they appointed a Dictator, who was to have supreme command of the army and power as though he was king in Rome, for six months.

Aulus Postumius was the name of the Roman who was chosen for this great trust.

Tarquin, his cruel son Sextus, and a band of Roman exiles marched to the battlefield, near Lake Regillus in the region of Tusculum. With them was their ally the King of the Latins, leading a great army.

The Romans, with Aulus at their head, advanced against the foe, and a great battle was fought.

Valerius, the Consul was on the field, and when he saw Sextus anger filled his heart, and he dashed forward to slay him. But the prince retreated, and Valerius followed until he was drawn into the lines of the enemy, and perished by the thrust of a spear.

Fiercely as the Romans fought, the day began to go against them. Then Aulus vowed that he would build a temple to the twin brothers, Castor and Pollux, if they would but come to his aid and give to the Romans victory.

Scarcely had the Dictator ended his prayer, when lo! two youths of more than human height and majesty appeared, clad in shining armour, and riding upon white horses.

Going to the head of the army, they led it afresh against the Latins.

The enemy, terrified by the splendour of the strangers, and startled at the suddenness of the new attack, were seized with panic, and fled.

On rushed the Romans in pursuit of the foe, on until they reached the camp of the Latins, which the strange horsemen were the first to enter.

The Latin army was now in utter confusion, while a great victory had been won by the Romans.

Aulus wished to reward the strangers to whom the victory was really due, but they were nowhere to be seen. Neither in the field nor in the camp was there any trace of the riders or their steeds.

But in Rome, where old men and women awaited, with anxious hearts, news of the battle, there appeared in the Forum, as the sun went down, two horsemen. They were mounted on pure white steeds, and they themselves were "exceeding beautiful and tall above the stature of men." But they bore upon them the stains of battle.

When they reached the spring that rises close to the temple of Vesta, they dismounted, and washed the foam from their horses, the stains from their clothes.

Men and women crowded around the strangers, eager to hear their tidings. Then the brothers told them of the glorious victory that had been won, after which they mounted their white steeds, and riding away, were seen no more.

When the Dictator returned to Rome, he told how he had prayed to the Divine Twins Castor and Pollux, and how he believed that they had indeed come to his aid.

Moreover, he was sure that it was they who had ridden to Rome with more than mortal speed to tell of the victory that had been won.

Then Aulus, with a glad heart, began to build the temple he had vowed to the Divine Twins, and the Romans kept a festival each year in honour of Castor and Pollux.

At this festival, sacrifices were offered in the temple, while a solemn procession of knights, clad in purple and crowned with olive, rode from the temple of Mars without the city wall to the temple dedicated by the Dictator to the Divine Twins. This temple is now being excavated in the Forum of Rome.

The Latins, after their defeat, refused any longer to fight for Tarquin, while they hastened to make peace with his enemies.

Alone and childless, for Sextus had fallen in battle, Tarquin went away to Cumæ, and there he, the last of the Kings of Rome, died.

Soon after this, Rome regained her dominions on the right bank of the Tiber. She had already ceased to regard the treaty which had forbidden her the use of arms.

CHAPTER XXVI

THE TRIBUNES

THE people of Rome were divided into two great classes, the patricians or nobles, the plebeians or common people.

After the death of Tarquin the Proud, the patricians began to oppress the plebeians even more than they had done in the time of the kings.

Sometimes the poor were forced to borrow from the rich, and the rich, although they lent their money, demanded such heavy interest that the plebeians were often unable to pay their debts.

Then the patricians swept down upon the miserable debtors, drove their wives and children from their home, and carried them away to work as bondsmen.

When at any time war threatened Rome, the plebeians were called on to fight, and while they were at war their fields lay untilled, unless they hired labourers to work in them. In either case the plebeians suffered. Did they hire labourers, they must borrow money from the patricians to pay them. Did they leave their fields untilled, they must borrow money to buy food and seed.

Driven at length to desperation, the plebeians rose against their oppressors, and at the very time that a hostile army was marching against Rome, they left the city, and encamped on a hill near the river Anio, about three miles away. Here they determined to build a city for themselves.

But the patricians could not hope to hold Rome against the approaching foe without the help of the plebeians. So the Senate sent a messenger to the "seceders," offering terms of peace and protection from the patricians, if they would return to Rome to fight against the common enemy.

The plebeians agreed to go back to the city, and for a time, at least, the patrician magistrates ceased to treat them unjustly.

To make them more secure, the plebeians were now, in 493 B.C., allowed to elect two magistrates of their own, who were to be called tribunes.

As the patricians were able to appeal to the Consuls, so the plebeians could now appeal to their tribunes against unjust treatment.

The tribunes were elected for one year, and during that year they were obliged to live in Rome, while their doors were to stand open day and night, that the plebeians might claim their protection at any hour.

THE TRIBUNES

This new law was made a sacred law, and the hill on which the seceders had encamped was named the Sacred Hill.

CHAPTER XXVII

CORIOLANUS AND HIS MOTHER VETURIA

MANY legends are told of the wars which the Romans now waged with a fierce tribe named the Volscians.

None, perhaps, is so well known as the story I am going to tell you of Gaius Marcius, who was named Coriolanus.

Marcius was only a lad of seventeen years of age when he fought in the great battle of Lake Regillus. For his courage in saving the life of a comrade on the battlefield he was crowned with a wreath of oak leaves, as was the Roman custom.

The young lad loved his mother Veturia well. When the battle was over, his first thought was to hasten to show her the wreath that his valour had gained, for he had no greater joy than to please her.

When the Romans went to war with the Volscians, Marcius was with the army which was besieging Corioli, their capital town.

CORIOLANUS AND HIS MOTHER VETURIA

One day, the defenders of the city, seeing that part of the Roman army had withdrawn from the walls, determined to venture out to attack those soldiers who remained.

So fierce was their onslaught, that the Romans began to give way.

Marcius, who was some distance off, saw what had happened, and with only a few followers rushed to the aid of his comrades, at the same time calling in a loud voice to those who were retreating to follow him.

Encouraged by the young patrician, the Romans rallied, and dashing after Marcius, they soon forced the enemy to turn and fly back toward the shelter of their city.

The Romans pursued the Volscians until they reached the gates, but they did not dream of entering, for within the city were many more of the enemy. Already the walls were manned, and a deadly rain of arrows was descending among them.

But Marcius, crying that the gates were open, "Not so much to shelter the vanquished as to receive the conquerors," forced his way into the city.

With only a handful of men, he succeeded in keeping the gates of Corioli open, until the main body of the army arrived, when the city was taken without difficulty.

The soldiers said, as was indeed the truth, that it was Gaius Marcius who had taken the city.

When the war with the Volscians ended, the Consul wished to reward Marcius for this and many another courageous deed. So he ordered that of all the booty that had been taken in the war, the tenth part should be given to the brave young patrician. He himself gave to Marcius a noble horse, splendidly caparisoned.

But Marcius refused to receive more than his proper share of the booty. He begged, however, for one favour. It was that a Volscian who had shown him hospitality and was now a prisoner, might be set free.

Shouts of applause greeted Marcius when the soldiers heard his request.

When all was again quiet, the Consul said: "It is idle, fellow-soldiers, to force and obtrude those other gifts of ours on one who is unwilling to accept them. Let us therefore give him one of such a kind that he cannot well reject it. In memory of his conquest of the city of Corioli, let him henceforth be called Coriolanus."

So it was that from this time Coriolanus was the name of the young soldier.

In Rome, as was usual after war, there was much misery, for the fields had been left unploughed, and no seed had been sown while the plebeians were away on the battlefield. Now the people were starving.

The Consuls sent to Etruria for food, and when it reached Rome it was divided among the people, but still there was not enough to satisfy their hunger.

While the people still cried for bread, the time to elect Consuls for the following year drew near.

Coriolanus was one of the candidates. He came to the Forum, clad in his white toga only, and drawing it aside he showed to the people the marks of the wounds he had received in fighting for his country.

But although at first they meant to elect Coriolanus, many of them remembered that he often spoke of their tribunes with bitter contempt. If he were Consul, he might try to do away with the tribunes altogether, and to whom then would the people be able to appeal against the oppression of the haughty patricians?

When the day came to elect the Consuls, the feeling against Coriolanus had grown so strong that he was rejected. This made him very angry with the plebeians, nor did he try to disguise his feelings.

Soon after the elections were over, large ships laden with corn reached Ostia. The senators were eager to feed the starving people, and as some of the corn was a gift, they were ready to give it to them without charging even a small sum.

But Coriolanus was indignant, and denounced in the Senate-house those who wished to treat the people so well. The plebeians had already grown more insolent than was fitting, owing to the favours bestowed upon them. "Before you feed them," said the haughty patrician, "let them give up their tribunes."

When the plebeians learned what Coriolanus had said, their anger knew no bounds. They would have forced their way into the Senate-house and torn him to pieces, had not the tribunes protected him and calmed the fury of the people.

"Do not kill him," said the tribunes, "for that will only harm your cause. We will accuse him of having broken the sacred laws, and you shall yourselves pronounce his sentence."

But when the tribunes summoned Coriolanus to appear before them, he mocked both at them and at the people.

A patrician appear before the tribunes to be judged! That was to Coriolanus a foolish idea.

But although the patrician ignored the summons, the tribunes and the people met and declared that Coriolanus was banished from Rome.

Then Coriolanus was forced to leave the city. Hastening to the Volscians, he threw himself upon the mercy of their chief, Attius Tullius.

Tullius was willing to help the banished patrician to punish Rome, and soon an army, led by the chief and by Coriolanus, was on its way to the city. Town after town fell into the hands of the advancing army. At length it encamped only five miles from Rome.

The Senate, in alarm at the success of the Volscians, sent to beg for peace.

CORIOLANUS AND HIS MOTHER VETURIA

But Coriolanus sent back the Roman ambassadors, saying that unless all the towns taken from the Volscians in the last war were restored to them, peace would not be granted.

Such terms were scorned by the Senate, and it sent other ambassadors to beg for easier conditions. But Coriolanus refused even to see these messengers.

Then the priests, clad in their sacred robes, walked in solemn procession to the camp of the enemy, to try to appease the anger of the haughty patrician. But the efforts of the priests were vain.

Meanwhile, the matrons of Rome had been beseeching Jupiter to come to the aid of the city.

When the priests returned, having accomplished nothing, one of these matrons said: "We will go to Veturia and Volumnia and beseech them to go plead with Coriolanus. He cannot refuse to listen to his mother and his wife, for he loves them well."

Veturia, who was stricken with grief that her son could betray his country into the hands of the enemy, needed no persuasion to go to speak with him.

Clad in black garments, she and Volumnia with her little children, followed by a band of Roman matrons set out for the camp of the enemy.

Coriolanus, when he caught sight of his mother, leaped from his seat, and running quickly toward her, would have kissed her, as was his wont.

"O my mother, thou hast saved Rome, but thou hast lost thy son."

CORIOLANUS AND HIS MOTHER VETURIA

But she, putting him aside, bade him first answer her question.

"Am I the mother of Gaius Marcius," she asked reproachfully, "or a prisoner in the hands of the leader of the Volscians? Alas! had I not been a mother, my country had still been free." As his mother said these words, his wife and children fell at his knees and clung to him. His mother's words did what nothing else had been able to do, for the proud patrician could not bear to listen to her reproaches.

With tears in his eyes he cried: "O my mother, thou hast saved Rome, but thou hast lost thy son."

Then he led the Volscian army away from the city, and restored to the Romans the towns which the enemy had taken.

Some legends tell that the Volscians were so angry with Coriolanus for deserting them, that they slew him as a traitor; but others say that he lived in exile until he was an old man.

Weary of exile, he is said to have cried: "Only an old man knows how hard it is to live in a far country."

CHAPTER XXVIII

THE ROMAN ARMY IN A TRAP

WHILE the Romans were at war with the Volscians, another tribe, called the Æquians, poured down from their mountain fastnesses and plundered and destroyed their land.

In 459 B.C. peace was made with these fierce mountaineers, and Rome hoped that her borders would no longer be disturbed.

But the Æquians were a restless people. They soon broke the treaty, and, led by their chief Clœlius, pitched their camp on one of the spurs of the Alban hills, and began to burn and plunder as of old.

The Romans, furious at this breach of faith, sent an embassy to demand redress.

But Clœlius mocked at the Roman ambassadors, and laughingly bade them lay their complaints before the oak-tree, under which his tent was pitched.

The angry ambassadors took the oak and all the gods to witness that it was not they but the Æquians who had broken the treaty and begun the

THE ROMAN ARMY IN A TRAP

war. Then hastening back to Rome, they told how insolently they had been treated.

An army, with the Consul Minucius at its head, was at once dispatched to punish the Æquians.

Clœlius was a skilful general, and as the Roman army advanced he slowly retreated into a narrow valley. The Romans foolishly followed the retreating Æquians, as Clœlius intended that they should.

When the enemy was in the midst of the valley, hemmed in by steep hills on either side, Clœlius ordered a band of soldiers to guard the end by which the Romans had entered. Minucius was caught in a trap.

But before the Æquian general had secured the end of the valley, five Roman soldiers had escaped, and these, putting spurs to their horses, rode swiftly to Rome to tell how the Consul and his army were ensnared.

As the terrible news spread, Rome was stricken with panic. She feared the enemy would soon be at her very gates, and their second Consul was far away, fighting against the Sabines.

In their dismay, the Senate determined to appoint a Dictator, who would have supreme authority as long as the country was in danger.

Neither the Senate nor the people had any doubt as to whom they should turn to in their trouble. There was one man only who could save the country. He was a noble patrician who had already held positions of trust in the State, and he was, too, a proved and experienced general.

Cincinnatus, or the Crisp-Haired, was the name of the man to whom the Senate now determined to send. This strange name had been given to him because his hair clustered in curls around his head. The family of the Cæsars also received their name from their curls.

When the messengers from Rome reached the home of the patrician it was still early morning, but Cincinnatus was already at work in his fields. For he, as many a noble Roman in the olden days, cultivated his own estate. As the heat was great, Cincinnatus had thrown aside his toga, and was digging with bare arms.

One of this household ran to the fields to tell that messengers had arrived from Rome and wished to speak with him.

So, putting on his toga that he might receive the messengers of the State in suitable guise, the simple-minded patrician hastened to the house.

No sooner did he hear that his country was in danger, and that he had been chosen Dictator, than he speedily went to Rome, where the people greeted him with shouts of joy.

Cincinnatus lost no time in assembling a new army. Going to the Forum, he ordered that the shops should be closed, and all business cease until Rome was safe.

THE ROMAN ARMY IN A TRAP

All who could bear arms were told to assemble without delay on the Field of Mars, bringing with them twelve stakes for ramparts and food for five days.

That same evening, before the sun sank to rest, the new army had left Rome, and by midnight it was close to the valley in which Minucius, with his legions, lay entrapped.

Here the Dictator commanded his men to halt and throw their baggage in a heap. Then he ordered trenches to be dug round the enemy's camp, as noiselessly as might be, and the stakes they had brought with them to be driven into the ground.

When this was done, Cincinnatus bade his soldiers shout with all their strength. The noise aroused the Æquians, who sprang to their feet, and in terror seized their arms.

But the legions of Minucius also heard the shouts, and recognizing their own war-cry, they also grasped their weapons and attacked the Æquians.

They, seeing that they were surrounded by the enemy, with no way of escape possible, surrendered to the Dictator, begging him to be merciful.

Cincinnatus spared the lives of Clœlius and his soldiers, but he made the men pass under the yoke, after which they were allowed to find their way back to their mountain retreats.

The yoke was formed of three spears, and as the soldiers stooped to pass beneath this rough erection they had to lay aside their cloaks and surrender their arms.

Clœlius and the other leaders of the Æquians were kept prisoners.

Then the Dictator having freed his country from danger, returned in triumph to Rome. At the end of sixteen days he resigned the Dictatorship, and went back to his home, honoured by the people and crowned with glory.

Soon he was again to be seen digging or ploughing in his fields, contented as of yore.

CHAPTER XXIX

THE HATED DECEMVIRS

THE tribunes, you remember, were appointed to protect the people from the cruelty of the patricians.

As they were chosen from among the plebeians themselves, they did not understand the laws of their country as well as did the nobles, who had ever guarded them as they might have guarded a mystery.

So when the tribunes tried to gain justice for those who appealed to them, they often found their plans thwarted by the patricians, because of their superior knowledge of the law.

Thus, in spite of all that the tribunes could do, the people still suffered under the oppressions of the nobles.

So restless and discontented did the plebeians become, that in 451 B.C. three patricians were sent by the Senate to Greece to find out how the people were governed in Athens.

The nobles of Greece were wiser and more cultured than those of Rome, and may have been supposed to have discovered how best to rule those under them.

Whether the three ambassadors drank deep of the wisdom of the Greeks or no, they returned to Rome with a new plan for the government of the country.

It would be well, said the ambassadors, if, for a time, there should be neither Consuls nor tribunes. In their place ten men or decemvirs (decemvirs being the Latin for ten men) should be chosen from among patricians and plebeians alike, to rule the country and reform her laws.

Until now the laws had been unknown to the people. But the ambassadors said that the reformed laws should be written on tables of brass and be hung up in the place of assembly, so that the people might read and understand them.

The new laws were called the Laws of the Twelve Tables, and for many long years they were obeyed. In the time of Cicero, schoolboys had to learn these laws as part of their regular lessons, while they were, as we would say, in the lower forms.

Like the Consuls, the decemvirs were elected only for one year, each of them during the year having in turn full authority.

At first the decemvirs tried to please the people. They worked hard to reform the laws, and before their year of office came to an end, ten of the twelve tables had been revised.

THE HATED DECEMVIRS

It was determined that the decemvirs should be re-elected for the following year that they might finish the code of laws which they had begun.

But Appius Claudius, who had been the chief among the first year's decemvirs, was not satisfied that this should be so, and he saw to it that more plebeians should be elected among the second year's decemvirs.

He hoped by doing this to persuade the people that he was their friend, but before long it appeared that he was a true friend to neither patrician nor plebeian.

The new decemvirs, with Appius Claudius at their head, soon struck dismay into the hearts of the people by going to the Forum, with a band of one hundred and twenty lictors. The lictors carried with them not only rods, but, as in earlier days, axes were concealed among the rods, which was a sign that the decemvirs had power over life and death.

Nor did the decemvirs scruple to use their power, banishing or putting to death those who displeased or opposed them, and seizing their property for themselves. When their year of office was nearly ended, the decemvirs had not finished the code of laws as they were expected to have done.

It was soon plain why they had seen no reason for haste, for, when the year came to an end, the decemvirs refused to resign.

Both patricians and plebeians were indignant, while the Senate, angry that the decemvirs did not consult it, had already, for the most part, left Rome.

To add to the confusion in the country, war now broke out with the Sabines and the Æquians.

One of the Roman armies was to be led by a plebeian tribune, who was loved by the people, for he had fought for his country in one hundred and twenty battles. On his way to join his army, this brave soldier was murdered, it was said by the order of Appius Claudius. The soldiers were furious at the loss of their leader, and the hatred against the chief of the decemvirs increased each day.

CHAPTER XXX

THE DEATH OF VERGINIA

A𝚙𝚙ɪᴜs Cʟᴀᴜᴅɪᴜs did not go to the war. He stayed in Rome, and before long roused the temper of the people beyond control.

Verginius, a brave plebeian soldier, was with the army, and in his absence he had left his beautiful young daughter Verginia in the care of her nurse.

One day as the young girl was on her way to school in the Forum, Appius Claudius saw how beautiful she was, and he determined to take her away from her father and Icilius, to whom she was betrothed.

But although he did his utmost to persuade the maiden to go home with him, Verginia refused to leave her father's house.

Then Appius Claudius grew angry, and vowed to himself that he would take her away by foul means, since fair ones had failed.

So the tyrant ordered a man, named Marcus Claudius, to declare that Verginia was not a free

THE STORY OF ROME

Roman maiden, as Verginius had pretended, but was a slave belonging to himself.

This Marcus did, and then, seeing the girl one day in the Forum, he tried to lay hold of her. But her nurse cried aloud for help, so that a crowd quickly gathered, and hearing what had happened, it vowed to protect Verginia, until her father and her betrothed returned from the camp.

Then Marcus did as Appius Claudius had secretly bidden him. He said that he did not wish to harm the maiden, indeed, he was even willing to take the matter to law.

So, followed by the crowd, he led Verginia before the judge, who was no other than Appius Claudius.

Here Marcus announced that he could prove to Verginius that the maiden was not really his child, but belonged to a slave who lived in his house. Meanwhile he demanded that the maiden should be given into his charge.

But the crowd did not believe what Marcus said, nor did they care to let the young girl leave her home in her father's absence.

"Send to the camp for Verginius," cried the people, heedless of the angry looks of the judge. "Verginia is a free maiden, and shall stay with her friends until she is proved a slave."

With an effort, Appius Claudius concealed his real feelings, and, speaking with the dignity of a judge, he said: "The maiden belongs either to

Verginius or to Marcus. As Verginius is absent, Marcus shall take charge of her until her father returns, when the case shall again come before me."

But to such an unfair sentence the people refused to submit. So fierce was their temper that they would have forced Claudius to leave the city had he not reluctantly allowed Verginia to stay with her friends until the following day. If Verginius did not then appear at his tribunal Marcus should claim the maiden without delay, said Claudius.

Icilius had by this time returned to the city, and he at once sent to the camp, beseeching Verginius to let nothing keep him from at once coming to Rome.

But Claudius also sent a messenger to the camp, bidding his officers on no account to allow Verginius to leave his post.

Fortunately, the messenger sent by Icilius reached the camp first, and Verginius was already hastening to the city when his officer received the order sent by Claudius.

The next morning Claudius went to the Forum, sure that before the day was over he would have secured Verginia.

What was his surprise and anger to see that Verginius, whom he had believed to be safely detained at camp, was already there by the side of his daughter, accompanied by many Roman matrons and a crowd of people.

The judge could hear the voice of Verginius as he drew near. He was speaking to the people, and Claudius knew too well how easily the passions of the mob could be roused.

"It is not only my daughter that is not safe," Verginius was saying; "who will dare henceforth to leave their children in Rome if I am robbed of my child?"

As the matrons listened they wept, thinking of the fate that might overtake their own dear daughters.

Claudius was now much too angry to try to humour the people.

Bidding Verginius be silent, he at once gave his verdict that the maiden should be given to Marcus, until her father had proved that she was free-born.

The people stood silent, stunned for the moment by the wickedness of the judge. But as Marcus drew near to lead Verginia away, her friends gathered around her, refusing to let the man come near her.

Then, in his rage, Claudius bade his lictors drive the people away, and they, raising their axes, soon scattered the crowd, for it was unarmed.

Verginius, turning quietly to Claudius, asked that he might at least speak apart for a moment to his daughter and her nurse. His request was granted. Then the poor father in his desperate sorrow knew that there was but one thing to be done. To trust his daughter to these wicked men was not to be thought of, so, drawing her into his arms, he snatched a knife from one of the stalls, and whispered in her ear: "My child, there is no other way to free thee." Swift and sure, even as he spoke, he plunged the knife into his daughter's heart.

Turning to the unjust judge, Verginius cursed him to his face; then breaking through the crowd, he sped to the city gates, and mounting a horse, rode in hot haste back to the camp.

Meanwhile, Icilius lifted the dead body of the maiden, and bade the people see what the tyrant Claudius had done.

In fierce anger, the crowd rushed upon the lictors and a band of armed patricians and drove them from the Forum. Claudius, covering his face with his toga, fled, and for the time escaped with his life.

Verginius had no sooner reached the camp than he told his piteous tale to the army. Willingly the soldiers marched to Rome, led by the miserable father, and joined by another army, at the head of which was Icilius.

Together they entered Rome, and the soldiers deposed the decemvirs, while each army elected ten tribunes. They then marched out of the city, followed by the people, and encamped, as once before, on the Sacred Mount, leaving Rome to the patricians.

The Senate saw that it was time to act, for the decemvirs, it was plain, still hoped to keep the power they had grasped. So it forced them to resign, and then sent to the Sacred Mount to ask the plebeians what sentence they wished the tyrants to suffer.

Icilius demanded that the decemvirs should be put to death, the others were content that they should be banished from Rome. But Appius Claudius was not banished with the other decemvirs. He was sent to prison, where some say that he killed himself, but others assert that his enemies put him to death.

The people were now ready to return to the city, having obtained from the Senate a promise that they should have their tribunes as of old, and that the sacred laws should be again established.

In 445 B.C., about four years later, the plebeians succeeded in gaining new privileges. A law was passed allowing them to marry patricians, and this greatly pleased the people.

For many years the plebeians had wished to be allowed to stand for the Consulship. Now it was arranged that, instead of Consuls, from three to six military tribunes should be appointed, and for this office plebeians might stand.

Two of the duties however that had belonged to the Consuls were not given to the military tribunes, but kept for two new officers, called censors. The censors were to be chosen from among the patricians.

CHAPTER XXXI

THE FRIEND OF THE PEOPLE

Ten years after the decemvirs had been banished, there was a severe famine in Rome. The misery was terrible—men, women, and little children were dying in hundreds for lack of bread.

Faint and stricken, those who still managed to exist looked to the Senate for help.

So Minucius was appointed Master of the Markets, and did his utmost to succour the people, buying large supplies of corn from foreign countries and selling it to them for a small sum.

Should a family be found to have in its possession more corn than it needed for a month, Minucius ordered the surplus to be sold to those who were starving. Slaves were put on the smallest possible allowance of food.

But, in spite of the efforts of Minucius, the misery in the city was but little less than before. The poor still suffered the awful pangs of hunger, and many threw themselves into the river Tiber to escape from their desperate plight.

When the famine was at its height, Mælius, a rich plebeian, full of pity for the suffering he saw on every side, sent to Etruria for large quantities of corn and divided it among the ravenous folk.

Sometimes he gave his bounty freely, at other times he took a small sum of money for his goods.

The patricians, who, needless to say, were not starving, were not pleased to hear of the generous gifts of Mælius. Instead of being glad that the poor hungry people were being fed, they murmured that he was doing what Minucius had been appointed to do. The truth was, that the patricians were seized with an ugly passion called jealousy, and the more the people showed their gratitude to their benefactor, the angrier, the more jealous grew the patricians.

It was certain that Mælius was trying to win the favour of the people for his own ends, said his enemies one to the other. What was his ambition, they wondered, and how could they thwart it?

Minucius, who was more suspicious of the good plebeian than any one else, informed the Senate that Mælius held secret meetings in his house, where he had concealed a large number of arms. Moreover, he declared that Mælius had bribed the tribunes, and soon the Republic would be overturned, while the traitor would reign as king.

The Senate, alarmed by such a report, did not stay to find out if it were true or false, but at once determined to elect a Dictator.

THE FRIEND OF THE PEOPLE

Cincinnatus was once again entreated to leave his plough, to come to Rome and save his country.

So, lest his country should be betrayed by the honest plebeian, Cincinnatus hastened to the city, and appointing one named Ahala master of the horse, bade him summon Mælius to the Forum. Here the Dictator awaited the traitor, sitting on his tribunal.

Mælius knew all that had been said against him, and not wishing to be accused of treason, he refused to go with Ahala, and appealed to the people he had helped to support him.

But Ahala, furious that the plebeian dared to ignore his summons, drew a dagger and stabbed Mælius to death.

The people, horrified at the fate of their friend, rushed to the Forum and demanded that the Dictator should punish Ahala.

But this Cincinnatus refused to do, saying that even if Mælius had not been guilty of treason, yet he had deserved death for disobeying the command of the Dictator.

Too weak from want of food to persist that their benefactor should be avenged, the people, so some stories tell, soon grew quiet, for Minucius promised that the corn still stored at the house of Mælius should be sold to them at a low price.

But other stories say that the people refused to be satisfied until they had driven Ahala from the city.

It was in such selfish, wicked ways that the patricians sought to ruin the plebeians when they saw them gaining power and influence in the State.

CHAPTER XXXII

CAMILLUS CAPTURES THE CITY OF VEII

When Rome was in danger, the people, as you know, were called from their homes, their shops, and their fields to fight for their country. If the army was sent to besiege a town, it was one which could be taken in a short time, so that the soldiers were soon free to go home to plough their fields and tend their shops.

These soldier citizens received no wages for fighting for their country. They were but doing their duty in defending her or in adding to her dominions.

But the Romans were now growing ambitious to win greater glory by their conquests than they had yet done. To do this they knew that they must have a regular army that could stay in the field as long as was necessary. This army, too, would have to be paid by the State. It was, partly, at least, through the influence of Camillus, who was soon to be made Dictator, that a standing army was raised. Under him the army began to grow in power, nor did it cease to grow until at length it was able to control Senate and people alike.

In 406 B.C. the Romans began their more ambitious wars by besieging a beautiful city called Veii. Veii was in Etruria, about ten miles north of Rome.

For many years the inhabitants of this city had made raids along the borders of Rome, plundering and burning the countryside, until the people fled from their homes at the slightest rumour of their approach.

To destroy Veii was the only way to put an end to these constant and irritating border raids, and the siege was begun.

The town was built on the summit of a steep rock, three sides of which it was impossible to scale, and she was strongly fortified. Her population was larger and richer than that of Rome, while her buildings were grander and more beautiful.

Camillus was made Dictator during the siege, which lasted for ten long years.

I need not tell you of all that happened in the course of these ten years, but of the taking of the city many legends are told. Here is one of them.

It was autumn, and many of the lakes and brooks were dry, for little rain had fallen during the summer. But in the Lake of Alba the water began to rise in a strange, mysterious way.

First it rose to the foot of the mountains which encircled the lake, and that was wonderful

CAMILLUS CAPTURES THE CITY OF VEII

enough, but when the water reached the summit of the mountains that was marvellous indeed.

No waves disturbed the peace of the lake, but by and by the sheer weight of the water broke down part of the surrounding mountains, which had acted as a dam.

Then a great flood of water spread over fields and groves, and the Romans whispered to one another, "It is a sign from the gods," yet no one could tell what the sign might portend.

In the camp before Veii and in the city itself every one talked of the strange omen.

One day a Roman soldier talked with a Veian soldier, who was said to know the meaning of omens.

It was plain that the Veian did not think that the omen boded ill to his city, but the Roman did not find it easy to find out all that the other knew. Until he had done so, he determined not to let him go.

So, telling the Veian stories about his own country, he drew the wise man unaware farther and farther from the gates of Veii. As they drew near to the Roman camp, the soldier, who was tall and strong, seized the Veian in his arms and carried him before his captain. Before long the captive had been persuaded to tell all he knew.

"The city of Veii shall never be taken," said the wise man, "until the waters of the Lake of Alba are dried up."

It seemed to the Romans that the soothsayer should be sent to the Senate, that it might hear for itself what he had to say.

But when the Senate had listened to the Veian's words it was still uncertain what to do; so it sent messengers to the oracle of Delphi, which was the highest authority it knew. The oracle sent back a plain message. "Shut up the water of the lake in its ancient bounds, and keep it from flowing into the sea"; and the Romans at once began to carry out its instructions.

Channels were dug, and soon, with the help of great engineering works, the water of the lake was carried away to irrigate the plain.

Meanwhile, Camillus, finding that he would never be able to take Veii by storm, ordered underground passages to be made between his camp and the centre of the city. So secretly were the tunnels dug that the enemy never dreamed what was going on beneath their streets and temples.

At length the passage was complete, and Camillus led a picked band of soldiers along the tunnel, until they stood beneath the temple of Juno, the goddess of Veii.

While the Dictator was stealing underground with his followers, the walls of the city were being once again attacked.

The Veians, still ignorant of the mine beneath their feet, rushed to defend their walls against the enemy.

CAMILLUS CAPTURES THE CITY OF VEII

As the conflict raged, the King of Veii hastened to the temple of Juno to offer sacrifices, and to beseech the goddess to grant him victory.

"The victory will be won by him who lays the sacrifice on the altar," cried the priest who stood by the side of the king.

Camillus, who was just beneath the altar, heard the priest's words. Instantly he broke through the floor of the temple and entered the sacred building with his followers, who shouted and waved their weapons above their heads.

The Veians fled from the temple in dismay, while Camillus hastened to seize the sacrifice and fling it upon the altar.

Then, knowing that victory was assured, the band of Roman soldiers rushed to the gates of the city and flung them wide that their comrades might enter.

A little later, and the Veians were overwhelmed, and Veii was at length in the hands of the Romans.

CHAPTER XXXIII

THE STATUE OF THE GODDESS

When Veii had fallen into his hands, Camillus allowed not only the soldiers, but the citizens of Rome to plunder the city, for he had agreed with the Senate that all the people should share in the spoil.

As he stood on a high tower watching the sack of the city which had resisted Rome for ten years, Camillus wept for pity. Then, covering his face with his toga, he prayed that if his great victory had made him proud, Jupiter would punish, not Rome or the army, but only him, and that "with as little hurt as might be."

Turning then to his right, as was the custom after prayer, the Dictator slipped and fell to the ground. This, he believed, was the "little hurt" sent to him by the god.

Many treasures were taken from the conquered city to Rome, but none more sacred than the statue of Juno.

THE STATUE OF THE GODDESS

Camillus ordered some young men to clothe themselves in white robes, and then to go to the temple to remove the statue.

It was a solemn moment when the youths stood before the image, scarce venturing to look upon it, lest they should be punished for their boldness.

One of them, half mocking, yet, it may be, half in earnest too, said: "O Juno, wilt thou go to Rome?"

Clear through the temple echoed the voice of the goddess: "I will."

Then reverently the young men lifted the image, but to their astonishment it was so light that they felt as though their arms were empty, and the goddess was walking by their side.

In safety they reached Rome with the wondrous image, and Camillus built a temple on the Aventine hill, in which henceforth the statue of Juno stood.

When the Dictator returned to Rome he enjoyed a great triumph. Dressed in the garments of Jupiter, he drove through the gates in a chariot drawn by four white horses, his soldiers following him, shouting the praises of their leader.

But the people of Rome were displeased with the Dictator, for none but kings might drive in a chariot drawn by four white horses.

Soon they even hated Camillus, for he sided with the Senate against those tribunes who had been faithful to the plebeians. Moreover, he had vowed to give a tenth of the spoil taken at Veii to the god Apollo. At the time that the city was sacked, it seemed that the Dictator had forgotten his vow. When he remembered it, the people had spent or parted with their share of the spoil, so Camillus forced them to give up the tenth part of their goods. At this the poor folk grumbled, as indeed they had some cause to do.

But much as the people hated Camillus, they could not do without him. When war broke out against a people called the Falerians, he was elected as a military tribune, and at once marched away with his army to besiege the strongly fortified town of Falerii.

In his heart Camillus hoped that if he was successful in taking the city, the Romans would forget their anger against him.

CHAPTER XXXIV

THE SCHOOLMASTER WHO PROVED A TRAITOR

THE Falerians were not disturbed when the Roman army pitched its camp without their walls, not even although they knew that so great a general as Camillus was at its head.

Their city was well fortified, and so, sure of being able to defend it, they guarded their walls, and then went on with their work and with their play as was their wont.

But there was a traitor within the walls of Falerii, and through his treachery misfortune well-nigh overtook the city.

The traitor was a schoolmaster. He thought that it would be an easy matter to betray the city to the Romans by the aid, unknown to themselves, of his pupils.

Before the siege began he had been used to take the children outside the city walls for their daily walks and exercises.

He continued to do so after the Romans had laid siege to the city, but at first he did not venture far from the gates, lest the children should be afraid.

But, little by little, as they became careless of the enemy, the schoolmaster took them nearer and nearer to the Roman camp. Then one day, before the boys were aware, their master had led them close to the enemy's lines and had asked to be taken before Camillus.

He was admitted to the presence of the tribune, and pointing to his pupils the traitor said: "I have brought you the children of Falerii. With them in your power, you will soon be able to make what terms you please with the citizens. They will give up their city without a struggle to secure the safe return of their children."

But Camillus was not the man that the traitor had dreamed. He looked with scorn upon the treacherous schoolmaster, then, turning to those who stood near, he said: "War indeed is of necessity attended with much injustice and violence. Certain laws, however, all good men observe, even in war itself, nor is victory so great an object as to induce us to incur for its sake obligations for base and impious acts. A great general should rely on his own valour and not on other men's vice."

Camillus then bade his officers strip off the schoolmaster's clothes and tie his hands behind him. The children were then given rods and told to beat their master back to the city.

Meanwhile, the Falerians had missed the children. Fathers and mothers, distraught with grief, rushed to the walls, to the gates, but nowhere was there any trace of their boys. Cries and lamentations filled the city.

Suddenly the cries were hushed. Hark! that was a joyful shout! And then another and yet another rent the air.

The children were there, in sight, running back, merrily as it seemed, from the direction of the enemy's camp.

Then silence fell upon the parents, for as the children came nearer a strange picture was visible.

Their boys had rods in their hands, and they were chasing and beating a miserable, naked man, who looked like the honourable schoolmaster. But surely they must be mistaken. . . .

A moment or two later the children rushed through the gates, and in breathless haste told to their parents all that had befallen them, and how Camillus himself had bidden them chase the traitor schoolmaster back to the city.

Not only the parents, but all the citizens of Falerii were so pleased with the kindness Camillus had shown to the children that they sent ambassadors to him, offering to give up to the Romans whatever he chose to ask.

Again Camillus showed how generous a foe he could be, for he made peace with the Falerians, and demanding from them only a sum of money, he took his army back to Rome.

But the soldiers, who had hoped to gain much booty in Falerii, were angry. When they reached Rome empty-handed, they grumbled against their general, and told the people he was not their friend, for he cared for nothing save his own welfare.

Then his enemies determine to get rid of Camillus. So they accused him of keeping more than his share of the spoils of Veii. Even now, so they said, valuable brass gates, to which he had no right, were in his possession.

Camillus had many friends as well as many enemies, and he entreated those who trusted him to prove that the accusations brought against him were false. But all they could promise to do was to help him pay, should the Senate insist on fining him.

But this did not satisfy the brave Roman, who knew that he was guiltless. He determined to leave the city for which he had done so much, without waiting to hear his sentence pronounced.

As he passed through the gates, he turned, and stretching out his hands toward the Capitol, he cried to the gods: "If not for evil I have done," he cried, "but through the hatred of my enemies I have been driven into exile, grant that the Romans may soon grow sorry and send for Camillus to help them when trouble befalls."

And his prayer was answered. For when, in 390 B.C., the Gauls descended upon Rome, soldiers

THE SCHOOMASTER WHO PROVED A TRAITOR

and citizens alike demanded that the Senate should send to Camillus and beseech him to come to help them in their dire need.

CHAPTER XXXV

THE BATTLE OF ALLIA

THE inhabitants of Gaul, who dwelt in the country we now call France, were tall, fair, blue-eyed warriors. Long before the time of which I am going to tell you, they had crossed the Alps and made themselves masters of Northern Italy.

Now, in 389 B.C., they turned to the south, crossed the Apennines, and came pouring down into the valleys of Etruria. The city of Clusium, only a few days' march from Rome, was the first to attract the barbarians.

There was peace at this time between Rome and Etruria, and the inhabitants of Clusium, in fear of the fierce-looking Gallic warriors, besought Rome to come to their aid.

The Senate at once sent three patricians as ambassadors to the Gauls, warning them not to attack the allies of Rome.

But the haughty barbarians, heedless of the ambassadors' words, at once demanded from the Etruscans land on which they and their families

THE BATTLE OF ALLIA

might settle. When their request was refused, they began to fight.

Now the Roman ambassadors had no right to join in the battle, for just as they were protected by their mission from being attacked, so they were forbidden to attack others.

But forgetting, in their anger with the Gauls, that they were ambassadors, the three Romans joined in the defence of Clusium, and unfortunately slew one of the Gallic chiefs and took his armour.

Brennus, the King of the Gauls, was so angry with the envoys that he at once withdrew from Clusium, and marched with his whole army through the valley of the Tiber toward Rome. He was determined to punish the city for the folly of her ambassadors.

The Romans at once marched out to meet the enemy, and in July, 390 B.C., near the Allia, about ten miles from Rome, a terrible battle was fought.

Although the Roman army was but forty thousand strong, while the barbarians numbered seventy thousand, yet the Romans had no fear. Against such uncouth foes they were sure to win the victory. Thus in their insolence and pride spoke the warriors of Rome.

But the battle day—it was the 18th of the month—was one that was never to be forgotten by the Roman legions.

Shouting their strange, fierce war-cries, the Gauls rushed upon the foe, while the Romans, dismayed at the wild appearance of the gigantic Gauls, and distracted by their war-cries, were seized with sudden panic. Without even attempting to fight, they turned and fled.

Pursued by the terrible barbarians, many of the fugitives plunged in despair into the river Tiber, and were drowned by the weight of their armour; many others were overtaken and slain. Only a remnant of the army reached Rome, for most of the fugitives who escaped took refuge at Veii.

The Gauls themselves were astonished at their easily won victory, for the fame of the Roman legions had reached even these barbarous tribes.

In Rome the Battle of Allia was henceforth a name of ill omen, nor would the Romans ever undertake a new adventure on the 18th of July, lest it should be doomed to failure, by the evil influence of that fatal day. For many long years, the Romans, who feared no other foe, trembled at the name of the barbarians.

CHAPTER XXXVI

THE SACRED GEESE

ROME, when she heard of the defeat of Allia was stricken with terror. Her walls were left unguarded, her gates open, for the one thought of the citizens was flight.

And in truth, so fearful were they lest the Gauls should reach the city and find them still there, that they crowded out of the gates, across the bridge to the Janiculum.

Some few sacred images they stayed to bury, and the vestal virgins tarried to take with them the sacred fire which must not be allowed to die, but many of the most sacred treasures of Rome were left to perish by the hands of the barbarians.

So the city was left desolate, her gates open to the enemy. Only in the Capitol, the temple of the gods, a band of armed men kept guard, and with them stayed the priests, who refused to leave the sacred building, and the Senate.

No others were left in Rome save some old patricians, who long years before had been Consuls, and had led the legions of the Republic to many a hard-won battlefield.

These clad themselves in their richest robes, then, after praying to the gods, they walked to the Forum and seated themselves, each in his ivory chair, there to await what the gods should send.

Three days after the Battle of Allia, the Gauls, having feasted as was their custom after a victory, appeared before the city.

The gates were open, the walls unmanned, and within the city all was silent as the grave. Was it a trap? Did an ambush lie in wait? Thus the Gauls hesitated, questioning one another.

At length they ventured into the city—not a single citizen was to be seen. On through the desolate streets wandered the bewildered warriors, until at length they stood in the Forum.

There, seated in chairs of ivory, silent and still as statues, sat a number of strange, venerable old men.

King Brennus himself came to the Forum to gaze at these still images of men, and was amazed to see them thus unmoved in his presence.

He noticed that "they neither rose at his coming, nor so much as changed colour or countenance, but remained without fear or concern, leaning upon their staves, and sitting quietly, looked at each other."

For a long time the Gauls gazed in silence at the quiet figures. Then, one of the soldiers, bolder

Seated in chairs of ivory, sat a number of strange, venerable old men.

than the others, drew near to Papirius, stretched out his hand, and slowly stroked the long white beard of the old patrician.

This was more than Papirius could bear. He, a Roman senator, to be touched by a barbarian! Quick as thought he raised his staff and struck the Gaul a blow.

The strange, silent images were alive then! They could move!

Swiftly the barbarian drew his sword, and a moment later Papirius fell from his ivory chair, wounded to death.

No longer awed by the silent images, the Gauls now fell upon the other patricians and killed them too. Then for days they sacked the city, and at length burned it to the ground, angry that the Capitol was held against them.

The Capitol stood on a hill, steep and impossible to scale, save at one point.

Again and again the Gauls tried to storm this one approach, but the brave defenders drove them back, killing some of their number. Then the Gauls determined to besiege the Capitol, but days and weeks passed, and still they seemed no more likely to take it than before. And now their provisions were beginning to run short.

Meanwhile, the Roman soldiers who had fled from Allia and taken refuge in Veii, began to be ashamed of themselves. Surely they ought to go to the help of their comrades who were so manfully

THE SACRED GEESE

holding the Capitol. If they had but a leader they would go.

Then all at once they remembered Camillus, who was still in exile. They would ask him to come back and lead them as of old to victory.

So they sent to beg Camillus to come to Veii and take command of the soldiers. But Camillus refused to come unless the Senate recalled him and asked him to deliver Rome.

At first it seemed that there was no way to reach the Senate. It was shut up in the Capitol. But a young soldier, named Cominius, hoping to retrieve the disgrace of his flight from Allia, offered to try to scale the rock and reach the citadel.

Disguising himself as a poor man, and carrying corks under his old clothes, he reached the Tiber as it was growing dark. The bridge, as he had expected, was guarded by the Gauls. To cross it was impossible.

So, taking off his clothes, he tied them on to his head, and laying the corks he had brought in the river, he swam with their help safely across and slipped unnoticed into the city.

Cominius, fortunately, was light and agile. He actually succeeded in scaling the rock on which the Capitol was built, as only a bold and skilful climber could. When he reached the summit in safety he called to the astonished guards and begged to be taken to the Senate.

It was pleased to see the brave youth, and after listening to his tale at once bade Cominius return and let Camillus know that Rome not only recalled him from exile, but appointed him Dictator. So Cominius hastened back to Veii with the good news, and because the soldiers were eager to fight, messengers were sent in hot haste to Camillus to tell him the decision of the Senate, and to bring him back to Veii.

Soon Camillus had twenty thousand men ready to follow him to Rome.

Meanwhile the Capitol was all but taken by the Gauls.

The morning after Cominius had clambered down the cliff, the barbarians noticed that the shrubs had been crushed, that bushes had had their branches torn, that the soil had been loosened on the side of the rock.

It was clear that some one had either climbed up to the Capitol, or had come down the terrible descent. And if that was possible, why should not they climb the cliff, and at last capture the Capitol?

So when night had come, the Gauls began their dangerous task. Up and up they climbed as noiselessly as might be, up and up, until they had nearly reached the top.

At the summit there was no wall, no sentinel. Even the watchdogs heard no sound and slept on undisturbed.

THE SACRED GEESE

Close to the top of the rock, however, stood the temple of Jupiter, Juno, and Minerva, the three guardian deities of Rome. Without the temple, geese, sacred to Juno, had their home. Although the defenders of the Capitol were starving, yet they never dreamed of touching the birds that were sacred to the goddess, "which thing proved their salvation."

Up and up climbed the Gauls, and no one heard them as they drew near to the summit of the rock, no one save the sacred geese. They, divine birds as they were, began to cackle and to flap their wings, and to make as much noise as geese can make.

Manlius, the captain of the guard, who slept near the temple, awoke startled to hear the din caused by the sacred birds. Springing swiftly from the couch on which he had lain wrapped in his military cloak, he seized his arms and ran to the top of the cliff. As he ran he shouted to his men to follow as quickly as they could.

As Manlius reached the edge of the rock, lo, the face of a Gaul peered at him over the summit.

The Roman was but just in time. Dashing his shield at the enemy, he hurled him down the cliff, and he, as he fell, knocked against those who were behind, so that they also were carried down the face of the rock, which they had climbed with so much difficulty. Thus the Capitol was saved by the sacred geese.

The defenders of the citadel were grateful to Manlius for acting so promptly, and although they were all suffering from hunger, each one agreed to give him, from his own slender store, one day's allowance of food. This consisted of half a pound of corn and a measure holding five ounces of wine.

At length a day came when the brave folk in the Capitol must either die of starvation or surrender. So the senators sent to King Brennus and offered to pay him a large sum of money if he would raise the siege.

As the Gauls too were suffering from famine, the king was willing to accept a ransom, but he demanded the large sum of one thousand pounds of gold.

Only by borrowing treasures from the temple, and receiving gifts of golden ornaments from Roman matrons, could the sum be found.

In bitterness of spirit the Romans went down to the Forum on the day appointed, and began to lay their treasures on the scales.

Suddenly they noticed that the weights which the barbarians were using on the scales, were false.

But when they complained, the king threw his sword into the scale, crying scornfully, "Væ Victis," "Woe to the Conquered."

At that moment, Rome was saved from the shame of paying a ransom, for Camillus with his army marched into the Forum.

THE SACRED GEESE

As Dictator, the supreme power was his, and he had the right to forbid even what the Senate had allowed.

He looked at the gold ornaments lying in the scales, and bade the Romans take them back, for, said Camillus proudly, "It is usual with Romans to pay their debts, not in gold, but in iron." By these words the Dictator meant that the Romans used their weapons to settle their quarrels.

Then, forcing the Gauls out of the city which they had ruined, Camillus and his army fought so fiercely against their enemy that not a single man was left alive to tell the tidings to his countrymen.

King Brennus himself was slain, and as he fell he heard the Romans shout in triumph the words he himself had so lately used, "Væ Victis," "Woe to the Conquered."

CHAPTER XXXVII

THE CITY IS REBUILT

When the Dictator had cut the Gallic host to pieces, he returned to Rome. The brave defenders of the Capitol went out to meet their deliverer, tears of joy streaming down their gaunt, hungry-looking faces. Scarcely yet could they believe that they were saved.

But when they saw the vestal virgins returning to their temple, bearing with them the fire they tended, still undimmed, and the priests also coming back to the city, they grew quiet and unafraid, for were not the ministers of the gods again in their midst?

Before aught else, the sacred places that had been pulled down must be restored. It was difficult amid the ruins of the city to find the very spot on which the temples had stood, but they were rebuilt as nearly as could be in the places where the people had been used to see them.

As the touch of the barbarian had made the sites unholy, they were dedicated anew to the gods, with solemn rites and sacrifices.

THE CITY IS REBUILT

Under the buildings which had been destroyed some relics were found, as by a miracle unharmed. One of these was the staff or crook used by Romulus when he dwelt upon Mount Palatine, a careless shepherd lad, while another was the Laws of the Twelve Tables.

But the ancient records of the history of the seven kings were never found, and this is why the story of the early days of Rome is so full of fancy as well as of fact.

When the sacred places were restored, many of the poorer citizens felt that they had done all that was needful. They shrank from the labour of rebuilding the city. Many of them, too, had houses of their own in Veii, which they had built while the Gauls were in Rome. They wished to return to their new homes and found a new city.

Camillus was grieved that the people should wish to desert Rome, the city of their birth, and he appealed to them by the things they held most sacred to remain.

Was it not in Rome that their beautiful temples stood? Was it not here that they had ofttimes heard the sacred voices of the gods? The people, touched by the words of Camillus, wavered. At that moment a band of soldiers halted without the Comitium or place of Assembly, the centurion calling to his standard-bearer: "Pitch thy standard here, for this is the best place to stop at."

Surely such words were not spoken by chance, thought the citizens. Surely they were words sent by the gods, bidding them to stay in Rome.

In this strange way the die was cast, and the people, throwing aside their indolence, began to build, pulling down the houses at Veii and bringing the stones to Rome to complete the rebuilding of the city.

Even with the help of material from Veii, the plebeians were forced to borrow money from the patricians before their houses were finished, and their shops and farms replenished.

As in earlier days, the patricians showed no mercy to their debtors, and when they could not pay, threw them into prison or sold them as bondsmen.

Now Manlius, who had saved the Capitol from the Gauls, was a rich man, and the troubles of the poor folk made him sad.

One day he saw a famous centurion, who had fought by his side in many a battle, being dragged from the Forum to prison, because he was unable at once to pay some haughty patrician what he owed.

Manlius could not look on at such cruelty and do nothing. He hastened to the spot, paid his old comrade's debt, and set him free. This was only one of the kindnesses by which he won from the grateful people the title, "Father of the Commons."

The patricians soon heard that Manlius was winning the hearts of the people. Jealous as ever, they determined to crush him.

THE CITY IS REBUILT

On one pretext or another he was arrested, and when he stood before the assembly of the people he was accused of treason, for he had, so his enemies said, tried to make himself king.

Manlius was standing in the Forum when he was accused, and looking up he could see the Capitol.

Pointing to the temple, Manlius appealed to the gods and to the gratitude of the Romans to save him. And the people, remembering all that he had done, refused to condemn him, in spite of the anger of the patricians.

But the patricians were still determined to destroy the Father of the Commons. The very name was an offence to them.

They succeeded in once more bringing Manlius to trial; but this time they arranged that it should take place in a grove, from which no glimpse of the Capitol could be caught.

Here he was sentenced to death, and as his crime was treason, it was decreed that he should be thrown down the Tarpeian Rock.

The struggle between the patricians and the plebeians lasted for nearly half a century after the death of Manlius.

But in the year 376 B.C., and for ten years afterwards, a wise man named Licinius did all that he could to make better laws for the people. The laws of this tribune were called the Licinian Laws.

Let me tell you three of the laws by which Licinius tried to gain fair treatment for the plebians.

He made it unlawful for the patricians to take an unjust rate of interest from the poor. As the patricians had grown rich with the money that they had extorted from the plebeians, they disliked this Licinian law. But to the poor it was of the greatest use.

Public land, which belonged to the poor as much as to the rich, had in the past been seized by the powerful and already wealthy patricians. This, said the tribune, should no longer be allowed. The land should henceforth be divided justly.

And of all these new laws, perhaps the most important was this, that one Consul should be chosen from among the plebeians. The patricians did their utmost to prevent this law from being passed, and when they were forced to yield, they did so with a bad grace.

To make it clear that they still had privileges which were not shared by the people, they decreed that certain new magistrates should be elected. These new magistrates were called prætors, and only patricians could be chosen for this new office.

Yet even so, the Licinian Laws improved the position of the plebeians, and were considered by them to be both wise and just.

CHAPTER XXXVIII

CAMILLUS SETS THE CAMP OF THE VOLSCIANS ON FIRE

WHILE Rome was still at work repairing the damage which the Gauls had inflicted on her city, the Volscians encamped within twenty miles of her gates. They hoped to attack the city while she was unprepared for war.

But an army at once set out to meet the enemy. Before the Romans were aware, however, their camp was surrounded by the Volscians, and they were unable either to fight or to retire.

Camillus, who had again been appointed Dictator, summoned every Roman who could bear arms to follow him. He then marched to within a short distance of the camp of the Volscians. Here he ordered fires to be lighted, that the imprisoned army might know that help was at hand.

But the Volscians saw the fires as well as the Romans, and at once began to strengthen their camp with a strong barricade, made out of the trunks of trees.

Then, knowing that their numbers would soon be reinforced, they were satisfied that the enemy could do them no harm.

But Camillus did not mean to wait until their allies joined them. He determined at once to set fire to the wooden barricade that the Volscians had built around their camp.

Ordering part of his force to attack the camp on one side, the Dictator withdrew the rest of the army to that side of the camp from which the wind blew. He then bade the soldiers fling lighted torches in among the wooden defences.

The flames, blown by the wind, quickly spread from stake to stake until they reached the camp itself.

There was no water at hand to quench the fire, and the Volscians were soon driven from their tents, to find themselves in the hands of the Romans, who cut them down without mercy.

Camillus then ordered the flames to be put out, that the soldiers might pillage what was still unconsumed by the fire.

Leaving his son to guard the prisoners, the Dictator was soon marching to Sutrium, which town was besieged by the Etruscans.

But before Camillus reached the city, he met a pitiful band of men, women and children, who had already been banished from the town by the victorious enemy.

CAMILLUS SETS CAMP OF THE VOLSCIANS ON FIRE

Their homes were plundered, their treasures were in the enemy's hands. With nothing left, save only the clothes they wore, they were wandering through the country in search of shelter.

Camillus was grieved for the misery of these poor folk. When he saw that his soldiers also pitied them, he determined still to go to the city, that he might wrest it once again from the Etruscans, and restore the Sutrians to their homes.

He foresaw that the victorious soldiers would be feasting, that the gates would be unguarded.

And so it was. Camillus had no difficulty in seizing the gates and manning the walls of Sutrium. Then he ordered his soldiers to fall upon the merry-makers, who were celebrating their victory with song and feast. Many of the Etruscans surrendered, while others waited like cowards to be slain. Sutrium was thus taken twice in one day.

CHAPTER XXXIX

THE BATTLE ON THE BANKS OF THE ANIO

THE battle on the banks of the Anio took place when Camillus was no longer young, and when he was attacked with illness.

Yet the Senate, anxious to have his help, would not listen as he pleaded that he was unable for the duties of a tribune.

But when war broke out with the Volscians and the Prænestines, it sent another tribune with Camillus, to lead the army, so that the old man's strength might be spared. Lucius Furius was the name of the tribune who accompanied Camillus.

The two tribunes encamped near the enemy, Camillus hoping to avoid battle until he was stronger.

But Lucius wished to win glory on the field, and was impatient to fight.

The old warrior, too generous to thwart the young tribune, agreed that he should lead the army

THE BATTLE ON THE BANKS OF THE ANIO

to the field; yet he feared that the rashness of Lucius might lead to defeat.

Owing to his feeble health, Camillus himself stayed in the camp, with only a small company of soldiers. But he could see all that was happening on the battlefield.

As he had feared, Lucius proved too rash a leader, and the Roman army was soon in dire confusion and flying toward the camp.

Such a sight was more than the brave old warrior could endure. Leaping from his couch, he bade those who were near to follow him.

Then as the fugitives saw their old general, who had so often led them to victory, forcing his way toward the enemy, shame stayed their flight.

Swiftly they rallied, and turning, followed Camillus, so that the Volscians and the Prænestines were in their turn forced to flee.

The next day Camillus led the whole army against the foe, and fought so fiercely that before long the enemy was in full retreat. Many of the fugitives sought refuge in their camp. But the Romans followed, and driving them from the shelter of the tents, put them to death.

Then, having won these three victories, Camillus returned in triumph to Rome, carrying with him much plunder.

But the old warrior was not yet to be allowed to rest.

In 381 B.C. war broke out in Tusculum, which town had long been faithful to Rome, and Camillus was sent to put down the rebellion. He was told to choose one of his five colleagues to help him.

Each tribune longed for the glory of accompanying Camillus, but his choice fell upon Lucius, who had so nearly lost a battle in the last war. Perhaps the great general wished to give the tribune a chance to retrieve his mistake.

When the Tusculans heard that Camillus was approaching their gates with a large army, they speedily repented of their rebellion and laid down their arms.

Ploughmen hastened back to their fields, shepherds to their sheep. Tradesmen, too, were soon again busy in their workshops, children were in their places at school, while the well-to-do citizens walked about the streets in their usual dress, unarmed.

When the tribunes arrived at Tusculum, they were welcomed by the magistrates with every sign of pleasure, and entertained as hospitably as though they were eagerly expected guests.

Camillus was too wise to be deceived by these simple folk, yet seeing their penitence, he was sorry for them.

So, instead of punishing them, he merely bade them send ambassadors to the Senate to beg for forgiveness, promising himself to speak on their behalf.

THE BATTLE ON THE BANKS OF THE ANIO

The Senate proved merciful. For the city was forgiven, and her inhabitants were made Roman citizens.

About five years later, in 376 B.C., the Latins were defeated so severely by the Romans, that they were glad to enter into alliance with their conquerors. Then for nearly ten years Rome enjoyed greater peace than had been her lot for long. It was during these years that Licinius made the laws of which I have told you.

But in 367 B.C., the Gauls, who were still dreaded by the Romans, marched with a large army toward Rome, laying waste the country through which they passed.

Camillus, although now eighty years of age, was again made Dictator.

Before leading his army against the dreaded foe, the Dictator ordered smooth and polished helmets of iron to be made. In other days he had seen that the swords of the Gauls swept down with relentless force on the heads and shoulders of the Romans. Now he hoped that their blows would glance off the smooth surface of the iron helmets, or be broken.

The Roman shields, too, were made of wood, but Camillus ordered their rims to be strengthened with bands of brass.

With his army thus equipped, the Dictator felt that victory was secure.

The Gauls, already laden with the plunder that they had taken on their march, were encamped near the river Anio.

Within sight of the camp was a hill with hollows, behind which it would be easy to hide from the enemy. To this hill Camillus led his men, carefully concealing the larger number of them behind these hollows so that from the Gallic camp the Roman soldiers seemed but a small company.

The Gauls were indeed completely deceived. It seemed to them that the Romans did not mean to attack them; that they had fled for safety to the hills.

Camillus, wishing to lure the Gauls into danger, never stirred, even when the enemy ventured close to his trenches in search of plunder.

Soon, careless of the enemy, the barbarians scattered over the country in search of forage, while those left in the camp spent day and night in song and feast.

Then the Dictator knew that the time for action had come.

He sent a small company of his men to harass the enemy, while early the following morning he marched with his whole army to the foot of the hill.

The barbarians were dismayed when they saw so great a host in battle array, and before they could form into their proper ranks the enemy was upon them.

Shouting their wild battle-cries, the Gauls then drew their swords and fought with fury. But

THE BATTLE ON THE BANKS OF THE ANIO

their swords were soon twisted or broken, as they slid off the polished helmets worn by the Roman soldiers. To complete their discomfort, the javelins which Camillus now bade his soldiers throw at the enemy's shields, stuck fast in them, until they grew too heavy to wield.

As their swords were useless, the Gauls sought to pull the javelins out of their shields, that they might use the Romans' weapons against the enemy.

But Camillus saw what they meant to do, and ordered his men to advance swiftly, and cut the Gauls to pieces before they could carry out their plan. The foremost were speedily hewn down, while those who could fled over the plains, for the hills were already held by the Romans.

So sure of victory had the Gauls been, that they had left their camp unguarded, and it too was soon captured.

Thirteen years before, the defeat at Allia and the sack of Rome had filled the Romans with a superstitious fear of the fierce Gallic warriors.

The battle now won by the banks of the river Anio for ever put an end to their dread of the barbarians.

Camillus returned once more in triumph to Rome, to find yet another service he could do for the country he had served so loyally and loved so well.

Civil war was on the point of breaking out, for the people, acting according to one of the Licinian laws, had chosen Sextus, a plebeian, to be Consul.

The Senate and patricians were not at all ready to carry out this law. Indeed, it seemed that they would rather fight than let the people have their will. As the plebeians refused to give up their new-won privilege, the city was in an uproar.

But Camillus had great influence with the Senate, and he persuaded it to yield to the just demand of the people. So the angry passions of the patricians and the plebeians were allayed, and Sextus became the first plebeian Consul.

In the following year, 366 B.C., a pestilence swept over Italy, and in Rome, among many who perished was the brave old soldier Camillus.

CHAPTER XL

THE CURTIAN LAKE

THE pestilence, to which Camillus fell a prey, did not cease until 361 B.C.

During the second year, the superstitious folk, of whom there were many, were startled by strange omens.

The Tiber overflowed its banks. This was perhaps not so unusual as to alarm the citizens of Rome, but when the waters streamed into the Circus it was certainly strange. For at that very time games were being held there, in the hope of propitiating the gods, so that the pestilence might be stayed.

But the flood speedily put an end to the games, and the people wondered if this was the answer of the gods.

The flood was alarming, but still more so was an earthquake that took place before the people had forgotten their fears. It is supposed that the earthquake gave rise to the well-known legend of the Curtian Lake.

For it was after the shock that a gulf wide and deep yawned in the Forum. The Romans believed that the gods who had sent the pestilence had now opened this terrible abyss in their market-place.

In vain the terrified people tried to fill up the gulf. However much they threw into it, there it was, deep, dark, mysterious as before.

Then the Romans went to their priests and begged them to learn from the gods how the gulf might be closed.

The answer, when it came, seemed almost as perplexing as had been the problem. "Never will the awful chasm disappear until into it has been thrown the best and truest strength of Rome."

What was the true strength of the city? With grave faces and anxious hearts the people pondered the answer of the gods.

Suddenly the truth flashed into the mind of a noble youth named Curtius, who was known among his fellows as a brave and gallant soldier.

"The true strength of Rome," said Curtius, "can lie in naught save in the arms and in the valour of her children. To think otherwise would shame us all."

So, believing that he had discovered the will of the gods, the noble youth donned his armour, mounted his steed, and plunged headlong into the abyss.

A great crowd had gathered in the Forum to see what Curtius meant to do. For a moment the people stood in silence, awed by the fate of the young Roman, and full of admiration for his deed.

Then, rousing themselves, they took offerings of gold and precious ornaments and flung them after the bold rider and his horse, and as they did so, slowly the gulf closed. And since that day the place where once the chasm yawned has been called the Curtian Lake.

Before the plague was subdued, in 361 B.C., the Gauls once more invaded Roman lands, and a terrible battle was again fought, near the river Anio.

Titus Manlius engaged in single combat with one of the barbarians, who was strong and tall as a giant. Yet so bravely did the Roman fight that the giant was slain. Then Manlius took from the neck of his foe a gold collar. As the Latin word for necklet is "torques," Manlius and his descendants were ever after called Torquati.

When the Gauls saw that their champion was slain, they retreated; yet for a year and a half they continued to harass the Romans. But in 358 B.C. they were defeated so severely that those who were left after the battle were glad to escape from the neighbourhood of Rome.

Ten years later, however, the Gauls were once again laying waste the plains and coasts of Latium.

Furius Camillus, son of the great Camillus, was Consul, and as his colleague had died, he alone was responsible for the safety of the State.

He, like his father, was a brave soldier, and his army soon scattered the Gauls.

During the battle, as Valerius fought in single combat with one of the strongest of the barbarians, a strange sight was seen.

A crow circled over the heads of the combatants, then suddenly it flew down and perched on the helmet of the Roman.

The clashing of swords, the cries of the barbarians, did not disturb the bird. It sat on the helmet of Valerius as still as though it was perched on a tree in the forest.

But by and by this strange crow began to watch what Valerius and the Gaul were doing. Seizing its chance, it darted again and again between the combatants, flapping its wings and tearing with beak and claws at the face and eyes of the barbarian.

Unable to see what he was doing with his sword, as well as unable to avoid the thrusts of his foe, the Gaul tried in vain to get rid of the bird.

At length, worn out with the unequal struggle, the barbarian fell, and Valerius was hailed as victor.

The crow, as though content with the result of the battle, now flew away and was seen no more; but from that time Valerius was called Corvus, corvus being the Latin word for a crow.

After the victory of Camillus, the Gauls left Rome undisturbed until the end of the third Samnite war, in 290 B.C.

THE CURTIAN LAKE

About the Samnite wars I am now going to tell you.

CHAPTER XLI

THE DREAM OF THE TWO CONSULS

THE Samnites were a rough and hardy race of warriors, whose homes were among the mountains of the Apennines.

In 343 B.C. they determined to wrest Campania, in the south of Italy, from the Romans.

The wars of the Samnites lasted for many long years, and when at length Rome conquered, she was mistress of Italy. But before she was victorious, the first, second, and third Samnite wars had been fought and won.

Of the first Samnite war little is known, save that it lasted for three years, and that the Romans won three battles.

During this first war, however, the Latins, who had allied themselves with Rome, revolted. They wished to be given the full rights of Roman citizens, and they demanded that one Consul, as well as half the members of the Senate should be Latins. Nor was this all. For they refused to be content

THE DREAM OF THE TWO CONSULS

unless Latium and Rome were henceforth counted as one Republic.

The Romans did not for a moment dream of granting such ambitious demands. Indeed, they resolved to punish the Latins for their presumption in making such large requests.

So they went to war and fought, until the Latins lost their last stronghold and were forced again to submit to Rome.

The Latins had gained little by provoking their former allies, for while some Latin cities were granted the rights of Roman citizens, all were forced to send soldiers to the Roman army.

Two famous stories are told of the war with the Latins.

The armies had encamped near to each other on the plain of Capua, in the south of Italy.

Manlius Torquatus was one of the Consuls, and he, with his colleague, had given strict orders that no soldier was to engage in single combat.

But the son of Torquatus chanced to be challenged by one of the enemy, and the temptation to fight was more than the young man could stand.

Was he victorious, what glory he would win! Was he beaten, he could but die! So, despite the strict order of the Consuls, young Manlius accepted the challenge.

Groups of Roman and Latin soldiers watched the combat with the keenest interest, and when at length, after a gallant fight, Manlius slew his opponent, a shout of triumph arose from his comrades. But the Latins looked on, sullen and ashamed, while their champion was stripped of his arms.

Flushed with victory, and thinking that his father would forgive his disobedience, the youth hastened to the tent of Torquatus, and laid the arms he had taken from his foe at his father's feet.

But discipline was dear to the Consul's heart, and he did not greet his son as he entered the tent, but turned coldly away from him. Had it been any other who had disobeyed, punishment swift and sharp would have descended on the culprit.

It made Torquatus angry to think that he should dream even for a moment of being more merciful to his own son than to another. He loved discipline, but he loved his son as well. So it was with a mighty effort that he resolved that, although it was his own son who had transgressed, punishment swift and sharp should be inflicted on him.

Cold and stern, the Consul's voice rang out, bidding the soldiers assemble in front of his tent, and there, before them all, he ordered that his son should be beheaded.

No one dared to dispute the order of the Consul, and the soldiers looked on in horror while their brave young comrade was put to death because of his disobedience.

The soldiers hated Torquatus for his severity, and never forgot it. But if they hated, they also

THE DREAM OF THE TWO CONSULS

The youth laid the arms he had taken from his foe at his father's feet.

feared, and never again were his commands disobeyed.

The second story is about a terrible battle that was fought close to Mount Vesuvius.

It was the night before the battle that the two Consuls, Torquatus and Decius Mus, both dreamed the same dream.

A man taller than any mortal appeared to each of the Consuls, and warned him that in the battle which was to be fought, both sides must suffer, one losing its leader, the other its whole army.

In the morning, when the Consuls found that each had dreamed exactly the same dream, they determined to appeal to the gods. Even as their dreams were alike, so also was the answer each received.

"The gods of the dead, and earth, the mother of all, claim as their victim the general of one party and the army of the other."

At all costs the Roman army must be saved. Of that neither Consul had any doubt. Nor did they shrink when they realised that to save the army one of them must perish.

So Manlius and Decius Mus agreed that the one whose legions should first give way before the enemy should give himself up to the gods of the dead.

When the battle was raging most fiercely, the right wing of the Latins compelled one of the

THE DREAM OF THE TWO CONSULS

Roman divisions to give way. The leader of the division was Decius Mus.

Without a murmur, the Consul prepared to fulfil the agreement he had made with Torquatus. By doing so he was sure that he would save the army from destruction.

Turning to a priest who was on the battlefield, he begged to be told how best to devote himself to the gods.

Then the priest bade Decius Mus take the toga that he wore as Consul, but which was not usually seen on the battlefield, and wrap it round his head, holding it close to his face with one of his hands. His feet the Consul placed on a javelin, and then, as the priest bade, he prayed to the god of the dead.

"God of the dead, I humbly beseech you, I crave and doubt not to receive this grace from you, that you prosper the people of Rome with all might and victory; and that you visit the enemies of the people of Rome .... with terror, with dismay, and with death.

"And, according to these words which I have spoken, so do I now, on behalf of the Commonwealth of the Roman people .... devote the legions and the foreign aids of our enemies, along with myself, to the god of the dead and to the grave."

When he had prayed, Decius Mus sent his lictors to tell Manlius what he was about to do.

Then, with his toga wrapped across his face, the noble Roman leaped upon his horse, and fully armed, plunged into the midst of the Latin army and was slain.

Inspired by the courage of Decius Mus, and knowing that the vengeance of the gods would now fall upon their enemies, the Romans fought with fresh courage.

At first the Latins were dismayed and driven backward. But they soon rallied, and fought so fiercely that it seemed as though the sacrifice of the Consul had been in vain.

But just as the Romans were beginning to give way, Manlius with a band of veterans rushed to their aid, and with loud cheers dashed upon the enemy.

The Latins, already weary, were not able to withstand this new shock. So the Romans were soon victorious, and slaughtered or took prisoners nearly a fourth part of the Latin army.

Torquatus now returned to Rome, expecting to receive a great triumph. But the citizens looked on his procession in silence and dislike, for he had come back from battle without his colleague.

In this the Romans were unjust to Torquatus, for had his legions been the first to flinch before the enemy, he would have faced death as bravely as did Decius Mus.

CHAPTER XLII

THE CAUDINE FORKS

ONE of the chief events of the Second Samnite war took place in 321 B.C., at a gorge or pass called the Caudine Forks.

Gaius Pontius, the general of the Samnite army, was encamped at Caudium. He had hoped to hold the passes which led from the plain of Naples to the higher mountain valleys among the Apennines.

But one day he thought of a better plan. If he could but entice the Roman army into the mountain passes, he would have them in a trap before they were aware.

So he sent two countrymen to Rome, bidding them report to the Consuls that the Samnite army had left Caudium and marched to Apulia, where they were besieging the town of Luceria.

The Consuls had no reason to doubt the truth of the countrymen's words, and as Luceria was held by allies of Rome, they resolved to send an army to her help, lest she should fall into the hands of the enemy.

So before long the Roman legions were marching toward Apulia. As the shortest way lay through the pass of the Caudine Forks, and as the Consul Postumius, who was at the head of the legions, believed that the Samnite army was far away, he did not hesitate to enter the gorge.

It was a deep and gloomy pass, between rugged mountains. As the Romans advanced, the gorge grew more narrow and precipitous, and they were glad when at length they approached the end of the dangerous path. But their pleasure was soon changed to anxiety, for the exit from the pass was barricaded with trees and great masses of stone.

Postumius began to suspect treachery. It was plain that the trees had but recently been cut down. Suppose the barricades were the work of the Samnites! The Consul at once ordered the army to retreat.

But long before the weary legions reached the opening by which they had entered the pass they felt sure that they were caught in a trap.

The Samnites were indeed guarding the entrance, and escape was impossible.

Nevertheless, the Romans made a gallant attempt to scale the side of the steep mountains that brooded over the gorge, and when they reached the opening they even tried to make their way through the enemy. But the Samnites killed or wounded all who tried to escape.

THE CAUDINE FORKS

When night fell, Postumius ordered his army to encamp in the valley at its broadest point, and here he awaited the will of Gaius Pontius.

But the Samnite general was in no haste to make terms with his prisoners. Each day that he delayed, famine would stare the Roman army more closely in the face. Before long it would be forced to agree to whatever terms he chose to dictate.

And, indeed, before many days had passed, the Romans were compelled to yield, crying to their foes: "Put us to the sword, sell us as slaves, or keep us as prisoners until we be ransomed, only save our bodies, whether living or dead, from all unworthy insult."

It was plain that the Romans feared lest they should be treated in the same way as they used their captives.

For the Romans dragged their prisoners in chains at the chariot wheels of their victorious generals. Often, too, their captives were beheaded in the common prison, and their bodies refused the rite of burial.

But Pontius used his power generously. If his terms were heard, yet they were just, and had in them no trace of cruelty.

"Restore to us," said the Samnite general, "the towns you have taken from us, and recall the Roman colonists you have unjustly settled on our soil. Then conclude with us a treaty, which shall own each nation to be alike independent of the other. If you will swear to do this I will spare your lives and let you go without ransom, each man of you giving up your arms merely and keeping his clothes untouched, and you shall pass in sight of your army as prisoners, whom we .... set free of our own will, when we might have killed them, or sold them, or held them to ransom."

The Consuls and officers of the army vowed to observe this treaty, and six hundred knights were given as hostages to the Samnites.

But Pontius, had he been wise, would have gained the consent of the Senate and people of Rome to his terms, before he was content.

To the Romans, the demands of Pontius seemed severe, but yet deeper was the humiliation they were to endure.

The entire army, along with the Consuls, were forced to pass beneath the yoke, in the presence of their foe. It was the only way of escape from the pass of the Caudine Forks.

Giving up their arms, and wearing only a kilt which reached from their waist to their knees, the vanquished army filed sullenly out of the gorge beneath the yoke.

This was no unusual humiliation, but was the custom in those days, and equal to our demand that arms should be laid down on the surrender of a garrison.

THE CAUDINE FORKS

Pontius was indeed strangely kind to his conquered foes, ordering carriages for the wounded, and giving them food to eat on the march back to Rome.

But nothing could comfort the Romans, whose pride had been gravely wounded by being forced to pass beneath the yoke.

In silence, shame written clear upon their faces, they marched gloomily along, with no desire to reach the end of their journey.

When they drew near to Rome, those who lived in the country slipped away to their homes, hoping that none would notice them. Those who lived in the city waited until it was dark that they might enter unseen.

The Consuls were not able to shun the attention of the crowd, for they entered the city during the day. But they, too, were so ashamed that they deemed themselves no longer fit to be Consuls, and escaping from the people as soon as possible, they shut themselves up in their homes.

Rome was a gloomy city for days after the return of the disgraced army.

The senators laid aside their gold rings, and no longer wore on their robes the red border which was the sign of their rank. In somber attire and with grave faces they sat in the Senate-house, or paced the streets, thinking of the disgrace that had overtaken their people.

Shops were shut, business was laid aside, while the citizens mourned alike for those who had returned as for those who had been slain.

Ere long new Consuls were elected, and they, with the Senate, agreed that the treaty made with Pontius must not be kept.

Postumius then offered to go back to the Samnites, with his colleague and officers, as a punishment for agreeing to so humiliating a treaty. To this proposal the Senate gave its approval.

The Consuls and officers were then stripped of all save the kilt which they had worn when they passed beneath the yoke, and thus, with their hands tied behind them, they were sent back to the Samnites.

"These men are forfeited to you in atonement for the broken treaty," cried those who accompanied the miserable penitents, when at length they stood in the presence of Pontius.

But the Samnite general refused to receive such atonement. "Either," said he, "you must put your army back in the Caudine Forks, or you must keep the treaty to which your Consuls agreed."

As the Romans refused to do this, the second Samnite war continued to be waged.

CHAPTER XLIII

THE DISGRACE OF THE CAUDINE FORKS AVENGED

A YEAR after the Romans had been, as they felt, disgraced at the Caudine Forks, they determined to blot out their humiliation.

The old annalists, whose one desire was to increase the glory of Rome, wrote of great victories and marvellous deeds achieved by the legions, but historians of a later day say that not all the stories told by these ancient writers are true.

It is one of these old annalists who tells that in 320 B.C. Papirius Cursor marched with an army into Apulia. He did not venture through the fatal pass of the Caudine Forks, but took his men along the coast. If this was a longer way it was at least safer than through the valley.

Reaching Luceria, Papirius took it from the Samnites, and not only so, but he recaptured all the arms and standards which the Romans had lost at the Caudine Forks. The hostages too, who had been taken to Luceria by the Samnites, the Consul found and set free.

Then, that the enemy might never dare to boast of the victory which they had won over the Romans, Papirius made seven thousand Samnite soldiers pass beneath the yoke.

And, by the favour of the gods, Pontius was commander of the city, so that the humiliation he had erstwhile forced upon the Romans he had now himself to endure.

After this victory, the Consul returned to Rome and enjoyed a triumph.

The chief object of the war was to secure Campania. After many battles, in which now one army, now the other was victorious, a decisive one was fought in 314 B.C., when the Romans utterly defeated the Samnites. The whole of Campania was now in the hands of Rome.

So as to protect her new possessions, the Romans sent a colony to Ponza, an island lying off the Campanian and Latin coasts. A new interest thus arose in the sea: in 312 B.C. commissioners were appointed to look after the ships of Rome and see that they were in good repair. The following year the Romans had a small fleet ready to sail along the coast of Campania.

Rome was not yet prepared to test her fleet by fighting at sea, but she was now able to send troops to the coast towns of her enemies.

It was about this time that the Consul Appius Claudius began to build the great road between Rome and Capua, which was called the Appian Way.

CHAPTER XLIV

FABIUS AMONG THE CIMINIAN HILLS

ONE of the most famous heroes of the second Samnite war was Fabius.

Before the disgrace of the Caudine Forks, Fabius, who was an ardent warrior, had fought a battle against the command of the Dictator, Papirius. That he was victorious did not make Papirius less angry with his disobedience. Indeed so angry was he, that he ordered that Fabius should at once be beheaded. But the soldiers threatened to mutiny if the order was carried out, and so for the time the life of the young soldier was saved.

Knowing that the Dictator would take the first opportunity to carry out the sentence he had pronounced, Fabius waited only until it was dark and then fled from the camp to Rome.

When he reached the city he summoned the Senate to meet, meaning to beg for protection from the wrath of the Dictator.

But before the Senate had assembled, Papirius, who had followed Fabius, dashed into the Forum and ordered the runaway to be arrested.

The father of Fabius then besought the tribunes to interfere between his son and the Dictator, declaring that if they did not do so, he would appeal to the Assembly of the people.

But although the tribunes disapproved of the severity of Papirius, they did not dare to interfere, for the power of the Dictator was supreme.

The people, however, who had now gathered in the Forum, speedily took the matter into their own hands. With one voice they begged Papirius to forgive Fabius for their sake.

Papirius, whose passion had had time to cool, was pleased that the people should ask him to be merciful, and he promised to pardon the disobedient soldier.

In 310 B.C., Fabius was elected Consul, along with Marcius. Together the two Consuls set out, each with his own army, to the relief of Sutrium, which town had already been besieged for a year by the Etruscans.

Roman troops had tried again and again, but without success, to raise the siege.

New hope was aroused in Sutrium when the citizens heard that both the Consuls were on the way to their relief. Before they had accomplished anything, however, Marcius was forced to leave his

FABIUS AMONG THE CIMINIAN HILLS

colleague to march against the Samnites, who were in Apulia, plundering the allies of Rome.

Fabius was left alone at Sutrium, but before long he had forced the Etruscans to raise the siege and had captured their camp, in which he found thirty-eight standards.

The Consuls then pursued the enemy across the Ciminian hills, which hills we now know as the mountains of Viterbo.

In these days of long ago, the Ciminian hills were densely-wooded, and strange stories were told of their mysterious shades.

No pathway was to be found through these hilly forests, while their unknown terrors were dreaded so much that even peaceful merchants never attempted to reach Etruria by passing through the Ciminian hills. This was the way that Fabius ventured in pursuit of the enemy.

The Senate at Rome no sooner heard of the Consul's daring, than it sent messengers to bid him be less reckless. But long before the messengers reached the edge of the thicket, Fabius was in the depth of the forests.

For weeks nothing was heard of the Consul and his army, and the Senate believed that they were lost. Fabius had, however, escaped from the thickly-wooded hills with but few adventures, and was safe in the rich plains of central Etruria. If he had not captured the Etruscans, he was now at least able to plunder their country.

THE STORY OF ROME

Meanwhile the dire tidings reached Rome that Marcius had been defeated by the Samnites, nor was it known whether the Consul had escaped with his life.

Bereft, for the time at least, of both Consuls, the Senate resolved to appoint a Dictator, and Papirius, they knew, was the man to inspire the people with the greatest trust.

But a Dictator must be appointed by one of the Consuls, and Marcius was either dead or in the hands of his enemies.

Fabius, of whose safety the Senate was now assured, would scarcely appoint Papirius to the supreme post of honour, for it was he who had hunted Fabius and condemned him to death in earlier days.

Nevertheless, the Senate determined to beg Fabius to forget the treatment he had received from Papirius, and for the sake of his country to appoint him Dictator. So messengers were sent to the Consul with the Senate's request.

Fabius had fought and won many battles, but never had he had a fiercer one to fight than while he listened to the message sent to him by the Senate.

His look indeed was forbidding, and gave the ambassadors little hope of success. Having heard what they had to say, he gave them no clue to his thoughts, for he dismissed them without a word.

But in the dead of night, he arose, as was the custom when a Dictator had to be appointed, and gave to his enemy the coveted post. By this act he made himself once more the subordinate of Papirius.

The ambassadors thanked Fabius for his noble deed, but showing no pleasure in their praise, the Consul, still without a word, sent them from his presence.

Fabius had won that night a more glorious victory than any he had ever gained on the battle-field, for he had conquered himself.

No sooner was Papirius appointed Dictator, than he marched against the Samnites and defeated them in a great battle. Marcius, who was alive, was thus set free to return to Rome. The Samnites were forced back into their own mountain country, and in 304 B.C. they made an honourable peace with Rome. Thus the second Samnite war came to an end.

Fabius meanwhile won victory after victory over the Etruscans, and in 304 B.C. they also made a peace with Rome, which lasted for several years.

Rome was now mistress of Italy, and in such respect was she held that no tribe henceforth dared to attack her, without first enlisting other powers to help them in their adventure.

CHAPTER XLV

THE BATTLE OF SENTINUM

THE peace made with the Samnites in 304 B.C. lasted for six years, after which the third war with these hardy mountaineers began.

One of the Consuls at this time was Cornelius Scipio, the great-grandfather of the famous Scipio who conquered Hannibal.

Now the Samnites had persuaded the Gauls to join them in their new attack upon Rome, and they, it is said, surprised and slew one of Scipio's legions. So dreadful was the slaughter that not a single soldier escaped to tell the Consul, who was some distance off with the main body of his army, what had happened.

Nor did the Romans know what had befallen their comrades, until the Gauls, elated with victory, galloped up to the camp of the enemy shouting their war-cries and carrying on the point of their lances the heads of those whom they had slain.

In 295 B.C. the Romans grew alarmed at the forces that had united against them, for the Samnites

THE BATTLE OF SENTINUM

had now not only the Gauls, but also the Etruscans and other tribes to strengthen them.

Fabius, whose courage had been tested in many a difficult position, was therefore appointed Consul for the fifth time, and sent with his colleague Decius to the war.

The leader of the Samnites, Egnatius, was at Sentinum in Umbria. He was anxious to fight without delay, for he knew how quickly the Gauls were used to desert their allies.

So he, as well as his men, was pleased when they saw that the Roman legions, with the two Consuls at their head, had reached Sentinum.

Yet for two days no battle took place. But as the armies faced one another, a stag chased by a wolf ran in between the two forces.

The Gauls, in their barbarous way, threw their javelins at the stag and killed it, while the Romans allowed the wolf to run safely through their ranks, for the beast was sacred to Mars, and its presence was to them a sign of victory.

"The Gauls have slain the stag which is sacred to Diana," cried the Roman soldiers. "It is certain that her wrath will fall upon them. As for us, the wolf bids us remember Quirinus, our divine founder. With his aid we have naught to fear."

The Consuls could no longer restrain the eagerness of their legions, and they at once led them against the enemy.

Fabius commanded the right wings, and faced the Samnites; Decius was opposite the Gauls. They, as was their way, rushed with loud war-cries upon the foe, spurring their horses forward with fury and driving their war-chariots upon the Roman cavalry.

Startled by the noise of the heavy chariots and by their strange appearance, the Roman horses turned and fled. In their flight they encountered the infantry, and dashing upon it, caused the legions to give way.

Decius tried in vain to rally his men. Then, in despair, he determined to do as his father had done, and yield himself up to death, that the army might be saved.

So, spurring his steed, he rode headlong into the midst of the Gallic warriors and was slain.

The soldiers, seeing that the Consul had sacrificed himself for their sake, took courage and turned to face the foe. Decius had, by his death, won a victory for his country.

Fabius meanwhile, had routed the Samnites, who now added to the confusion by rushing past the Gauls, in a desperate effort to reach their camp.

As the Samnites fled, the Gauls formed themselves into a dense mass, for they feared that they would now be attacked by Fabius.

The Consul, however, contented himself by sending a detachment of his men to harass the Gauls in their rear, and another to attack them in front.

THE BATTLE OF SENTINUM

Then vowing to build a temple to Jupiter and to offer him all the spoil if he was victorious, Fabius himself followed the Samnites and cut them down ruthlessly, until at length Egnatius, their brave commander, fell. Resistance was now at an end, yet those who were still alive refused to surrender. Forming themselves into a compact body, they marched away and struggled back to their own country.

The Gauls too were utterly crushed, and the glory of the battle of Sentinum belonged to Rome.

CHAPTER XLVI

THE SON OF FABIUS LOSES A BATTLE

The year 295 B.C. in which the battle of Sentinum was won, was a year long remembered by the Romans for its glorious victories.

But three years later their armies were defeated by the Samnites.

Fabius, the son of the Fabius who crossed the Ciminian hills, led the Roman legions against the foe. The young Consul believed that the Samnites had been so severely beaten during the last few years, that he need take no great precautions before attacking them.

It was after a long march that Fabius encountered a small detachment of the enemy. His men were weary, but he determined to pursue the foe, and succeeded in making it slowly retreat.

The Consul pushed on still more eagerly, to find himself, before he was aware, close to the entire Samnite army, which was drawn up ready for battle.

THE SON OF FABIUS LOSES A BATTLE

A terrible struggle took place. But the Romans, exhausted and unprepared, were slain in great numbers. Indeed had night not fallen, the whole army would have been destroyed.

At Rome, the dreadful tidings roused great indignation against Fabius. It was even proposed in the Senate that the young Consul should be recalled and have his Consulship taken from him, a disgrace unheard of until now.

But his father pleaded that his son might be spared so heavy a punishment. If he was allowed to keep his command, Fabius even offered to go to the war and serve under his son.

So unselfish an offer could not be refused, and the veteran general was permitted to join the army. He lost no time in setting out, and he took with him large reinforcements, for every man was willing to follow the brave old chief.

The Roman soldiers were themselves anxious to retrieve their defeat. Encouraged by the presence of the general, who had so often led them to victory, they fought fiercely and defeated the Samnites, taking Pontius, their leader, captive.

When young Fabius returned to Rome, his former defeat was forgotten in the joy of this great victory, and he enjoyed a triumph.

Some histories tell that the leader of the Samnites, whom Fabius had captured, was the same Pontius who thirty years before had spared the lives of the Roman soldiers at Caudium.

If that was so the generous treatment of the Samnite chief was now cruelly requited. For as Fabius drove in his chariot through the streets of Rome, Pontius, loaded with chains, walked in the procession. At the foot of the Capitol he was taken, with other captives, to the prison beneath the Capitoline hill and beheaded.

A year or two later, in 290 B.C. the third Samnite war drew to a close. The last battle was won by a famous Consul, named Dentatus.

The Samnites, hoping to bribe the Roman, sought for him in his country home. They found him, like Cincinnatus, living quietly on his farm, cooking for his dinner turnips which he had himself sown in his fields.

Dentatus had little to say to the Samnite ambassadors, when they offered him bribes to desert his country, save to tell them that he did not consider it a great thing to possess gold. "To rule those who have it, is what I value," he added sternly. And as the ambassadors withdrew they saw, as in a picture, their own army defeated, and the Romans, with Dentatus at their head, marching home victorious.

The Consul did indeed defeat the Samnites, so that they were forced to sue for peace and retire once again to their mountain strongholds.

Yet even now their hardy spirits were not subdued, and again and again you will read of them coming down from their fastnesses to strike a blow at Rome. And they were wise in their warfare, choos-

THE SON OF FABIUS LOSES A BATTLE

ing always the time when Rome was already surrounded by other foes.

CHAPTER XLVII
PYRRHUS, KING OF THE EPIROTS

ALONG the southern coast of Italy, many of the towns were Greek, and had not yet become subject to Rome.

But as Rome became more and more powerful in the south of Italy, many of these Greek towns, when attacked by an enemy, appealed to her for help.

Tarentum, the chief of these towns, was jealous of Rome, and chose to send to Greece or Sicily when help was needed.

During the second Samnite war, Rome had made a treaty with the Tarentines, promising that no ships of war should enter the Gulf of Tarentum.

But in the autumn of 282 B.C. ten Roman warships suddenly appeared before the harbour, to the indignation as well as to the dismay of the Tarentines.

Should the warships be allowed to enter the inner harbour, their town would be in the hands of

PYRRHUS, KING OF THE EPIROTS

Rome. So the Tarentines speedily manned their ships and boldly sailed to attack the enemy.

On this occasion the Tarentines showed themselves good fighters, and soon they had sunk four of the Roman warships and taken one, while the other five escaped.

The admiral of the fleet was killed, and many soldiers and sailors were made prisoners. Of these, the Tarentines sold the sailors as slaves, the soldiers they put to death.

Knowing that the defeat of the Roman fleet would be avenged, the Tarentines grew reckless.

Thurii, a town not far off, had received help from Rome and had had a Roman garrison imposed upon it. The Tarentines now marched to Thurii, expelled the garrison, and prepared to defend themselves from the consequences of their act.

But Rome was at war with the Samnites, and was not yet ready to punish Tarentum.

She merely sent an embassy to demand that the prisoners taken from her fleet should be given up, that the garrison should be restored to Thurii.

The Tarentines not only refused to do as Rome demanded; they treated the embassy with insults.

This was more than the Senate could brook. The Consul Æmilius was at once sent with his legions into the country of the Tarentines.

Æmilius offered the people peace on the same terms as the embassy, but again the citizens flouted the offer. Then knowing that the legions of Æmilius had come to support the demands of Rome, they sent in hot haste to Pyrrhus, king of Epirus, begging him to come to their aid.

The Consul seeing that his terms were rejected, did indeed begin to plunder and lay waste the country, while the Tarentines looked but the more eagerly for the answer of Pyrrhus.

Nor was it long in coming. In the early spring of 280 B.C. the king of Epirus reached Tarentum.

Epirus, the region over which Pyrrhus was king, lay in the north-west of Greece, among wild mountains and narrow valleys.

The Epirots were proud of their king, and because of his courage on the battlefield they called him the "Eagle."

Pyrrhus knew the name his soldiers had given to him, and he said to them, "It is by you that I am an eagle, for how should I not be such, while I have your arms as wings to sustain me."

The king had one peculiarity, which added to the terror he at times inspired. When he opened his mouth no row of upper teeth was to be seen. Instead of teeth, one single long bone was visible, with small lines to mark where the separate teeth should have been. Such was the king who had hastened to the aid of the Tarentines.

PYRRHUS, KING OF THE EPIROTS

So eager had Pyrrhus been to set out, that he had refused to wait for a fair wind, and a terrible storm had overtaken his fleet and scattered it, while he, with only a small part of his army, had been driven ashore some distance from Tarentum.

With his army Pyrrhus had brought twenty elephants, for, the king had been in Africa and had learned there how useful these huge animals could be on the battlefield. But he had reached Tarentum with only two elephants and a few soldiers.

After many difficulties, however, his whole force had succeeded in rejoining him, bringing with it the other eighteen elephants. To the Tarentines, as to the Romans on the battlefield, these elephants were a new and awe-inspiring sight.

The king had been but a short time in Tarentum before he found that the people he had come to help were lazy, and more fond of pleasure than of war.

They would be well pleased to stay at home to feast, to talk of the great battles they would fight, while their new ally was in the field, enduring hardships and struggling with the Roman legions.

The king of the Epirots was used to having real soldiers around him, and he determined, if it was possible, to turn the foolish, indolent Tarentines into an army of trained, resolute men.

So he ordered the theatres, the baths, and the other places of amusement to be closed, and then he called upon all who were old enough, to enrol their names for service.

Then began a strange state of affairs in Tarentum. The city was turned into a military camp. Discipline was strict, and the recruits grumbled that they were under arms all day, guarding the walls, or watching in the market-place.

The most indolent actually made up their minds to escape, forgetting that Pyrrhus was training them that they might be able to defend their own homes. There seemed no trace in these indifferent citizens of the spirit that had made them sail against the Roman fleet and turn the Roman garrison out of Thurii.

"Not understanding what it was to be commanded, these called it mere slavery not to do as they pleased."

CHAPTER XLVIII

THE ELEPHANTS AT THE BATTLE OF HERACLEA

WHILE Pyrrhus was training the lazy Tarentines, the new Consul, Valerius, was advancing with his army toward the city, burning and plundering the country through which he passed. So Pyrrhus resolved to leave Tarentum and go to meet the enemy. Assembling his troops he marched away toward the town of Heraclea, which stood on the bank of the river Siris, where he determined to pitch his camp.

Across the river lay the Roman army, and the king rode along the bank on his side of the Siris, admiring the order and discipline of the enemy.

"We shall see presently what they can do," he said to a friend who rode by his side.

Wishing to keep the Romans from crossing the river until his reinforcements arrived, Pyrrhus ordered soldiers to guard the passage.

But Valerius did not mean to wait for the king to strengthen his force, and he at once sent his cavalry higher up the Siris to cross at a ford, while he, with his infantry, tried to cross the river in spite of the guard set by Pyrrhus.

The king immediately advanced with three thousand horse, hoping to scatter the Romans ere they succeeded in reaching the opposite bank.

But protecting themselves with their shields, the Roman soldiers were soon scrambling out of the river.

Pyrrhus, ordering his men to form in closer ranks, then led them against the enemy. His armour, richer and more beautiful than that of his soldiers, at once attracted the attention of the Romans and drew on him the most determined attacks.

His friends, seeing the danger to which the king was exposed, begged him to beware.

One of them, pointing to a barbarian who rode upon a black horse with white feet, said, "Sire, yonder fellow fixes his whole attention on you alone, taking no notice of others. Be on your guard against him."

The king answered, "It is impossible for any man to avoid his fate, but neither he nor any other Italian shall have much satisfaction in engaging with me."

At that moment the Roman, spurring on his horse and lowering his spear, dashed upon the king.

Pyrrhus fell to the ground, for his steed was pierced by the enemy's spear.

THE ELEPHANTS AT THE BATTLE OF HERACLEA

The armour of Pyrrhus was richer and more beautiful than that of his soldiers.

Quick as lightning, Leonnatus, who had warned Pyrrhus of this very soldier, killed the Roman's horse, and before he or any other of the enemy could reach the king, his friends had dragged him to a place of safety. He was then persuaded to change his armour with one of his officers named Megacles.

The Romans now fiercely attacked Megacles, and at length they succeeded in dragging him from his horse and in wounding him to death.

Then the victors seized his helmet and cloak and hastened with them to their general, to show that they had indeed killed the king.

The royal trophies were placed on the point of a spear and carried along the lines of the Roman army, that all might see that the king was slain.

While the Romans shouted for joy, the Greeks looked on in dismay, thinking that their Eagle king was no longer alive.

But Pyrrhus soon learned what had happened, and dashing to the front, he rode bare-headed before his men, shouting to them to follow him.

The Consul now determined to bring forward the force he had kept in reserve, thinking that it would decide the day. But Pyrrhus too had a reserve force, and a more terrible one than his enemy. This was his twenty elephants, which, with towers on their backs filled with armed men, he now let loose upon the foe.

CHAPTER XLIX

PYRRHUS TRIES TO FRIGHTEN FABRICIUS

AFTER the great victory of Heraclea, Pyrrhus sent his minister Cineas to Rome to offer terms of peace.

Cineas was an orator. By the magic of his word he could sway men's minds and wills, and it was said that he, by his tongue, had won more cities than Pyrrhus by his sword.

Between the eloquence of Cineas and the fear of another defeat, the Senate wavered—almost it was tempted to accept the terms offered by the conqueror of Heraclea.

As the Senate hesitated, Appius Claudius, who was now old and blind, appeared before the Assembly, leaning upon the arms of his sons. He had heard that the Senate thought of accepting the terms of the conqueror, and old and feeble as he was, he had come to protest against so disloyal a deed.

"Hitherto, Fathers," said the old man, "I used to mourn that I was deprived of the light of the eye; now, however, I should consider myself happy, if, in addition to that, I had lost the sense of hearing, that

I might not hear the disgraceful counsels which are here openly proposed to the shame of the Roman name. . . . Whither have your pride and your courage flown?"

Weak as the old man was, he spoke with such passion and such wisdom, that when he ended, there was not a single member of the Senate who was not prepared to vote that war should continue until Pyrrhus had been forced to withdraw from Italy.

Cineas, as he listened to the passionate words of Appius Claudius, knew that his cause was lost. He was indeed bidden to hasten back to his master and say that the Romans would never make peace with him, no, not if he "should have defeated a thousand such as the Consul Valerius."

Meanwhile Pyrrhus had marched north, to Capua, hoping to seize the town, only, however, to find that Valerius had already taken possession of it.

Disappointed as he was, the king continued his march until he was within twenty-three miles of Rome. And as he marched Valerius followed, harassing his rear on every possible occasion.

Then Pyrrhus, hearing that a Dictator had been appointed and was ready to oppose him, retreated to Tarentum, where he spent the winter months.

The victory of Heraclea had been followed only by a useless march.

PYRRHUS TRIES TO FRIGHTEN FABRICIUS

During the winter an embassy, led by Fabricius, came from Rome to Tarentum, to offer an exchange of prisoners.

Cineas advised the King to try to bribe the Roman. So Pyrrhus offered Fabricius splendid gifts, but he answered proudly, "If I am base how can I be worth a bribe, if honest how can you expect me to take one? Poverty with honesty is more to be desired than wealth."

Then Pyrrhus, finding that the advice of Cineas had been useless, determined to try a plan of his own. Perhaps he would be able to frighten Fabricius into doing as he wished, and this is the strange way he chose.

He ordered his largest elephant to be placed in the room in which he and the Roman were to meet. The elephant was to be hidden by a curtain, which at a signal from the king was to be drawn aside.

So the next day when Pyrrhus and the ambassador met, their conversation was suddenly interrupted, and the Roman to his astonishment found himself standing close to a huge beast, whose trunk and tusks would have looked formidable enough even to a strong soldier, while Fabricius was an old man.

But when the elephant began to trumpet, the Roman only laughed, and without stirring he said, "The beast cannot move me to-day more than your gold yesterday."

Fabricius had easily guessed the meaning of the strange interruption, and of the appearance of the huge animal in the king's sitting-room.

Pyrrhus saw that it was hopeless to try to come to terms with the Roman, and he again prepared for war.

Early in 279 B.C. he marched into Apulia, and there, near the town of Asculum, another great battle was fought.

The Romans had learned to dread the terrible war-elephants which accompanied Pyrrhus on the battlefield. To cope with them, they had wagons built, with spikes fixed to the wheels. These wagons were filled with soldiers, who carried javelins, ready to throw at the dread beasts.

But Pyrrhus made these precautions of little use, for he sent the elephants to a part of the field where no wagons had been placed.

Long and terrible was the struggle between the two armies.

The elephants, with archers scattered among them, advanced in a closely-formed body upon the Romans, while the Greeks, using their swords, seemed heedless of their wounds, so only they might get to close quarters with the enemy. But here, as at Heraclea, the elephants dashed upon the Romans before they were aware, and they were forced to flee.

Pyrrhus and many of his officers were wounded, and although the day was theirs, they were soon glad to retire to Tarentum, until their wounds were healed.

The victory of Asculum seemed of as little use as that of Heraclea, for when his wound was healed, Pyrrhus found that so many of his men had perished, that he could not again take the field until reinforcements arrived from Epirus.

So in the spring of 278 B.C. the king once again tried to make terms with Rome.

But the Senate still heard the brave words of Appius Claudius ringing in its ears, and it refused even to discuss terms of peace with the victor.

Meanwhile the people of Tarentum showed their dislike to the discipline of the king more and more plainly. Their ingratitude and the approach of the hostile armies of Rome made Pyrrhus glad to leave Tarentum.

So he sailed to Sicily, where the Greek colonies were in danger from the Carthaginians, who had come from Africa in hope of new conquests.

He spent two years in the island, where at first he won great victories. But here, as in Italy, he seemed unable to reap good from his conquests.

Moreover his officers, although they began by behaving well to the Sicilians, soon showed themselves to be both greedy and cruel. In 276 B.C. the people resolved to endure these foreign soldiers no longer, and they hounded them out of the island.

Pyrrhus then went back to Italy, where both the Tarentines and the Samnites were becoming alarmed at the growing power of Rome.

CHAPTER L

PYRRHUS IS DEFEATED

PYRRHUS found it no easy task to return to Italy, for the Romans had made a league with the Carthaginians, whose fleet was now watching the shore, to prevent him from landing.

But the soldier-king was not easily daunted, and although in a battle with the Carthaginian fleet he lost a number of his ships, he succeeded in reaching Italy.

When the king now marched for the second time into Tarentum, it was at the head of as large an army as he had brought with him from Epirus.

But although in numbers his army was as strong as before, in real strength it had lost much. For the king's own faithful veterans had perished on the battlefields of Heraclea and Asculum, and their place was taken by hired soldiers. And of true courage and devotion to their leader, what did these hired fighters know?

The king himself, too, had lost hope of achieving great things in Italy, and Cineas was no longer living to cheer him with his outbursts of eloquence. Yet his name alone, had he but known it, still awoke terror among the legions of Rome, and made them shrink from meeting him again in battle.

Meanwhile the Consul Dentatus, with his army, had already left Rome, and was marching along the Appian Way toward Maleventum. Here he took up a strong position on the hills, hoping to fight as soon as his colleague joined him.

Pyrrhus knew that his cavalry and elephants could be of little use on the hilly ground on which the Romans had taken up their position, yet, rather than wait until Dentatus was strengthened by the arrival of his colleague, he at once offered battle.

All might have gone well for the king had not one of his young elephants been wounded. In its pain and fright it rushed wildly hither and thither among the other elephants, seeking its mother.

The beasts were soon thrown into utter confusion, while the hired soldiers were seized with panic, and proved useless in quelling the disorder.

Two of the elephants were at length killed by the Romans, while four were captured and led in the triumph of Dentatus, when he returned victorious to Rome.

For the king was utterly defeated and forced to escape, with only a few followers, to Tarentum. In 274 B.C. he sailed back to Epirus, having lost all hope of gaining a kingdom in Italy. But he left a garrison in Tarentum, under one of his officers.

PYRRHUS IS DEFEATED

The town, however, was blockaded by the Carthaginian fleet and besieged by the Consul Papirius, and soon, being in a sorry strait for want of food, it was forced to surrender.

Latin colonies were then sent to settle in many towns that had until now been held by the Greeks, and soon Rome was mistress from the river Rubicon to the extreme south of Italy.

CHAPTER LI

THE ROMANS BUILD A FLEET

THE Romans had conquered Pyrrhus with the help of the Carthaginians. Now that they no longer needed the help of their new allies, the Romans would have been glad had the Carthaginians sailed away to their home in Africa. But this they did not seem to think of doing.

In Sicily they took possession of many Greek towns, and this made Rome jealous. Their fleet, too, was often seen sailing along the coasts of Italy.

Like the Vikings of the North, the Carthaginians would suddenly swoop down upon some undefended coast town and plunder it and the surrounding district. Farm-houses were burned, plantations destroyed, and men and women dragged away to be sold as slaves, long before the Romans had been able to gather an army and march to the spot to punish the offenders.

But such insolence Rome could not brook, and she declared war against the bold intruders. This was the beginning of the first Punic war, which was the name given to the struggle between the Romans

THE ROMANS BUILD A FLEET

and Pœni or Carthaginians for the empire of the world.

On land the Romans quickly showed that they were more powerful than their former allies, and in about three years the Carthaginians had been forced to sail away to the shores of Africa, while those who stayed behind held only a few sea-coast towns in Sicily.

But the Carthaginian fleet was as powerful as ever, and the Romans saw that they would never get rid of their enemy, until they, too, had a fleet, and could cope with them on sea as well as on land. So, although they knew little about ships and none of them were sailors, the Romans determined to build a fleet.

The Carthaginian warships were large vessels with five benches, built one above the other. The five benches were provided for five sets of rowers.

These large five-decked boats were called quinqueremes, *quinque* being the Latin word for five, and *remus* for an oar.

One day, one of these Punic vessels was stranded on the Italian coast. Here was the very model the Romans needed. They seized it, and sent it to Rome as a copy for the ships that were to form the new fleet.

When the quinquereme reached Rome the shipwrights at once set to work. Forests were hewn down, timber was sawn, and in two short months the Romans had built and launched one hundred ships, large and solid as those of the Carthaginians.

And what was perhaps even more wonderful was that there were sailors ready to man the fleet. For while the ships were being built, the men chosen to form the crew had been placed on benches on dry land. These benches were arranged in the position they would have on board.

Here the landsmen, who had still to be changed into sailors, had practised the movements of the oars, and had learned to keep time as they would have to do when actually at sea. A musical accompaniment had helped them to pull the oars together.

But these hastily trained sailors could not hope to handle their vessels as skilfully as the well-trained mariners of Carthage. So the Romans added to each ship a solid wooden bridge, with a spike at the end. When the enemy's ship drew near, the Romans meant to drop the bridge, which was attached to the masts, on to the deck of their foe. The spike, sinking into the deck by the force of the fall, would hold the ship, while the Romans would rush across this rough drawbridge and fight with their enemy at close quarters, as though they were on land.

In 260 B.C. the new fleet put to sea under the command of the Consul Duilius, and before long it met the enemy on the northern coast of Sicily.

The Carthaginians had no fear of the newly built ships and quickly trained sailors. Their captain

THE ROMANS BUILD A FLEET

even thought the usual manoeuvres unnecessary, and sailed toward the Roman fleet in a careless way, thinking to charge prow to prow. To his surprise he found his vessels suddenly gripped by the ships of the enemy, and unable to move.

The bridges, of which I told you, could be wheeled round the masts and dropped just where they were needed, and the Romans, aided by the careless attack of the Carthaginians, had dropped their bridges at the right moment and secured the enemy's ships.

Before the Carthaginians had recovered from their surprise, the Romans had rushed on board, sword in hand, and ere long had captured many of the crew and taken possession of, or destroyed, fifty of the Punic vessels.

Even the flagship, a huge vessel of seven rows of oars, which the Carthaginians had once taken from Pyrrhus, was abandoned to the victors.

This, the first great victory at sea, caused much joy in Rome, and Duilius was awarded a triumph.

It is said that to the end of his life, the Consul was accompanied by a flute-player and a torchbearer as he returned home from banquets, in memory of this glorious victory.

Three years later another great battle was fought at sea, both sides claiming the victory.

But the Romans were ambitious and inspired by their success, they determined to sail to Africa and attack the Carthaginians in their own country.

So they began to build a larger fleet of three hundred and thirty ships. When it was ready they sent on board two armies, of about 40,000 men, under the command of the two Consuls, Regulus and Manlius.

As the Roman fleet sailed along the south coast of Sicily, it was met at Ecnomus by an even larger Carthaginian fleet, under the command of Hamilcar and Hanno.

The Punic generals had been sent to scatter or destroy the Roman fleet before it reached Africa.

CHAPTER LII

THE BATTLE OF ECNOMUS

THE Romans no sooner saw the Carthaginian fleet than they knew that it would be necessary to fight before they could sail on their way.

As the enemy's ships were drawn out in a long weak line, the Consuls determined to charge through its centre.

No sooner had the Romans begun the attack, than Hamilcar ordered his ships to row away, as though they had been put to flight.

As the Carthaginian had foreseen, two divisions of the Roman fleet followed, one of them having Regulus on board.

On sped the Punic ships, eager to separate the Roman divisions from the rest of the fleet. When the enemy was some distance off, Hamilcar ordered his ships to turn, to attack the vessels that had followed them.

But at close quarters, as the Carthaginians should have known, the Romans were more than a match for their foe.

The bridges of the Roman ships fell, grappling the enemy's vessels to their own, and in a fierce hand-to-hand fight Hamilcar and his ships were soon overpowered.

Regulus then hastened to the help of his fourth division, which had been attacked by Hanno, and was now fighting desperately between two divisions of the enemy. Here, too, the Consul was successful, and forced Hanno to retreat.

Meanwhile, the third division of the Roman fleet had been driven toward the coast, but had suffered little damage, for the Carthaginians feared to approach too near lest they should find themselves grappled by the Roman bridges. These they were learning to dread.

The two Consuls soon set the third division free, and before long they had taken sixty-four of the Carthaginian ships with their crews, while more than thirty vessels had been sunk.

As for the Romans, they had lost only twenty-four ships, and these were sunk not captured.

The victory of Ecnomus left the way to Africa open, and after putting in on the Sicilian coast for repairs, the Roman fleet sailed away toward the Gulf of Carthage.

CHAPTER LIII

THE ROMAN LEGIONS IN AFRICA

THE Roman soldiers did not wish to sail to a strange land. Their dislike to the voyage grew as they listened to bewildering tales of these unknown regions.

So they began to grumble, saying that the heat would overpower them, that they would be lost in the great forests of which they had been told, and that huge and poisonous serpents would certainly strangle them. Even one of the tribunes was disloyal, and encouraged the soldiers to complain.

But Regulus paid no heed to the distress of the soldiers, and the fleet sailed on, until it reached the coast of Africa.

The soldiers disembarked, and in a short time they found how foolish had been their fears. Instead of being lost in dark and fearful forests, they found themselves in a country that was beautiful and glad as a garden.

Figs, larger than the Romans had ever seen, grew in abundance; harvests, more plentiful than they had deemed possible, waved golden in the fields. Houses, surrounded by vineyards, oliveyards and rich pasture land, roused the envy as well as the delight of the soldiers.

Over this beautiful country the Roman army was soon scattered to plunder and to destroy. Houses were burned, fields were trampled down, cattle was stolen, and it is said that 20,000 persons, many of whom had lived in comfort all their lives, were now captured and sold as slaves.

And while their land was destroyed and their people were taken prisoners, the Punic army kept to the hills, and left the enemy unmolested.

Then the Romans, knowing that on such steep ground neither cavalry nor elephants would be of much use to the enemy, attacked the Carthaginian army and defeated it.

After this victory, Manilus, with one army, was recalled to Rome.

Regulus continued to ravage the country unchecked, for the Carthaginians, after their defeat, were unable to hinder his onslaughts. The Consul indeed is said to have boasted that he had taken and plundered more than three hundred walled villages.

To add to the misery of the people, the wild tribes of the desert also began to attack the defenceless village folk, and to rob their homesteads.

Then, from far and near, the wretched inhabitants flocked into Carthage for shelter and protection, until the city was so full that there was scarcely enough bread to feed the hungry multitude.

The Senate of Carthage sent, in despair, to Regulus, to beg for peace.

But the Consul received the ambassadors with scant courtesy, while the terms he offered were intolerable.

Among other things, he demanded that the Carthaginians should make neither alliance nor war, unless by the permission of Rome, that they should never send more than one ship of war to sea for their own ends, while if Rome demanded help they must be ready to provide her with a fleet of fifty vessels. The Consul also said that they must agree to pay, not only the expenses of the war that was going on, but a yearly tribute to Rome as well.

When the ambassadors protested that it would be impossible for Carthage to accept such degrading terms, Regulus drove them from his camp, rudely saying, "Men who are good for anything, should either conquer or submit to their betters."

The Senate, with one voice, agreed that the terms offered by the Consul deserved no consideration.

It was plain that Regulus would not help them, and so the people, in their despair, turned to their gods. Lest the city of Carthage itself should fall into the hands of the enemy, they must be appeased with sacrifices.

In the temple, one of the gods stood with arms outstretched, while at his feet a furnace flamed.

Into the cold and lifeless arms little children of noble rank were laid. But the god was unable to hold the treasures given into his keeping, and they rolled out of his arms and fell into the furnace below. By such terrible sacrifices the Carthaginians strove to appease their gods.

After the sacrifices had been offered the Senate determined to send for hired soldiers to Greece, that the army might be strengthened. Among those who came to fight for the Carthaginians was a Spartan officer, named Xanthippus.

As he belonged to Sparta, Xanthippus, like all the youths of his land, had been trained from the age of seven to endure hardships, and to suffer pain without a murmur.

CHAPTER LIV
REGULUS IS TAKEN PRISONER

XANTHIPPUS had fought in the wars of Greece, and he was a skilful as well as an experienced soldier.

He had been but a short time in Carthage before he saw that the Punic army had made a mistake in fighting among the hills.

So wisely did he speak to the officers, showing them how they could yet conquer the enemy, that he inspired them with confidence.

Before long he was appointed, by the Senate, commander of the entire Carthaginian army. Under the training of the Spartan, the troops speedily regained their lost courage, and soon they were clamouring to be led against their cruel foe.

Xanthippus, secure in the enthusiasm of his troops, led them to an open plain. Their number was not large, but he could depend on his cavalry, which was four thousand strong. A hundred elephants too, if carefully guided, might well cause havoc among the enemy.

Regulus would perhaps have been glad to avoid a pitched battle. But if the Punic army was now strong enough to stop the raids of his followers, his food supply would soon come to an end. So as a battle was inevitable, the Consul marched to within a mile of the enemy.

When the Carthaginians saw the dreaded Roman legions so near, they were well nigh panic-stricken. But Xanthippus was at hand to allay their fears, and confident in their leader, the men's courage was soon restored.

Then the Spartan gave the signal to advance. At the same moment, the Romans, clasping their spears, rushed to meet the enemy that they had grown used to conquer.

A line of elephants was ranged in front of the Carthaginian army, but the left wing of the Romans slipped past the animals and attacked the Punic infantry.

It was on the point of giving way when Xanthippus, riding quickly up, rallied it. Then flinging himself from his horse, the Spartan fought in the midst of his infantry, as a common soldier.

The Carthaginian cavalry meanwhile had swept the Roman horsemen from the field, and was now charging the legions at the rear.

Then the elephants, already roused to fury by the noise of battle, reached the main body of the Roman army and trampled and crushed the bravest to the ground.

REGULUS IS TAKEN PRISONER

Those who succeeded in escaping from the elephants found themselves in front of the unbroken ranks of the Punic infantry, and were soon cut to pieces.

Only two thousand of the Roman army escaped. Regulus himself fled from the field, followed by about five hundred soldiers, but he was pursued and taken prisoner.

In a short time after this great victory, which was gained in 255 B.C., the Romans lost all that they had formerly gained in Africa.

In Carthage, and throughout the land, joy and gratitude were unbounded. People crowded into the temples with offerings and thanksgiving, for the foe who had used them so cruelly was crushed.

Xanthippus, to whom the glory of the victory belonged, went back to Greece, loaded with gifts from the grateful Carthaginians.

The Consul was kept a prisoner for five years. During these years the war between the Romans and Carthaginians was carried on in Sicily, the Romans in the end making themselves masters of the island.

Then the Carthaginians, disheartened and tired of war, determined to beg for peace.

Ambassadors were sent from Carthage to Rome, and with them went Regulus, having first taken an oath that if he did not prevail on the Senate to grant terms of peace and an exchange of prisoners, he would return to captivity.

When the ambassadors reached the gates of Rome, Regulus refused to enter the city, saying that he was no longer worthy to be counted a citizen. Nor could he be persuaded to see his wife or his children.

As Regulus would not enter Rome, the Senate agreed to meet him without the walls. It believed that he had come to ask that peace should be made with the Carthaginians.

But the Roman had never meant to urge the Senate to make peace. Although he knew that he must go back a prisoner to Carthage if the war was continued, yet he besought the Senate to fight until Africa was subdued, for his pride in his country was greater even than his love of liberty.

And so, the Senate having agreed to carry on the war, Regulus, true to his oath, went back to Carthage, knowing that torture and death awaited him.

The legends say that the Carthaginians were so angry that Regulus had not even tried to make peace, that they did indeed torture him.

So cruel were they that they shut their prisoner up with an elephant, so that at any moment he might be trampled or crushed to death. He was starved, his eyelids were cut off, and he was laid in the scorching sun, where no shade tempered the burning rays. At length the unfortunate Roman was placed in a box, in which he could not move without his body being torn by the nails with which it was studded.

REGULUS IS TAKEN PRISONER

It is also told that when the tale of what Regulus had suffered reached Rome, two noble Carthaginian prisoners were given to his widow and her sons, that they might avenge on these the cruelty done to Regulus.

But these terrible stories of vengeance and torture are now thought by many historians to be untrue.

CHAPTER LV

THE ROMANS CONQUER THE GAULS

THE first Punic war ended in 242 B.C., leaving the Romans in possession of Sicily, while the second Punic war did not begin until twenty-three years later.

For a little time Rome was at peace, and in 235 B.C. the gates of the temple of Janus were closed for the first time since the reign of the peace-loving King, Numa Pompilius.

But ten years later, the Gauls once again threatened to invade Rome. They were always foes to be dreaded, and some of the old superstitious fears, which had apparently vanished for ever, began once more to spread among the Roman legions.

Omens of ill too were rife. The Capitol was struck with lightning, so the Sibylline books were opened, and behold, it was written, "When the lightning shall strike the Capitol and the temple of Apollo, then, must thou, O Roman, beware of the Gauls."

THE ROMANS CONQUER THE GAULS

After that the simplest event seemed to the Romans to forebode evil. And while they brooded over the meaning of a strange light in the sky or a cloud of curious aspect, a large Gallic army was marching through Etruria, upon Clusium, a town only three days' march from Rome. This was the very way their fathers had taken long years before.

When the Consuls were absent from Rome, or already engaged with other matters, prætors were sent to lead the Romans against the foe.

In this case it was a prætor who was sent with a reserve corps to track the enemy. He succeeded in following the Gauls to Clusium, and believed the enemy was in his grasp.

But during the night, the main body of the Gauls slipped quietly out of their camp and marched some distance off, leaving only the cavalry to guard the tents. They hoped to entrap the Romans.

The prætor, finding only a small force of cavalry in the camp, ordered an attack. As the Gallic horse retreated, the Romans followed, to find themselves, almost at once, face to face with the whole force of the barbarians.

A fierce struggle followed, in which six thousand Romans were slain. Those who were left alive entrenched themselves with the prætor on a hill, and were at once surrounded by the Gauls.

Meanwhile Æmilius, one of the Consuls, found himself free to hasten to Clusium with a large army. Here he heard of the disaster that had befallen the arms of Rome, and he resolved to restore her fortune.

The prisoners on the hill were soon cheered to see the watchfires of their comrades, and they were sure that in the morning the Consul would scatter the barbarians.

But the Gauls had no wish to encounter Æmilius while they were laden with prisoners and booty. So they began to march northward, followed by the Consul, who harassed their rear, and wrested what booty he could from the retreating-foe.

Suddenly the barbarians were ordered to halt. Their chiefs had seen another army approaching. If they were Romans, the Gauls saw that they were caught in a trap.

It was indeed a Roman army that was marching toward them, led by Regulus, the son of the Consul who had perished at Carthage. He was on his way to Rome when he unwittingly startled the Gauls by his appearance.

With an army marching straight toward them and another in their rear, there was nothing left for the Gauls to do save prepare for battle.

One part of the Gallic army continued to face northward, ready to destroy, as they hoped, the troops led by Regulus. The other turned to the south, to face Æmilius, who was eager to attack the warriors. A short time before it had seemed as though they were going to escape the punishment he was anxious to inflict.

THE ROMANS CONQUER THE GAULS

Those who advanced upon Æmilius were the fiercest of all the fierce Gallic tribes. They wore neither armour nor clothes, but their bodies were covered with ornaments.

The chiefs wore the richest jewels, for they were adorned with heavy collars and bracelets of twisted gold, the sight of which filled the Romans with greed. Their savage war-cries filled them with fear.

Amid the blowing of horns and trumpets, the Gauls, still shouting their wild battle-cries, dashed upon the enemy, while they, remembering the dread day of Allia, fought with all their might.

Toward the north, the battle also raged. Regulus himself led his cavalry, but he was slain almost at once. The barbarians cut off his head, and in their savage way held it aloft on a spear, that his followers might see what had befallen their leader. With no one to command them, the cavalry withdrew, to allow the infantry to advance.

But the Gauls soon found that their weapons were of little use against the shield or helmet of the enemy. Their swords, of which the steel was badly tempered, bent at the first stroke and glanced aside, leaving the Roman's shield or helmet unglazed.

Fierce was the struggle between the two forces, but ere long the barbarians found that the day was going against them. The knowledge made them fight but the more desperately.

Slowly but steadily the Roman legions now began to close in, shutting the Gauls together in their midst, until at length they were hemmed in so relentlessly that it was not possible for them to use their arms. Then the Romans slaughtered them without mercy.

Forty thousand were killed, ten thousand taken prisoners, while one of the Gallic kings was captured alive. The other perished by his own hand.

All the booty that the Gauls had taken from the Romans, when they enticed them out of the camp at Clusium, was now recaptured. The Gauls themselves were robbed of their ornaments and their land was invaded by the victorious armies.

Æmilius then led his troops back to Rome and was given a great triumph, while the people thanked the gods that their city was safe from the barbarians.

For three years the war with the Gauls continued, until, from the Apennines to the Alps, the whole plain of Northern Italy had been subdued and was subject to Rome.

CHAPTER LVI

THE BOY HANNIBAL

The Carthaginians, as you know, had been turned out of Sicily at the end of the first Punic war. They had, too, lost more than Sicily, and were eager to atone for their losses by gaining territory in other lands.

Their thoughts turned to Spain, where already they had a few colonies.

So while the Romans were busy fighting against the Gauls, and too engrossed with the barbarians to trouble about the ambitions of the Carthaginians, they sent their general Hamilcar Barca to Spain, to add to the power and dominion of Carthage.

This was in time to prove the cause of the second Punic war.

Before setting out for Spain, Hamilcar went to the temple to offer a sacrifice to the supreme god of his people, at the same time beseeching him to grant success to his adventure.

As he turned away from the altar he caught sight of his little son Hannibal, then a boy of nine years old, who was watching his father with eager, awe-struck eyes.

Bidding those who stood near to withdraw, Hamilcar called the boy to him, and asked if he would like to go with him to Spain.

To go with his gallant father! To be a soldier like him!

There was no need for the child to answer, his eager face told his father all he wished to know.

So then the great general solemnly led his little son to the altar and bade him lay his hands upon it, as he swore never to be the friend of the Romans.

Hannibal took the oath as his father bade him, and never, in all the years to come, did he forget it. His hatred of the Romans grew with his strength, and when he became a man, his chief aim was to thwart their plans and overthrow their power. So it happened that when Hamilcar set out for Spain, Hannibal went with him.

In the camp the boy soon learned to love the hardships as well as the joys of a soldier's life.

His father himself saw that he was trained as a good soldier should be. In the end he gave his life to save his son from danger on the battlefield. After his father's death, Hannibal served under his brother-in-law, Hasdrubal, for eight years.

While he was still young, he was given a command in the army, and none was ever loved by his men as was he.

In battle, the young leader was always to be found at the point of danger, and every hardship, in the camp as on the field, he shared with his men. Nothing seemed able to daunt his spirit. In disaster as in success he remained cheerful and confident. And he complained of no trouble when it could help his cause.

Until he was twenty, Hannibal lived his hard and happy soldier life. Then young as he was, a great responsibility was laid upon him.

Hasdrubal was killed in his tent by a slave whose master he had murdered, and the army shouted with one voice, that no one but Hannibal should become their commander.

And at length, the government of Carthage reluctantly agreed that the young soldier should be appointed. Until now this important post had been filled by men of greater age and wider experience than Hannibal.

But the new general soon showed the stuff of which he was made. He was young and energetic, and in two years he had taken many towns and added to the power and possessions of Carthage in Spain.

But Saguntum, a town on the east coast of Spain, defied Hannibal's efforts and remained unconquered. As the inhabitants watched the growing power of the young Carthaginian leader, they grew afraid, lest they in the end should be forced to yield. So they appealed to Rome for help.

In the winter of 220 B.C. a Roman embassy was therefore sent to Spain, bearing a message from the Senate for Hannibal.

The young leader received it with no goodwill. Did it not come from the country he had sworn to hate, and had not his hatred grown, until now it had become the burning passion of his life?

But although the Roman ambassadors found Hannibal in no pleasant mood, they did not attempt to pacify him. Haughtily they gave their message that he should not attack Saguntum, or dare to cross the river Ebro, beyond which the Carthaginians had not yet advanced.

Hannibal listened with undisguised disdain to the demands of the Senate, and dismissed the ambassadors from his camp without an answer.

In the spring of 219 B.C., it was plain that he went to defy Rome, for he laid siege to Saguntum.

For eight months the city held out. When their provisions failed, and starvation stared them in the face, they still refused to surrender, believing that Rome would send help.

But at length all hope of relief faded. Then the Spanish chiefs determined to die rather than fall into the hands of the enemy. So they ordered a fire to be kindled in the market-place, and into it they flung all the treasures which were left in the city. After the

"I carry here peace and war, choose, men of Carthage, which ye will."

treasures were consumed, they themselves leaped into the flames and were burned to death.

When tidings of the fall of Saguntum reached Rome, she sent an embassy to Carthage, at the head of which was a noble named Fabius.

Fabius demanded that Hannibal and his officers should be given up, otherwise Rome would declare war against Carthage.

While the Carthaginians hesitated, Fabius rose, and gathering up the folds of his toga, as though in them he held the fate of the city, he cried, "I carry here peace and war. Choose, men of Carthage, which ye will."

"Give us whatever ye wish," answered the Senate.

Then shaking out the folds of his toga Fabius answered, "Then here I give ye war," and without another word he left the Senate-house.

"With that spirit with which ye give it, shall we wage it," cried the Carthaginians, while the ambassador strode away.

As the shout of the Assembly followed him, Fabius knew that the men of Carthage did not dread his gift.

CHAPTER LVII

HANNIBAL PREPARES TO INVADE ITALY

THE Romans thought it would be an easy matter to send an army to Spain to punish the young general for his daring defiance of the Senate. But as they soon found, it was not so simple as they had deemed.

Hannibal had ambitions beyond the wildest imaginations of the Romans, and before they had sent an army to Spain, he had left the country to invade Italy, for this was his great ambition.

In order to reach Italy, he determined to lead his army across the Alps, a feat that no one without the genius and the daring of the Carthaginian general could have ever hoped to accomplish.

The Gauls, who had so lately been at war with Rome, promised to join Hannibal's forces. When he was assured of the help of the barbarians, Hannibal called his soldiers together and told them his plans.

"The Romans," he said, "have demanded that I and my principal officers should be delivered up to them as malefactors. Soldiers, will you suffer such an indignity? The Gauls are holding out their arms to us, inviting us to come to them and to assist them in revenging their manifold injuries. And the country which we shall invade, so rich in corn and wine and oil, so full of flocks and herds, so covered with flourishing cities, will be the richest prize that could be offered by the gods to reward your valour."

As you know, Hannibal was the idol of his men, and when he had spoken a loyal shout arose. It was plain that his soldiers would follow him to death.

Hannibal thanked his troops for their devotion, told them the day on which they were to march, and then dismissed them.

He himself went to the temple to pray to the gods for the success of his invasion of Italy.

Day and night he brooded over his plans, so that even when he slept his mind was possessed by them.

One night he dreamed that he was in the presence of the gods of Carthage. The deities bade him invade Italy, and one of them, they promised, would be with him as his guide.

In his dream he and his divine leader then set out. "See that thou look not behind thee," said the god. But in spite of this command Hannibal looked back and a terrible dragon, covered with innumerable scales, met his gaze. As the monster moved, it dragged in its path, woods, orchards, houses.

"What is this that I see?" asked Hannibal.

"Thou seest the desolation of Italy," answered his guide. "Go thy way straight forward and cast no look behind."

Thus encouraged by his dream, Hannibal went back to his army more confident than before, and marched into Italy to perform his boyhood's vow.

CHAPTER LVIII

HANNIBAL CROSSES THE ALPS

In the spring of 218 B.C. the Carthaginian army set out on its great undertaking, thirty-seven elephants in its train.

Hasdrubal, one of Hannibal's brothers, was left behind to guard the towns that had been taken in Spain.

Meanwhile the Roman Senate, knowing nothing of Hannibal's movements, sent Sempronius, one of the Consuls, into Sicily with an army, while the other, Cornelius Scipio, was ordered to lead an army into Spain to punish Hannibal.

But while Rome was thus hoping to secure the general who had flouted her, he was already marching through Gaul. At the river Rhone he was met by his first difficulty, for some of the tribes that were unfriendly to the Carthaginians had gathered on the opposite bank to oppose his passage.

Hannibal at once sent a body of his troops higher up the river, with orders to cross, and, stealing unnoticed into the camp of the enemy, to set it on fire. When the general thought that there had been time for this to be done, he began to cross the river with the main body of his army, in boats and canoes. On the opposite bank, the barbarians were drawn up in battle array.

Hannibal did not fear them. Already his quick eyes had seen a column of smoke rising from the Gallic camp, and he knew that when the flames burst out, the Gauls would not stay to oppose his passage across the river.

As Hannibal had foreseen, so it happened. The Gauls, to their dismay, soon saw that their camp was on fire, and many of them at once rushed away to try to save their goods. Those who did not desert their post were too few to prevent Hannibal and his army from landing in safety.

It was no easy matter to get the elephants across the river. Huge rafts were moored to the bank and covered with earth to make them seem part of the land. The animals were then persuaded to venture on board.

When the rafts began to move, some of the elephants grew restive and jumped into the river, drowning their drivers. The beasts themselves, however, reached the other side in safety.

By this time Rome had discovered Hannibal's movements. Scipio, who had not yet sailed for Spain, was sent toward the Rhone to keep Hannibal from crossing the river. But as you know, he was already too late to do so.

However, he sent out a company of cavalry to find out the movements of the enemy and to report to him. The cavalry soon came across a number of Hannibal's men, who, after crossing the Rhone, had been sent forward to reconnoitre.

Scipio's horsemen drove them back toward their camp, then sped swiftly to the Consul to tell him that Hannibal was across the river and had now encamped on its banks.

No sooner had Scipio heard this, than he hastened in the direction of the river, only to find that the Carthaginians had marched away three days earlier. But from the direction in which the enemy had gone, Scipio learned that they intended to cross the Alps and descend into Italy by one of the passes used by the Gauls in other times.

It was incredible, yet it was true. Scipio did not dare to follow Hannibal into the dangerous passes of the Alps, so he marched into Italy, to be ready to meet the bold invader when he descended into the valley of the river Po.

Among the mountain passes, the Carthaginian army was meanwhile struggling against terrible difficulties.

It was already October, and snow had fallen and lay thick in the passes, so that often no footpath was to be seen. Guides proved false, mountain tribes hostile.

It was almost impossible to find food or shelter for the great army he was leading, yet Hannibal went before his troops fearless, undaunted. Neither cold, nor hunger, nor treachery could change his purpose.

The hostile tribes were guarding many of the defiles through which the army must pass, but it was only during the day that they were to be seen. When darkness fell they slipped away to their own homes, which were scattered among the mountains.

One evening, Hannibal with a band of lightly armed troops, seized the posts that had been held by the barbarians through the day.

When morning dawned, the general ordered his army to advance along the narrow and difficult defile, while he stayed above the pass, to keep the enemy in check.

At first the barbarians looked at the slowly moving army in astonishment; then, seeing how easy it would be to attack and plunder it, they rushed down the mountains and dashed upon the startled Carthaginians. Hannibal had been unable to hinder their descent.

In the narrow pass all was soon in utter confusion. The cattle, laden with baggage, stumbled, fell and slipped over the track, while the horses, wounded by the darts of the enemy and mad with fear, plunged into the depths below.

Hannibal saw the havoc that was being done in the valley, and despite the danger, he now charged down upon the barbarians, and succeeded in driving them away. But in the struggle, as he had foreseen, many of his own men were lost.

Soon after this desperate adventure, the army emerged from the pass, and ere long reached a town which Hannibal took by storm.

Here he found many of his own men, as well as much baggage, which had been captured by the hostile tribes.

In the town there was also a good supply of corn and cattle, so that the exhausted army was fed and rested, before it again began its perilous march.

It seemed as though the natives had now determined to be friendly. When the army had marched steadily on for four days, many of the tribes came to meet it, with branches of trees in their hands and on their heads wreaths, in sign of friendship. They even brought with them cattle to provide the army with food, and offered hostages, to prove that they were sincere.

Yet Hannibal did not trust them. He accepted their offers of help, but as the army approached another dangerous pass, he was careful to send the baggage and cavalry on in front.

The cavalry left the defile safely, but as the foot soldiers were still toiling along the dangerous way, the faithless barbarians attacked them from above, rolling huge stones and great masses of rock upon them.

HANNIBAL CROSSES THE ALPS

A great number of soldiers were killed, and it was with difficulty that Hannibal regained his cavalry on the following day.

But the worst of the ascent was now over, and the army reached the summit of the Alps, after a march of nine days.

The soldiers, who had come from the warm and sunny climates of Africa and Spain, were unused to snow and frost, and they grumbled at every discomfort.

Hannibal soon roused them to a braver spirit. Calling them together he bade them look at the valley beneath. "That valley," he said, "is Italy. It leads us to our allies, the Gauls, and yonder is the way to Rome."

After resting for ten days, the army began the descent, and although no hostile tribes added to the difficulties, the downward way proved even more dangerous than the ascent.

Snow had completely covered the path, and the soldiers unawares stepped off it, to be hurled down the precipice into the chasm below.

At one spot it is said that the road was broken away by an avalanche, and in front of the army yawned a hideous gulf. But even such a disaster proved powerless to daunt Hannibal.

Encouraged by their general, the men were soon at work bridging the chasm. Before a day had passed the cavalry and baggage were sent across in safety. But it took three days to make a bridge strong enough and wide enough to bear the elephants.

At length, all obstacles were overcome, and Hannibal led his army into Northern Italy. But in the terrible journey across the Alps he lost three thousand men.

CHAPTER LIX

THE BATTLE OF TREBIA

AFTER the hardships they had endured while crossing the Alps Hannibal and his army were forced to rest. But in a short time Hannibal was ready to lead his men along the left bank of the river Po, having sent a corps of cavalry forward to reconnoitre.

Scipio, you remember, had determined to await Hannibal in the valley of the Po, and he was now also marching along the left bank of the river.

As he crossed the Ticinus, a tributary of the Po, he suddenly found himself face to face with the cavalry of the enemy.

A fierce struggle at once took place, but before long the Roman soldiers turned and fled, in spite of all the Consul could do to rally them. He himself showed the greatest courage, fighting in the forefront of the battle and so being wounded. Had it not been for the bravery of his young son, he would indeed have been captured or killed.

Seeing that his father was wounded and surrounded by the enemy, the lad, who was only sixteen years of age, dashed into their midst. He was followed by his men, who were ashamed to linger behind their young leader. His daring attack scattered the foe, and the Consul was carried off the field in safety. This lad of sixteen was the Scipio who afterwards became known as Scipio Africanus, the conqueror of Hannibal.

The battle at the Ticinus was in reality only a skirmish. But Scipio was warned by this defeat to be cautious, and he determined to withdraw across the Po. There he would await his colleague Sempronius, who had been recalled from Sicily, when it became known that Hannibal meant to invade Italy.

Although the fight at Ticinus was only a skirmish, yet the victory of Hannibal's cavalry encouraged many Gallic tribes to throw off their fear of Rome and join the Carthaginians.

Even those Gauls who had joined the Roman camp were eager to escape, and one night more than two thousand of them mutinied, and, overpowering the sentinels, left the Romans to join Hannibal.

After the flight of the Gauls, Scipio thought it would be wise to move to a safer position, so he marched to the upper Trebia, another tributary of the Po. Here he was joined by Sempronius.

Hannibal was eager to fight while the Gauls were still faithful to him, for he, as well as the Romans, knew their unstable character. Scipio on the other hand, wished to delay meeting the enemy, for he was still wounded. Moreover, he thought that if a battle did not take place soon, the Gauls would be more than likely to forsake their new ally.

THE BATTLE OF TREBIA

But Sempronius, who had entire charge of both the Roman armies since Scipio was wounded, could brook no delay.

The Carthaginian general had already discovered that it would be easy to tempt the second Consul to fight. He therefore determined to entice him to cross the river Trebia.

It was winter. Heavy rains and sleet had fallen, and the river was flooded, when, early one bleak morning, Hannibal ordered his brave young brother Mago, with a large number of troops, to lie in ambush in a dried-up watercourse, where they were hidden by high banks and tall bushes. Until a signal bade them dash out upon the enemy, they were not to stir.

Meanwhile a body of Carthaginian cavalry had been sent across the river, close to the Roman camp. The cavalry was to tempt Sempronius to leave his camp and offer battle.

The Consul no sooner saw the enemy, than without waiting for his men to have breakfast, he ordered the horsemen to advance at once, and the infantry to follow as soon as possible.

Cold and hungry, the Roman army obeyed, and the Punic cavalry retreated across the river before the enemy.

The Roman foot soldiers were ordered to follow, although the water was cold as ice, and reached almost to their shoulders. When they scrambled up on the other bank, they were chilled to the bone as well as faint for want of food. More miserable bedraggled Roman soldiers had never been seen. They were scarcely fit to attack a small body of the enemy, much less to face the main body of the Carthaginian army, which, well fed and warm, awaited them in battle array.

Hannibal, with his usual care for his soldiers, had seen that they had a good meal, after which he had bade them rub their bodies with oil in front of the camp fires, before they buckled on their armour.

It was soon plain that the Romans were not fit to cope with the comfortable Carthaginian troops.

Yet in spite of the elephants, that trampled them underfoot, and in spite, too, of the Punic cavalry which was stronger than their own, the Roman legions held their ground.

It was only when the signal had been given, and Mago, with two thousand men rushed from his ambush, and attacked them in the rear, that the Romans gave way.

Then they turned and fled towards the Trebia, hoping to be able to cross it and to regain their camp. But many of them were cut down before they reached the river, while, of those who attempted to recross the cold and swollen waters, many were drowned.

Only ten thousand in the centre of the Roman army succeeded in keeping their ranks unbroken. These brave soldiers pushed their way through the enemy and retreated to Placentia, a town on the river

THE BATTLE OF TREBIA

Po, which had already been taken and fortified by their own legions.

Before the day was over the Carthaginians, too, had suffered severely from the weather. Showers of rain and snow forced them at length to give up the pursuit of the Romans and hasten to their tents for shelter and warmth. Many of the elephants perished in the storm.

When Rome heard of the defeat of her two armies, and that both her Consuls were shut up in Placentia with a remnant of their soldiers, she was dismayed at the greatness of the disaster. Moreover, she was well aware that this victory would make the Gauls cleave more steadfastly than before to the successful general.

Thus the year 218 B.C. drew to a close, while signs of evil omen added to the anxiety of the citizens of Rome.

Rain fell; no gentle, refreshing showers, but rain of red-hot stones. In the market-place a bull ran up the third story of a house and leapt from thence into the street. And who ever heard of a child of six months old being able to speak! Yet one of just such tender age was heard to shout "Triumph."

Even the least superstitious saw in these strange portents the hand of the gods, and they trembled for what might next befall.

CHAPTER LX

THE BATTLE OF LAKE TRASIMENUS

EARLY in 217 B.C. Hannibal broke up his camp in the valley of the Po.

The Gauls in large numbers were still with him, but he had lost many of his own loyal soldiers, since he had crossed the Rhone a year earlier.

Now, with the first sign of spring, he marched to the river Arno. Here his difficulties began.

The country through which Hannibal wished to take his army was in a state of flood. As the snow melted on the mountains, streams of water poured down into the valley, and these streams, along with the heavy rains of spring, had made the ground like a vast swamp.

Many of the Carthaginians sank deep into the marsh, and they and their beasts perished.

For three days, part of the army was forced to wade through the floods, and, when night fell, there was no dry spot on which to pitch its tents. The soldiers had perforce to rest as well as they could on

THE BATTLE OF LAKE TRASIMENUS

the bodies of their poor fallen steeds or amid the baggage which had been left behind by their comrades.

Damp and hardships of this kind made many of the soldiers ill, while Hannibal himself lost the sight of one eye, through an attack of inflammation.

But it was the Gauls who suffered most, and they were less willing than the well-trained Carthaginian troops to endure hardship. Had it been possible they would have deserted, but Hannibal, knowing their fickle ways, had ordered his brother Mago with the cavalry to ride at the rear of the army.

As the march continued, it seemed that Hannibal was on his way to Rome. He passed the Roman camp where Flaminius, one of the new Consuls, was in command, and then continued southward, with no army now to hinder his approach to the city.

But what the great general was really trying to do was, not to reach Rome and besiege it, since for that he had not the necessary machines, but to entice the Roman army from its camp and force it to fight. All unwittingly, the army fell into the trap which the Carthaginian set.

Flaminius had been sent into Etruria to see that Hannibal did not march upon Rome. As he had allowed the enemy to pass his camp unhindered, he determined to atone for his error as well as might be, by following swiftly and destroying it.

The Consul was urged to wait until his colleague Servilius joined him, but this he was much too impatient to do.

Hannibal meanwhile had reached the Trasimenus Lake. Between the lake and the mountains ran a narrow road. The general saw at once that this was the very place in which to entrap the Roman army. So he sent his men to command the heights that overlooked the path.

That same evening, Flaminius encamped a short distance from the lake. He could see the narrow road stretching out before him.

Early in the morning the Romans were again on the march, hastening after the enemy that was, as they believed, on the way to Rome.

Unaware of evil, they marched along the narrow road by the side of the lake, scarce able to see a step before them, so heavy hung the mist on the pathway and along the foot of the mountains.

But up on the heights, where Hannibal had posted his men, the sun was shining bright.

The Consul was glad of the mist. He would be able to approach the enemy unseen and attack it suddenly, while it was in marching order and unprepared for battle.

On and on tramped the Roman soldiers, and although they knew it not, they were tramping to destruction.

THE BATTLE OF LAKE TRASIMENUS

Hannibal waited until the rearguard had entered the defile, and then he gave his men the signal to attack.

Suddenly the Romans seemed to see the mist break and scatter before their eyes, pierced by the terrible battlecry of the Gauls and by the quick tramp of Hannibal's cavalry as it dashed out of the silence, upon the startled foe.

Javelins and arrows, hurled by unseen hands penetrated the mist as it again closed around them, while great stones came crashing down upon them, too huge to be withstood by shield or helmet.

In vain Flaminius strove to rally his panic-stricken troops. They but rushed the more wildly hither and thither, falling now upon the enemy, now upon each other, in their despair. The Consul himself fought bravely, but he soon fell wounded to death.

Thousands of his soldiers were slain. Some threw themselves into the lake, hoping to swim to safety, but their armour weighed them down and they were drowned. Others waded out as far as they dared into the water, only to be followed by the cavalry of the enemy and slaughtered without mercy.

It was useless to cry for quarter that day, for it was a day of vengeance and of sacrifice to the gods of Carthage. In three short hours, the Roman army was not only defeated; it no longer existed.

Only a body of six thousand men escaped. It had been at the vanguard of the army, and had cut its way through the enemy to the top of the hills.

Here the survivors stayed until the mist lifted, knowing nothing of what had befallen their comrades, until it was too late to go to their aid. So they then entrenched themselves in a village not far from the lake, but Hannibal's cavalry soon surrounded them and forced them to surrender.

In the battle of Lake Trasimenus the Carthaginians lost but fifteen hundred men, and of these the larger number were Gauls.

Fugitives from the army soon reached Rome, and threw the citizens into consternation by the terrible and different tales they told.

The following day tidings of the awful slaughter at the edge of Lake Trasimenus reached the Senate.

Then the people thronged into the Forum and surrounded the Senate-house, demanding to know what really had happened.

In the evening, when the people's patience was all but at an end, Marcus, one of the prætors, mounted the public platform and cried in a loud voice, "We are beaten, O Romans, in a great battle, our army is destroyed, and Flaminius the Consul is slain."

At the words of Marcus the city became a scene of wild despair. Many men and women who had lost their husbands and sons called down the

THE BATTLE OF LAKE TRASIMENUS

"We are beaten, O Romans, in a great battle, our army is destroyed."

curses of the gods upon their enemy, others wept and prayed in the temples and forbore to curse, for all the bitterness of their loss.

Amid the tumult, the Senate alone remained calm. Day after day, from early morning until late in the evening, it sat to consider how it might best save the city from the mighty conqueror.

Three days passed, and then even worse tidings arrived.

The Consul Servilius had sent his cavalry to prevent Hannibal's advance on Rome, but it had been either captured or put to the sword. Servilius without his cavalry was powerless to prevent the Punic army from advancing upon the city.

In a short time indeed, Hannibal, at the head of his triumphant army, was scarcely two days' march from Rome.

Flaminius was dead. Between Servilius and the city was the Carthaginian army.

Being bereft of both her Consuls, Rome determined to appoint a Dictator.

CHAPTER LXI

HANNIBAL OUTWITS FABIUS

THE Senate had restored some sense of confidence to the stricken people by its gravity and calmness. It had also reassured them by destroying the bridges by which the city could be approached and by strengthening her walls.

Soldiers who had been deemed too old to follow the army were now called together, and armed with weapons which had hung for years in the temples—trophies these from many a hard-fought field.

But most important of all, a Dictator was chosen to guide Rome in the crisis that had befallen her.

Fabius, the noble patrician who was elected, was a wise man, and one who was not easily swayed by others. He was, however, neither a brilliant nor an enterprising soldier.

Minucius, one of the people's favourites, was appointed to be the Dictator's master of horse.

Now many of the people believed that disaster had overtaken the army because Flaminius had marched to the war without first offering sacrifices

THE STORY OF ROME

to the gods. And also because he had treated their warnings with contempt.

For as he rode off to join his troops he was thrown from his horse, while a standard that had been thrust into the ground was found to be so firmly embedded that the standard-bearer, with all his efforts, could not dislodge it. These omens Flaminius had treated with scorn, merely remounting his steed and ordering the standard to be dug out of the ground.

Fabius the Dictator, therefore, determined before he did aught else, to pacify the anger of the gods and at the same time to please the people.

So he ordered white oxen to be offered in the temples, as an atonement for the neglect shown to the gods by Flaminius. The people flocked gladly to these sacrifices, bringing with them their own offerings to lay on the altars, while they prayed for the goodwill of the god of battle.

A vow, too, was made by the whole of the people, to keep "A holy spring."

This vow said that "every animal fit for sacrifice, born in the spring of the year 216 B.C., and reared on any mountain or plain or river bank or upland pasture throughout Italy, should be offered to Jupiter."

There was no need to offer children to the gods in sacrifice, for they, when they grew old enough, offered their lives, and that right willingly, on the battlefield to the god of war.

When the religious rites were ended, Fabius prepared to meet the enemy.

Two new legions were soon raised, and Servilius was ordered to bring his two legions to Rome, so that Fabius had four legions to lead to battle.

The Dictator had his own idea of how best to beat Hannibal, and to this idea he remained faithful, although his own followers as well as the enemy derided his policy.

Fabius had determined not to meet the Carthaginians in a pitched battle. They had already been victorious too often in such a struggle. He intended to harass the rear guard of the enemy and to cut off the parties Hannibal sent out in search of food or forage. This discreet policy proved pleasing neither to Hannibal nor to his own troops, but of this Fabius recked little.

After deciding on these tactics, the Dictator led his legions into Northern Apulia and encamped near to the enemy. In vain Hannibal tried to tempt Fabius to fight. He wantonly burned the homesteads and destroyed the vineyards of the Italians, that the Dictator might grow indignant and hasten to their help. But seemingly untouched by the desolation of his country, Fabius continued to follow his own method of warfare.

This method of delay has since his time become a byword, and is known as "The Fabian Policy." He himself was named, or perhaps I should say he was nicknamed, Cunctator, The Delayer.

Minucius, the master of the horse, eager for battle, encouraged the soldiers in their discontent with the Dictator, until they even dared to say that Minucius was more fit to command Romans than Fabius.

Then Minucius, seeing the men were in his favour, grew more daring, and ventured to jest at the Dictator because he encamped always on the hills, while the enemy was in the plains. "It is," said the officer, "as if Fabius has taken us to the hills as to a theatre, to look at the flames and desolation of our country." Or he would mockingly declare that the Dictator was leading them up to heaven, having no hopes on earth, or even that he was trying to hide them in the clouds from the Carthaginians.

These words were told to Fabius, and his friends urged him, as they had often done before, to fight.

But the Dictator answered, "I should be more faint-hearted than they make me, if through fear of idle reproaches I should abandon my own convictions."

Such words showed the true bravery of the Delayer's spirit.

Soon after this, Hannibal, who had been despoiling the beautiful country of Campania, determined to march back to Apulia, with the booty he had secured. He had with him great herds of cattle which formed a large part of the spoil.

HANNIBAL OUTWITS FABIUS

To reach Apulia, the Carthaginians would have to march through a narrow defile, and Fabius believed that now his patience was going to be rewarded. He would catch Hannibal in a trap.

But Fabius had scarcely realised the man with whom he had to deal. Hannibal in a trap like that which he had himself often set for the Romans! That surely was not easy to believe.

Knowing the country well, the Dictator did not on this occasion delay, but sent a company of four thousand soldiers to guard the exit by which the enemy must leave the pass, on its way to Apulia. He, with the main body of his army, stationed himself on the summit of a hill, close at hand.

Hannibal guessed what the Romans had done, and he made up his mind to frustrate their plans; moreover, he determined to do so by a trick. He seemed to treat the Dictator and his arrangements with scarcely the requisite gravity.

First he ordered two thousand of the oxen he had captured to have torches or dry faggots fastened to their horns.

Then when it grew dark these faggots were lighted, and the beasts were driven toward the mountains where the Roman soldiers were encamped. Hannibal and his army followed slowly behind the oxen.

The beasts moved heavily along, the lights on their heads making them appear like a mighty army, marching through the night. By and by the fire burned the horns down to the quick, and the poor animals, in horrible pain, ran hither and thither, tossing their heads and thus setting fire to the trees which they happened to pass.

On the crest of the hill, the Roman army saw the moving lights, but as Fabius issued no orders, the soldiers stayed in the camp.

The company guarding the pass also saw the lights and thought that they were moving toward the mountains. Thinking their comrades would be in danger, they deserted their post and ran to give them help.

Hannibal's soldiers at once seized the forsaken exit, and the Carthaginian army passed out of the defile unharmed.

Before morning dawned Fabius discovered how he had been outwitted by Hannibal. Yet fearing lest his men should fall into an ambush if he sent them in pursuit of the enemy before it was light, he still kept his army idle in camp.

When it was daylight it was too late to do the Carthaginians much harm, although the Dictator ordered his army to attack them in the rear.

CHAPTER LXII

FABIUS WINS TWO VICTORIES

Rome was not long in hearing how Hannibal had tricked the Dictator, and the people were roused to fury because Fabius had allowed their great enemy to escape.

Now it was necessary at this time for Fabius to leave the army and return to Rome to celebrate a religious rite.

Minucius was left in command of the legions during the absence of the Dictator. Before he left, Fabius bade the young officer on no pretext to risk a battle while he was away.

But no sooner had the Dictator gone, than Minucius, hearing that a large body of the enemy had left their camp in search of forage, fell upon a company of those that were left behind. He killed many of them, and retreated without losing any of his own men.

When tidings of this success, slight though it was, reached Rome, the people were both excited and elated. And as was perhaps natural, they began to compare Minucius and his triumph with the Dictator and his policy of delay.

If Minucius had been commander, Hannibal would have been beaten long ago, so grumbled the people. Surely it was ignoble to camp on the hills in safety, while the country was being destroyed by the enemy.

So great was the discontent of the people that at length the Senate decreed that Minucius should be given power equal to that of the Dictator. This had never been done before, as the Dictator always held the supreme power alone.

When Fabius returned to camp he showed no chagrin at the new arrangement, but gave to his former master of the horse complete control of two legions, while he himself kept command of the other two. This was, he believed, wiser than that two generals should rule the entire army.

Hannibal was well pleased when he heard how the Roman command had been divided. For he foresaw that it would be easy to draw the young impetuous general down from the heights.

So, as his way was, he carefully laid an ambush, and then sent out a small party to take possession of a hill that lay not far from the enemy's camp.

Minucius rose, as a fish rises, to the bait. He sent out his light troops and cavalry to scatter the enemy. Then when he saw the great Carthaginian general himself march to the help of his men, he

FABIUS WINS TWO VICTORIES

ordered his whole army to hasten forward to the attack.

No sooner did Hannibal see that his ruse had been successful than he gave a signal to the men lying in ambush, and they, springing from their hiding place, with loud cries attacked the Romans in the rear.

In vain did Minucius try to rally his terrified followers. They were soon in utter confusion. Nor, now that battle had actually been given, did the new general show himself a capable or wise soldier.

Just as the Romans were on the point of flying from the field, Fabius, who, foreseeing what would happen, had ordered his army to be ready, cried, "We must haste to rescue Minucius, who is a valiant man and a lover of his country."

Then speeding to the battlefield with his men, he led them so bravely, and at the same time so warily, that Hannibal was soon forced to sound a retreat.

To his friends the Punic general remarked, "Did I not tell you that this cloud which always hovered upon the mountains, would at some time or other, come down with a storm upon us?"

After Hannibal had withdrawn his troops, Fabius went back to his camp without saying a harsh or reproachful word to Minucius.

He, the more ashamed, that Fabius treated him so generously, called together his discomfited army, and told them that he was sorry that he had ever spoken against the Dictator.

"Some reason," he said, "I may have to accuse fortune, but I have many more to thank her; for in a few hours she hath cured a long mistake, and taught me that I am not the man who should command others, but have need of another to command me.... Therefore in everything else henceforth the Dictator must be your commander; only in showing gratitude towards him, I will still be your leader and always be the first to obey his orders."

Then he bade his men follow him to the camp of Fabius, carrying with them their standards.

As Minucius drew near to the tent of the Dictator, Fabius came out to meet him.

Ordering the standards to be laid at the feet of the man he had disdained, Minucius said, "You have this day, O Dictator, obtained two victories, one by your valour and conduct over Hannibal, and another by your wisdom and goodness to your colleague."

Then thanking Fabius for saving his life and the lives of those under him, he flung himself into the arms of the Dictator, calling him father.

The soldiers of each army, touched by the example of their leader, forgot their jealousy and also embraced one another with tears of joy.

CHAPTER LXIII

THE BATTLE OF CANNÆ

WINTER was nearly over, and spring, the usual time for the new Consuls to begin their duties, was at hand. Fabius therefore resigned his Dictatorship, as the Consuls would be able to carry on the war.

The people had chosen Varro, a man hated by the patricians, to be one of the Consuls. He was the son of a butcher, so it was declared; but be that as it may, his birth had not kept him from holding positions of trust in the state.

His colleague was Æmilius, a member of a noble family, who had, three years earlier, held the post of Consul.

Spring passed, and in summer of the same year, 216 B.C., Hannibal again marched into Apulia and seized the citadel of Cannæ, where the Romans had stored a large quantity of provisions for the army.

This, Hannibal was well aware, would force the Romans either to retreat or to give battle, for their army now consisted of eight legions, and with-

THE STORY OF ROME

out food, and a large supply of food, the Consuls would be compelled to take action.

Now Æmilius and Varro commanded the army on alternate days. The patrician Consul, who before leaving Rome had said: "I will rather seek in my conduct to please and obey Fabius than all the world besides," urged Varro not to fight on the plains of Apulia.

Fabius, he knew, would never have risked a battle on the plains, where the cavalry of Hannibal would have every advantage. And his cavalry was without doubt his greatest strength.

But Varro refused to listen to the advice of his colleague. When it was his turn to command, he drew up his army close to the village of Cannæ, and hung his scarlet coat outside his tent. This was a signal that the Consul meant to fight, and Hannibal at once ordered his men to prepare for battle.

As the wind at the time was blowing violently, carrying with it a cloud of dust, the Carthaginians took up their position with their backs to the storm, so that the dust swept harmlessly past them. But it dashed into the faces of the Roman legions, wellnigh blinding them.

In the centre of his army, and a little in advance, Hannibal had placed the soldiers on whom he could least depend. The bravest and most loyal men were in the wings.

This he did because he foresaw that the Romans would first attack the centre, and as the less

THE BATTLE OF CANNÆ

resolute soldiers fell back, they would press forward. Then, as they continued to push back the Carthaginian centre, Hannibal meant to bid the men on the right and left wings to close in and envelop the enemy.

So when the Romans charged the centre of the Punic army, pushed it well back and were already beginning to think of victory, the wings closed in and charged upon their flanks. Then the centre, seeing how it was supported, took fresh courage, and charged the front of the enemy with sudden determination.

Slowly but surely the Roman infantry was pressed closer and closer together, until they were unable to strike a blow, unable even to move.

Those on the edge were cut down at once, while thousands in the centre were compelled to stand and look on, awaiting their fate.

For a whole day the slaughter never ceased, and when the sun sank there was no longer any Roman army left. Hannibal had cut to pieces well-nigh the whole eight legions, which was the largest army that Rome had ever sent to the field.

Æmilius had been wounded at the beginning of the battle. In spite of this he had tried to remount, to rally his men. But he was too severely injured to be able to sit in his saddle, and he fell again, unnoticed, and was slain.

Minucius, who was on the field, was also killed, as well as eighty senators who had taken part in the battle.

The plebeian Consul, Varro, escaped, with about seventy horsemen, to the town of Venusia, where scattered troops of soldiers gradually rejoined him.

Maharbal, the mast of Hannibal's cavalry, begged to be sent at once to Rome. "If you will let me lead the horses and follow quickly, you shall dine in the Capitol in five days," he said with perfect confidence.

But Hannibal refused to march on Rome, and offered her terms of peace instead.

Then Maharbal turned sadly away, muttering, it is said, these words: "You know how to win a victory, Hannibal, but not how to use it."

The terms offered by Hannibal, Rome in her pride refused, although the loss of her eight legions had left her wellnigh helpless in the hands of her conqueror.

Hannibal seemed indeed not to know how to use his victory. He turned away from Rome, and marched to the wealthy city of Capua, in the south of Italy. The gates were thrown wide to the victorious general, and here he entered and set up his camp.

CHAPTER LXIV

THE DESPAIR OF ROME

AFTER the victory of Cannæ, Hannibal was deemed more than a mere man. Surely he must be endowed with the power of the gods, or he would never be able to sweep eight legions from his path, as he had done on this last dread battlefield.

Even a number of young Roman knights, of the best patrician families, were so sure that nothing could now save their country, that they determined to fly to the coast and thus escape to another land, where they might yet win honour by their arms.

But Cornelius Scipio, although but a lad like themselves, drew his sword and boldly declared that he would kill any one of them who refused to swear never to forsake his country. His courage made the young knights so ashamed that they gave up their selfish plan.

In Rome itself the people had been more confident than of late years, for was not Varro at the head of their army, and had he not been heard to say that he would conquer Hannibal in a day?

Tidings of the disaster at Cannæ reached the city first as a mere rumour, but even so it filled the hearts of the people with dread forebodings. Rumour said that the whole army was annihilated, that both Consuls were slain—the citizens in despair watched and waited for certain news of the battle.

At length a horseman was seen riding in hot haste toward the city. The people's hopes rose at the sight. For a moment they forgot the rumours that had made them so uneasy, forgot all, save that their favourite Varro had been fighting for them. So they rushed toward the messenger, shouting with expectant voices: "Is it victory of which you have to tell—victory?"

But even as they spoke the people knew how foolish were their hopes. For the face of the rider was pale and stricken with pain, and the folk shrank back, fearful now to hear the truth. And the messenger seemed in no haste to tell his tidings.

But Fabius the Delayer came to him and bade him speak, saying that if he had bad news, they were prepared to listen.

So, amid a sudden silence, the terrible tale was told, nor when it was ended was there a house to be found in Rome that was not filled with mourning. Henceforth the people trembled at the very sound of the conqueror's name.

After the first shock of the tidings, the people awoke to fresh fears. Suppose Hannibal was already marching upon Rome?

THE DESPAIR OF ROME

In a panic they flocked to the gates, longing to escape from the city that they believed was doomed.

Again it was Fabius who came and talked to the terrified folk, and by his calmness allayed their fears. In these troublous days the Delayer proved indeed so strong and wise that, before long, even those who had been used to mock at his slowness were glad to turn to him for counsel.

It was Fabius who ordered guards to be placed at the gates, that the frightened inhabitants might not desert their city. It was he who ordered the women not to wail and sob in the streets, but to go quietly to their homes to mourn there for their dead.

Meanwhile messengers were sent along the Appian and Latin roads to gather tidings of Hannibal's movements. And soon they returned to tell that the conqueror was not on his way to Rome, but was still in Apulia, dividing the spoil of the battle.

Varro, who was in Venusia, had with much difficulty gathered together the remnant of the army. He was now bidden by the Senate to bring it back to Rome.

It was a command he had dreaded. He had left Rome in joy, proud of the confidence of the people, he was going back shamed and, in his own eyes, disgraced. How would he be received by the Senate, by the people?

When he reached the gates of the city he would not enter, but awaited without the judgment of his fellows.

Then the Senate, knowing that the Consul loved his country and mourned for the humiliation he had brought upon her, went down to the gates to welcome him, followed by many of the people.

Fabius was among the senators, and from none of their lips did Varro hear a word of blame for the disaster of Cannæ. But they praised him for gathering together the remnant of the army, and thanked him, too, that after so great a loss "he had not despaired of the safety of the Commonwealth, but had come back to Rome to help them in their plans to deliver their country from the Carthaginians."

Meanwhile Hannibal had marched to Campania, and been gladly welcomed to its chief city Capua. Here, after their many hardships, he and his army enjoyed through the winter months comfort and ease. It is even said that the great general relaxed the severity of his discipline for a time.

But Capua was punished for opening its gates to Hannibal, for two Roman armies, under Fabius and Marcellus, were sent to besiege the town. The siege lasted during 212 and 211 B.C.

In the latter year Hannibal determined to march to Rome, for by doing so he thought he would force the Roman armies to leave Capua.

THE DESPAIR OF ROME

So at length what the citizens had often feared actually came to pass. The dreaded Carthaginian was on his way to Rome, and the people were sure that their city would be razed to the ground, while they themselves would be carried away as slaves.

But although Hannibal encamped three miles from the city, and rode round part of her walls, he did not attempt to lay siege to her. He knew that he had not the materials needed to reduce so strong a fortress as Rome.

Hannibal did not achieve all that he had hoped from his march. The siege of Capua was not raised, although Fabius, it is true, was recalled from before her walls.

So the Punic general, having accomplished little, set out, meaning to return to Capua. He was followed by a Roman army, of which he took no notice until five days later.

Then, hearing that Capua was still besieged, he was angry, and vented his wrath upon the army at his rear. Waiting until it was dark and their camp was set up, Hannibal stormed it, and drove the Romans away in utter confusion. As he knew he was not strong enough to relieve Capua, he did not return to the city, and she, thus deserted, was forced to surrender to the Romans.

But thirty of the noblest senators of Capua resolved to die rather than fall into the hands of those they had betrayed, for they feared their vengeance. So they met together for a last solemn feast, after which they each took poison, and so escaped from their enemy.

The senators who had chosen to trust to Roman justice were loaded with chains and sent as prisoners to two different towns.

Fulvius, who longed for a sterner punishment, determined to inflict it himself. He followed the prisoners with a body of cavalry, and reached the first town early one morning. Twenty-eight of the wretched prisoners were at once ordered to be brought before him, that they might be scourged and put to death. Then, hastening to the other town, he ordered twenty-five senators to be put to death, without the trial they had a right to expect.

It is told that before his vengeance was complete Fulvius received a letter from Rome, ordering the punishment of the senators of Capua to be delayed until she herself was able to judge them. But Fulvius, suspecting what was in the letter, left it unread until his horrible work was done.

Meantime, Hannibal was looking for reinforcements from Africa, and he wished to secure a good harbour where they might land in safety. So in 210 B.C. he attacked the citadel of Tarentum, and took it, only, however, to lose it the following year, when it was retaken by Fabius. Hannibal had now no port at which troops might land.

If he was yet further to subdue Italy he must wait until his brother Hasdrubal could bring him fresh troops from Spain.

CHAPTER LXV

THE DEFEAT OF HASDRUBAL

EARLY in the spring of 207 B.C. Hasdrubal was on his way from Spain to join Hannibal in Italy. He had with him a large army and much money to enable his brother to carry on the war.

Hasdrubal crossed the Alps with less difficulty than Hannibal, for it was springtime and the passes were not covered with newly fallen snow. The native guides, too, proved friendly.

He was also greatly helped by the bridges which Hannibal had built, and by the cuttings he had made through the rocks. Even now, after seven years, the bridges were still trustworthy, the cuttings clear.

While he awaited his brother, Hannibal encamped near Venusia, on the borders of Lucania and Apulia, and here he hoped Hasdrubal would join him. But the Romans were watching the brothers, and they hoped to be able to keep them apart.

One Roman army, under the Consul Claudius Nero, had already had skirmishes with the Carthaginians, and was now encamped not far from

Venusia. As Claudius had lost fifteen hundred men in these skirmishes, he did not again venture to attack the enemy.

The other Consul, Livius, was stationed near the river Sena, to stop Hasdrubal should he attempt to march southward to join his brother.

But Hasdrubal intended to march not to Venusia, but into the Umbrian country, where he wished Hannibal to go to meet him. To let his brother know his plans, he wrote a letter, and entrusting it to four soldiers, he bade them deliver it to no one save the Carthaginian general himself.

The soldiers mounted their horses and rode away, promising to deliver the letter to Hannibal. They knew that they were risking their lives, for at any moment they might fall into the hands of the Roman soldiers, of whom the country through which they had to pass was full.

They reached Apulia without difficulty, but not finding Hannibal, they rode toward Tarentum, and were captured by a band of Roman soldiers, who demanded what they were doing in that part of the country.

The soldiers' answers were not very clear, and they were threatened with torture unless they frankly told the object for which they were riding toward Tarentum.

In their terror the men acknowledged that they were looking for Hannibal, and that they carried with them a letter from his brother Hasdrubal.

THE DEFEAT OF HASDRUBAL

The soldiers were then hastily dragged before Claudius, and in a short time the letter was in the Consul's hands, the letter that the men should have guarded with their lives.

Claudius was exultant! He knew the secret that was meant only for Hannibal. Now at length the Carthaginians would meet the fate they deserved. The Consul laid his plans with care, and carried them out with complete success.

A messenger was sent to Livius to warn him that Claudius intended to join him with a company of his army.

When night fell the Consul and his men stole quietly out of their camp, so quietly that Hannibal did not know that they had gone. Claudius had left soldiers to guard the camp, so that the great general might suspect nothing.

As the Consul and his soldiers passed along the road, the Italian townsfolk and village folk alike, came out to welcome them. It was plain that they trusted that the Romans would banish the invaders who had poured down into Italy from the Alps.

Men left their work, women their homes, children their play—all were eager to see the Consul pass. To show their goodwill many of them brought food for the soldiers.

Thousands of men joined the army as volunteers, and they, and the regular soldiers, were so eager to reach the camp of Livius that they would hardly interrupt their march to eat and drink.

The Roman camp lay to the south of the river Metaurus, and not far off was the camp of Hasdrubal.

Claudius had arranged to reach his colleague at night. He arrived as quietly as he had left his own camp, and his men were at once scattered among the tents in which the soldiers of Livius were already for the most part asleep.

As the camp had not been enlarged, the Consuls thought that Hasdrubal would not notice that the army of the enemy had been increased.

But Hasdrubal had fought with Romans in Spain, and he knew their signals. So the following morning, when he heard two trumpets sound instead of one, as had been the case on other days, he was aware that the second Consul had joined the camp. And when the army was drawn up, Hasdrubal would have been unobservant indeed if he had not seen that the number of Roman soldiers was greater than before. How it was that the camp remained unchanged may have proved a puzzle which Hasdrubal had no time to solve.

The new soldiers were haggard and worn, as though they had marched far and fast, or as though they had been on the battlefield, and, seeing this, Hasdrubal grew alarmed.

Had Hannibal by some strange chance been at last defeated, and were these the exhausted but triumphant troops?

THE DEFEAT OF HASDRUBAL

Had his letter failed to reach his brother? Nay, worse still, had it fallen into the enemy's hands?

In his uncertainty Hasdrubal determined that when night fell he would withdraw his army to the other side of the river. It would be safer there until he heard from Hannibal.

So when it was dark the camp was broken up, and the army set out with guides to ford the river.

But the guides proved faithless, and fled, leaving Hasdrubal and his men to wander up and down the river bank in search of a ford. Thus much precious time was wasted.

When morning broke, Hasdrubal was still but a short distance from the enemy's camp, and the Romans, who were early astir, were soon able to overtake him.

Hasdrubal saw that he could not avoid a battle although he would fain have done so until his troops had rested. He had not, indeed, time to throw up fortifications before the enemy was upon him.

But Hasdrubal was a brave soldier, and he made up his mind to fight to the death.

His army he arranged in the best possible position, and his elephants he hoped would prove of great service. They, however, grew restive, and as often happened, did as much harm to their friends as to their foes.

After a fierce struggle, Claudius succeeded in attacking the brave Spanish soldiers both in the rear and in the flank, and they, overcome by the numbers that attacked them, fell, after a bold and desperate struggle.

When Hasdrubal saw that the Spaniards, on whom he chiefly relied, were being slaughtered, he knew that the day was lost.

For himself, he resolved neither to leave the field, nor to be taken alive. Putting spurs to his horse, he galloped wildly into the midst of the enemy and was slain, still grasping his sword in his hand.

Not only were ten thousand of Hasdrubal's soldiers slain, but many were taken prisoner. The spoil was enormous, for Hasdrubal had plundered the country as he had passed through it, and he had also been carrying large sums of money to Hannibal.

Perhaps it was little wonder that the Romans felt that even the awful battle of Cannæ was now avenged.

CHAPTER LXVI
LIVIUS AND CLAUDIUS ENJOY A TRIUMPH

HANNIBAL had not discovered that the Consul had left Venusia before he had returned.

As soon as the battle of Metaurus was over, Claudius had marched back to his camp, carrying with him the head of Hasdrubal. This, with cruelty unworthy of a conqueror, he ordered to be thrown into Hannibal's camp.

Two prisoners he also set free, that they might go to the Carthaginian camp and tell how their comrades had been slain.

In this terrible way Hannibal first knew what had befallen his brother and the army he had brought from Spain.

Claudius, before he marched to the camp of Livius had sent to Rome to tell the Senate what he hoped to do. As the news of his hasty march became known, the greatest anxiety was felt.

No one was able to work. The Forum, indeed, was crowded with people; but they assembled, not to do business, but to talk of the desperate action of the Consul, of the hopes and fears that clustered around his deed.

After a time the women betook themselves to the temple, and spent the hours in prayers to their gods, that now at length they would send victory to Roman arms.

As hope was changing into fear, a messenger was seen spurring his horse toward the city. When he rode in at the gates the people crowded round him to try to gather his tidings.

Good! It seemed that the news was good. The face, the whole bearing of the messenger proclaimed it so, yet the people were afraid to believe. They had grown used to such evil tidings. How could they believe all at once that the gods had at length sent them victory! Yet so it was.

The messenger made his way through the crowds to the Senate-house, and then for a little while the people were left to their vague hopes and fears.

At length the door of the Senate-house was opened, and down the steps into the Forum stepped one of the senators, to tell the breathless multitude that the tidings were good indeed. Hasdrubal was slain and his army was destroyed.

Then at last the people believed, and a great shout rent the air, a shout of triumph.

Public thanksgivings were at once ordained, to last for three days. The people in their joy never

A messenger was seen spurring his horse toward the city.

stayed to think that Hannibal was still alive, and in their land unconquered.

Hannibal, indeed, stayed in Italy four years longer, yet he fought no more great battles there. The towns, too, that he had won were, one after another, gradually reconquered by Rome.

After the defeat of Hasdrubal, Hannibal withdrew to Lacinium with his troops. They remained loyal to their great leader in his misfortune as in his prosperity.

Claudius and Livius, to whom the great victory was due, were both given a triumph.

But as the battle had been fought in the province of which Livius had charge, and as it was he who had commanded on the battlefield, he entered the city on a triumphal car drawn by four horses, his army marching in the procession, while Claudius rode on horseback by the side of the car, and his army, being needed on the field, was not with him.

But it was the Consul who rode on horseback at whom the people for the most part gazed, and it was for him that the crowd cheered its loudest. For the people knew that it was Claudius whose decision had made the battle so complete a triumph.

CHAPTER LXVII

THE CAPTURE OF NEW CARTHAGE

From the time that Hannibal entered Italy, it seemed as though the Romans needed all their strength to meet so powerful a foe. They did, indeed, have as many as eight legions on the battlefield of Cannæ. Yet, at the same time, they had sent officers and soldiers to Spain, and were fighting against the Carthaginians in that country, as well as in Italy.

Publius Scipio had, you remember, been ordered to march to Spain in 218 B.C. to punish Hannibal for defying the demands of Rome. But as he found that Hannibal was crossing the Alps, he awaited him in the valley of the Po, sending his brother Gnæus to Spain in his stead.

In about twelve months Publius was able to join his brother, and for four years they fought together against the Carthaginians. Then in 213 B.C. the Romans found that the enemy was making a determined effort to push their possessions beyond the river Ebro.

Such presumption must be punished, and Publius with an army set out to repulse the enemy. But in the battle that followed he fell, mortally wounded. Gnæus also was slain about three weeks later.

The loss of the Scipios was a serious blow to Rome, for their influence in Spain had made the Roman name powerful. Nor was it easy to find an officer to send to Spain in the place of the brothers, for every soldier wished to stay in Italy to fight against Hannibal, the arch enemy.

At length Cornelius, the son of Publius Scipio, offered to take up the work that had fallen from his father's hands.

Cornelius Scipio was only twenty-four years of age, but he had already shown that he was brave and skilful. On the battlefield of Ticinus he had by his prompt action saved his father's life, and after the slaughter at Cannæ he had prevented a band of young knights from forsaking their country.

In Rome, Scipio was a favourite with the people, partly, perhaps, because of his good looks, and partly because, although he was so young, he was grave and dignified, and his serious ways became him well.

His offer to serve in Spain was accepted, the people electing him for the post with goodwill. The few who were anxious lest he was too young for so great a charge were soon reassured, for his speech, when he addressed them, was wise as well as confident. And the trust of the people was justified.

THE CAPTURE OF NEW CARTHAGE

Scipio arrived in Spain about 210 B.C., and finding that a town, which the enemy had named New Carthage, was of great importance, he determined to attack it.

Although the Carthaginians had three armies in Spain, each of their camps was at some distance from new Carthage.

So confident, too, were the Punic generals of the strength of the town, that it was guarded by a garrison of only one thousand men. As for the inhabitants, they knew little of the use of arms, being for the most part fishermen and mechanics.

Yet New Carthage was supremely important. She was the nearest port to Carthage, and it was at her harbour that reinforcements and stores from Africa were landed. Here, too, the Carthaginians kept their magazines, their money, and their Spanish hostages.

The city was surrounded by high, strong walls, save at one place, where it was protected by an inland sea or lagoon. Here the walls were low and guarded less vigilantly, for the sea was believed to make the city secure from attack.

But Scipio had been talking in his grave and pleasant way with the fishermen of New Carthage, and he had learned quite simply what he wished to know—that the sea was shallow enough at times to make it possible to reach the low and well-nigh unguarded wall.

When Scipio, his plan determined, ordered his soldiers to march, they knew nothing of what their young leader meant to attempt. Only to Lælius, his most trusted friend, did he confide his scheme, bidding him take the Roman fleet to the harbour of New Carthage on a certain day.

Lælius was to join in the assault upon the city; if it failed, he was to be ready to carry off the troops in his ships.

Scipio's orders were obeyed. The fleet reached the harbour at the same time that the Roman army encamped without the city walls.

Mago, who was in command of the garrison, was surprised when he saw the Roman fleet in the harbour, the Roman army close to his gates. He at once ordered the walls to be manned, and about two thousand of the citizens to be armed.

A party of soldiers then sallied out to drive off the enemy, the armed citizens joining in the attack. They were, however, beaten back by the Romans. In a panic the citizens crowded together in the narrow gateway, each trying to regain the safety of the streets. So foolish was their haste, that many of them were trampled underfoot and wounded, if not killed.

The Roman soldiers all but succeeded in pushing their way into the city, along with the desperate citizens. They did not quite succeed, but they managed to fix the scaling ladders against the walls. This proved, however, of little use, for the ladders, they found, were too short for the height of the

THE CAPTURE OF NEW CARTHAGE

walls, while they suffered greatly from the arrows and missiles which fell in their midst.

It was afternoon when the Romans withdrew, and the garrison believed that they were safe for another day. But a few hours later the besiegers again attacked the walls.

This second attack was only a ruse to distract the defenders of the city from a more serious undertaking.

Scipio had seen that the water in the lagoon was ebbing, and would soon be shallow. So he now ordered his men to step boldly into the water and carry their ladders to the low and carelessly guarded wall.

His order was speedily carried out. The ladders were soon in position, and the next moment the Roman soldiers were climbing up into the city.

Meanwhile the garrison was busy repulsing the attack upon her high and strongly guarded walls.

But the Roman soldiers, having scaled their ladders, leaped into the city, killing the few guards whom they encountered. Quickly they made their way toward the gate, which was being assaulted from without. When they reached it they flung it open, and their comrades poured into the city, the garrison was overcome, and New Carthage was in the hands of Scipio.

The young general was modest, and refused to claim all the glory of the victory. Part of it, at least, was due to Neptune, the god of the sea, for he, said

Scipio, had come to him as he slept and bidden him enter the city by the lagoon.

There was much booty to be gathered in the conquered city, and in the harbour a fleet of both warships and merchant vessels was captured.

But the chief value of the victory was that the Romans had now possession of a town in the very centre of the enemy's country, as well as of its best port.

In 206 B.C. Scipio returned to Rome, able to say that he had left no Carthaginian soldier in Spain.

But Scipio had done more than drive the enemy out of Spain. He had tried to win two powerful allies for his country, in Africa, and he had succeeded in gaining one.

Syphax, King of Western Numidia, had been now on the side of Rome, now on that of Carthage. Scipio sailed to Africa to visit Syphax, and before he left him he believed that he had secured his fidelity to Rome.

But although the king was charmed with the Roman, and said of him that he was "even more admirable in conversation than in war," when Scipio's influence was removed he proved fickle as ever. In the end he went over to, and remained on, the side of the Carthaginians.

The ally whom Scipio gained was an African prince named Masinissa. He had come to Spain with a body of Numidian cavalry, and promised that it should be at the service of Scipio when he landed in Africa.

For this was now the young general's great ambition—to carry the war with the Carthaginians into their own country.

CHAPTER LXVIII

SCIPIO SAILS TO AFRICA

It was not usual to award a triumph to a Roman citizen who had been neither a prætor nor a Consul.

Yet it may be that when Scipio returned to Italy in 206 B.C. he hoped to receive this honour, for he had served the State loyally and successfully.

The people clamoured for the honour to be given to their favourite. So the Senate assembled in the temple of Bellona, which stood outside the walls of the city, to meet Scipio, and hear what he had accomplished in Spain.

If a triumph was to be awarded to him, he must, as was the custom, stay without the city gates until he entered it to celebrate the great occasion.

It was a noble record to which the Senate listened. Scipio had fought with four generals and four armies, and had been victor in every battle and over each general. Nor was a single Carthaginian soldier left in Spain.

In spite of the splendour of his achievements a triumph was not decreed to the young soldier.

SCIPIO SAILS TO AFRICA

Partly, perhaps, because among the senators were some who did not care to forsake old customs, while others did not wish to encourage so ambitious a youth as Scipio. They did not know to what his ambitions might lead, and they were afraid.

But although Scipio entered Rome as a private citizen, he did so with all the pomp and splendour that he could muster. And the people flocked around him, and cheered him, it may be, the more lustily that he had been denied the triumph which would have been his had he held the rank of Consul.

Soon after this the election of Consuls for the year 205 B.C. took place.

From far and near the people flocked to Rome, not only to vote, but to see the man who had driven the Carthaginians from Spain.

In spite of the opposition of the Senate, Scipio was one of the Consuls chosen. The Senate feared that he would now persist in his wish to carry on the Carthaginian war in Africa. They had already done their utmost to discourage this, his great ambition.

Still, as the colleague of Scipio had duties which would keep him in Rome, it was plain that if one Consul was sent to a foreign province that one must be Scipio.

Some of the senators hesitated to let the province be Africa. It seemed to them too great a risk to send an army to Africa while Hannibal was still in

Italy. At the head of those opposed to Scipio was Fabius the Delayer, who was as cautious as of old.

To those who feared Hannibal's presence in Italy, Scipio explained, that to carry the war to Africa would be the quickest and surest way to get rid of the great general. For he would certainly be recalled to help in the defence of his own country. And in this, as you will hear, Scipio proved correct.

So determined was the new Consul to go to Africa that at length he declared that if the Senate refused to send him, he would appeal to the people in a popular Assembly.

With this threat, for such it really was, the Senate was indignant. It knew too well what the result of an appeal to the people would be.

After violent debates between Scipio's friends and those who were opposed to him, the Senate reluctantly gave the province of Sicily to the young Consul. And with Sicily he was given permission to cross into Africa, should he think "the best interests of the State demanded it."

The permission was shorn of all graciousness, for the Senate refused to allow Scipio to levy troops. Only the soldiers already serving in Sicily were put under his command.

But Scipio was not easily thwarted by difficulties. The Senate could not refuse to let him enrol volunteers. And no sooner was it known that the Consul wished for soldiers, than many flocked to his standard. For to fight under so brave and gallant a

SCIPIO SAILS TO AFRICA

captain as Scipio was an adventure all good soldiers welcomed.

A year was spent in Sicily, where Scipio trained his volunteers. In the spring of 204 B.C. his ambition was fulfilled, for he set sail for Africa.

In his fleet the Consul had four hundred transports and forty warships, while his army was said by some to consist of twelve thousand five hundred men, by others, to reach any number within thirty-five thousand.

The fleet had assembled at the seaport town of Lilybæum, and the citizens were full of interest and excitement at the novel sight.

A great crowd gathered in the harbour in the early morning of the day fixed for the departure of the fleet. Then as a herald commanded silence, a sudden hush fell upon the people while the Consul offered a solemn prayer to all the gods and goddesses of Rome, beseeching them to grant him "protection, victory, spoils, and a happy... return, after inflicting on the Carthaginian people all those evils with which they had threatened the Commonwealth of Rome."

When the prayer ended, trumpets sounded, and the fleet sailed away amid the cheers of the onlookers.

The Carthaginians knew that Scipio was sailing to their country with an army, yet they sent no fleet to stay his course. Unhindered by the enemy, undelayed by any storm, Scipio landed on the coast of Africa at the Fair Promontory, close to the port of Utica.

CHAPTER LXIX

THE ROMANS SET FIRE TO THE CAMP OF THE NUMIDIANS

No sooner did Scipio land in Africa, than he was joined by his ally Masinissa, with about two hundred of his famous Numidian cavalry.

Masinissa had been expelled from his lands by Syphax, and he was glad to throw in his fortune with the Romans. To Scipio he was a valuable ally, for he knew the war tactics and habits both of the Numidians and Carthaginians.

The Carthaginians had gathered a large army to oppose the invaders. It was led by Hasdrubal, the son of Gisco. King Syphax with his Numidian troops had joined Hasdrubal, and the two armies were encamped near Utica, to which town Scipio had laid siege.

The Roman general, pretending that it might be possible to arrange terms of peace, sent ambassadors, during a short truce, to the camp of Syphax. But his true reason for doing so was that they might find out something of the numbers of the enemy and of the position of its camp.

As was therefore to be expected, the negotiations were of no use, and were soon broken off.

The Punic army believed that the attack on Utica would at once be renewed. It did not dream that its camp was in danger.

But Masinissa knew that the camp was guarded carelessly. He also knew that the tents in the camp were huts, built of wood, and covered with branches of trees or with rushes. So he advised Scipio to plan a night attack on the camp, and to set fire to the huts.

One night Scipio resolved to do as Masinissa had suggested. He ordered his men to have supper early. The bugles sounded at the hour usual for the evening meal, that the enemy's attention might not be attracted by any departure from the daily routine. But on this night the bugle was not the signal for supper, but the call to march.

It was cold and dark when, soon after midnight, the whole Roman army drew near to the camp of the Carthaginians, having marched a distance of seven miles.

Masinissa at once ordered every exit to be closely guarded, then he stealthily set fire to the huts on the edge of the camp.

The flames spread rapidly from one wooden hut to another until, before the Carthaginians were aware, their whole camp was in a blaze.

ROMANS SET FIRE TO THE CAMP OF THE NUMIDIANS

Late as it was, some of the officers were still feasting when the smoke and the noise of crackling wood roused them to a sense of danger.

They rushed out, still carrying in their hands the cups out of which they had been drinking, to see the tents blazing fiercely.

Others sprang out of bed and hastened toward the tents, and although all were startled and dismayed, none of them seemed to think that an enemy had done this thing. They simply imagined that the fire was an accident, caused perhaps by some careless soldier.

The whole camp was now in confusion. Many perished in the flames, while many others were trampled to death in the crowd.

Those who tried to escape were seized by Masinissa and his men and were slain, almost before they realised that they were in the hand of the enemy.

Hasdrubal and Syphax saw that it was hopeless to try to save the camp or the soldiers. Accompanied by a few horsemen, they succeeded in slipping away unnoticed by Masinissa or his soldiers.

Carthage was angry with Hasdrubal when she heard of the loss of her army, and condemned him to death. But he had ridden into the neighbouring districts, and was already enrolling volunteers, for he was determined still to serve his country. In thirty days another army, under the same leaders, was ready to meet the enemy.

Scipio, leaving troops to support the fleet, which was now blockading Utica, at once marched against Hasdrubal and Syphax. On the Great Plains a terrible battle was fought, in which the Romans were victorious. Hasdrubal escaped from the field, and Syphax hastened away to his own kingdom of Numidia.

When Hasdrubal at length ventured to enter Carthage, his enemies tried to take him prisoner. But he hid himself in the mausoleum or tomb of his family. Then, determined never to be taken alive, he took poison and died.

The people, in their rage at being thus cheated of their victim, dragged Hasdrubal's body into the street and placed his head in triumph on the top of a pole.

King Syphax was followed to Numidia by Masinissa and a detachment of Roman soldiers.

The king again faced his enemies, but once more he was defeated, and being captured he was taken to the Roman camp. Masinissa now recovered his own dominions, as well as part of the kingdom that had belonged to Syphax.

From this time the African prince grew more and more powerful. Led by him, the Numidians now fought for the Romans, so that Carthage found herself left alone to fight against two powerful enemies.

CHAPTER LXX

HANNIBAL LEAVES ITALY

CARTHAGE might now have despaired, had not Hannibal been alive. His name, she knew well, could still inspire the Roman legions with terror, his presence would, she believed, ensure their defeat. So messengers were sent to Italy to bid him hasten to Carthage.

The great general left Italy sorrowfully, for the hopes with which he had entered her had not been fulfilled.

In spite of all the great victories he had won, Italy had slipped from his grasp. Perhaps it was true, as Maharbal had said, "Hannibal knows how to win victories, but not how to use them."

But if Hannibal left the country reluctantly, the people rejoiced at his departure. They could never feel secure while he was in their land. His name, indeed, still made the Romans tremble.

Before the great general left, he ordered bronze tablets to be made, and on these he ordered to be engraved the battles he had fought in Italy, as well as a full account of the war. These records were written both in the Greek and the Punic language.

A famous historian, who was a boy when Hannibal was fighting in Italy, saw these tablets when he grew to be a man, and so he was able to write a true account of the second Punic war.

But all the history that Polybius wrote was not carefully preserved. So that after the battle of Cannæ we have no records save those given to us by Roman historians. And what they, in their pride, wrote, was not, many people think, the same as Hannibal recorded on his bronze tablets.

After the capture of King Syphax, a short truce had been arranged between the two powers, while an embassy went from Carthage to Rome to try to obtain peace.

But the truce was broken by the Carthaginians, and for this the Romans made them suffer heavily.

Some ships, laden with provisions for the Roman army, were on their way from Sardinia to join Scipio's fleet, when a storm blew them on to an island in the Bay of Carthage. The Carthaginians seized some of the ships, being unable to resist the temptation to get food, of which they had had but little for some time.

Scipio was indignant at this breach of the truce, and he at once sent to Carthage to demand that the booty should be restored.

But there were some in Carthage who wished the war with Rome to go on, and they were more powerful than those who longed for peace. So the war party arranged that the Roman ambassadors should be sent back by ship to Scipio, with a safe conduct, indeed, but without an answer to his demands.

They were taken safe to within sight of their own ships, then their escort withdrew, while the admiral of the Punic fleet, having been secretly instructed, at once tried to take the ambassadors prisoners.

Two of the crew were injured, some were even killed, while the ambassadors escaped with difficulty.

After so evident an insult to the messengers of Rome, Scipio at once prepared to carry on the war.

By the autumn of 203 B.C. Hannibal was in Carthage, and the people, full of confidence in their great general, were eager that he should at once take the field.

But Hannibal roughly bade the citizens "attend to their own affairs, and leave him to choose his own time of fighting."

He then begged for an interview with Scipio, and tried to arrange terms of peace. But the Consul refused to have anything to do with such terms, saying that the truce had been broken, his envoys insulted, and the Carthaginians must suffer the consequences of such deeds.

Scipio was indeed impatient to fight, that the war might the sooner come to an end.

It was already the month of October, 202 B.C., and although the people of Rome had decreed that Scipio should still continue in Africa, the Senate was anxious that one of the new Consuls should be sent to join him, and share his power.

Claudius, the hero of Metaurus, was one of the new Consuls, and he was ordered to cross to Africa with a fleet of fifty quinqueremes.

Scipio resented this, for if the war with Carthage ended successfully after Claudius reached Africa, it was he, as Consul, who would enjoy the triumph at Rome.

Now the invasion of Africa had been Scipio's own scheme, and he wished to have the glory of its success himself alone. So before the end of October he hastened to lead his army to battle in the neighbourhood of Zama.

CHAPTER LXXI

THE BATTLE OF ZAMA

HANNIBAL was not ready for battle when the Roman army drew near to him at Zama. He had but just determined to change his camp and move to a better position in which to face the enemy.

Before he had time to carry out his plan, the enemy was upon him, and he was forced to fight in a position with which he was not satisfied.

The elephants belonging to the Punic army no longer terrified the Romans as they used to do, for they had grown accustomed to the animals on many an Italian battleground.

Besides, they had now learned how to elude the onslaught of the heavy beasts, by simply leaving spaces between their companies, through which the elephants could run without causing much damage. These spaces were at the beginning of the battle filled with soldiers, who irritated the elephants with darts and then stepped swiftly aside.

But at Zama, the elephants did not even attack the enemy. Startled by the noise of trumpets and the blowing of horns, they rushed back, instead of forward, upon the Numidian cavalry, which was stationed on Hannibal's left wing. Masinissa seized the opportunity, and before the cavalry had rallied from the shock of the elephants, he charged and put it to flight. The Carthaginian cavalry on Hannibal's right was at the same time routed by Lælius.

Two bodies of heavily-armed troops still faced the Romans.

First came the mercenaries hired by Hannibal. Fiercely they fought and well, although they were no match for their enemy. Nor did they once falter until they began to fear that the Carthaginians were failing to support them.

Then they turned, stricken by sudden panic, and anxious only to force their way through those behind, who they believed had betrayed them.

As the Romans followed them in their flight, all was soon in confusion, the mercenaries and Carthaginians being slain, not only by the Romans, but by each other.

Hannibal, meanwhile, was with a band of veterans whom he had held in reserve.

Those soldiers who had escaped from the Romans now tried to steal in among these veterans, but Hannibal, who had no mercy for cowards, ordered his men to lower their spears and push them away. The desperate wretches then escaped from the battlefield as best they might.

Scipio was now ready to advance against the veterans, and here the struggle was long and stern.

THE BATTLE OF ZAMA

For these Carthaginian soldiers were inflexible against every attack. Not one man flinched, but each stood steadfastly at his post until he was killed. Only when Laelius and Masinissa returned from pursuing the enemy's horse and fell upon Hannibal's rear was the battle won.

The number of the slain was terrible. Twenty thousand Carthaginians were said to have fallen, and almost as many to have been taken prisoner, while the Romans did not lose more than fifteen thousand men.

Hannibal escaped to Carthage, leaving his camp to be seized by the enemy.

CHAPTER LXXII
SCIPIO RECEIVES A TRIUMPH

AFTER the battle of Zama, in 202 B.C., the war was at an end, for the Carthaginians had no longer any army.

They had, indeed, no choice now, save to accept the terms Rome might offer, unless they were prepared to see Carthage itself besieged.

Since submission was inevitable, the Carthaginians resolved to yield with as good a grace as possible. So they decked one of their ships with olive branches, and sent ambassadors on board to sail toward Utica. They hoped that the ambassadors would thus meet Scipio, who was on his way to the town of Tunes.

But the Roman general haughtily refused to receive them until he reached his destination. Then his interview with the suppliants was brief, his answer to their petition for merciful terms, proud.

"You deserve nothing at our hand but condign punishment," he told them, "yet Rome has determined to treat you with magnanimity, on condition that you receive the terms offered to you."

SCIPIO RECEIVES A TRIUMPH

The crestfallen ambassadors had no retort to such imperious words, for they knew that they were helpless to resist, however hard the terms might prove. But the conditions, although severe, yet at least still left Carthage a free nation.

To begin with, the Carthaginians were made to suffer for their rashness in breaking the truce.

The ships and provisions which they had taken must be restored. All captives and runaway slaves must be sent back. The elephants, without which the Carthaginians would feel uneasy on a battlefield, were all to be given up to the Romans, as well as the warships, save only twenty. But this was not all. The conquered people must promise to wage no war in foreign countries; and, more bitter still, they must not even fight in Africa itself without first asking Rome for permission to do so. Masinissa was to have all his land and property given back to him.

These, with a few other conditions, completed the demands of Rome.

Among the Carthaginians there were some bold, reckless spirits who would have refused to accept such terms. For these would cripple their commerce, and also leave them powerless to resent the encroachments which Masinissa would certainly make upon their frontier.

But Hannibal was present at the conference that was being held, and he told his rash countrymen that they should be grateful that the terms were not even more severe.

His progress was as that of a king.

SCIPIO RECEIVES A TRIUMPH

When one of the senators still urged that the Romans should be defied, Hannibal caught his robe and pulled him to his seat while he was speaking. His only apology for such conduct was to say: "I have been so long with my army that I have forgotten the habits of civil life."

Since no other way was possible, the terms were accepted, and Scipio, having finished his work in Africa, was now ready to return to Rome.

When he reached Italy his progress was as that of a king. In towns and villages he was hailed as the deliverer of Rome. Had he not forced Hannibal to leave Italy, and had he not even defeated the bold conqueror of Cannæ?

His triumph was the most magnificent that had ever yet been seen. For several days, too, games were held in the city, and for these festivities Scipio himself supplied the money.

That his great victory might not be forgotten, Scipio was now given the name of the country which he had conquered, and he was henceforth known as Scipio Africanus.

CHAPTER LXXIII

FLAMININUS IS COVERED WITH GARLANDS

TEN years before the struggle with Hannibal ended, Rome had declared war against Philip, King of Macedonia. This was the beginning of a war that ended with the conquest of the East.

But the Romans soon found that, with Hannibal in Italy, they would have neither time nor troops to spare for Macedonia. So for a time King Philip was left undisturbed, although he had dared to defy the Romans, and in 215 B.C. to make a treaty with Hannibal. Before the battle of Zama too, he sent four thousand Macedonian soldiers to help the Carthaginians in their struggle against Rome.

But when peace was made with Carthage, the day of reckoning with King Philip speedily came. A Roman army of twenty thousand men was sent across the Adriatic to punish him.

The Consul Flamininus was made commander of the Roman army in Greece in 198 B.C., and in the autumn of the following year he met Philip at Cynoscephalæ, where a great battle was fought.

FLAMININUS IS COVERED WITH GARLANDS

In the morning, before the struggle began, a thick mist hid the armies from one another. Flamininus, wishing to find out the position of the enemy, sent a detachment of cavalry and infantry to reconnoitre.

Suddenly the detachment found itself face to face with the Macedonian reserves, which were stationed on the ridges of the hill named Cynoscephalæ, or Dogshead, as the difficult name is translated in our language.

The Macedonians, being on a higher slope of the hill than the Romans, were at first the more successful.

In their triumph at having worsted even a detachment of Romans, they sent messengers to tell King Philip of their success, and to urge him to bring up the main body of his army without delay.

The king hesitated. He had not expected to meet the enemy that day, and had sent off a large number of his men to forage. His army, too, was on rough and even precipitous ground, which was quite unsuitable for the movement of the phalanx, which needed a wide open space in which to move.

The Macedonian phalanx was as important a part of Philip's army as the elephants had been in that of Hannibal. It was formed by sixteen thousand men in close order, sixteen rows deep, and the men were armed with long spears. These spears were held in such a way that those of the first five ranks reached to the front row, so that a wall of solid steel seemed to stare the enemy in the face.

The eleven ranks behind held their weapons in a slanting position over the heads of those before them, and thus shielded their comrades from the darts aimed at them.

Now the men forming the phalanx marched so close together that they could turn neither to flank nor rear, but must move straight forward. Their spears, which varied from sixteen to fourteen cubits, could only be used for the one forward movement.

In the days of Pyrrhus, the Romans had dreaded the attack of the phalanx, but now they had lost all fear of this body. They were lightly armed, could move swiftly, and had grown used to annoy and defeat it.

On this misty autumn morning, then, in 197 B.C., Philip reluctantly yielded to the wishes of his soldiers, and ordered his army to move to the ground, from which the advanced guard of the Romans had already been driven.

Here he arranged his right wing in the form of a phalanx, and himself led it to charge the left wing of the enemy.

As the solid mass of men moved down the slope of the hill, it gathered force, and struck with such weight against the Romans that they were scattered.

Before, however, Philip's left wing could form, owing to its steep and difficult position, Flamininus was upon it, and his men fought with such vigour and determination that the Macedonians were put to flight.

Then one of the tribunes ventured on a daring deed, one which, as it proved successful, really settled the battle.

Instead of joining the rest of the army in pursuit of the left wing of the enemy, he led his men to the rear of King Philip's right wing.

All at once the king saw that something was wrong. His men, who had scattered the left wing of the Roman army, seemed in difficulty. They began to throw away their weapons, to fly from the field. And not only so, but the Romans, who shortly before had been worsted, had now once again turned to face the foe.

Quickly Philip climbed higher up the hill, and then he understood what had happened. For he saw that his men had been attacked in the rear by the Roman tribune, and that they had been seized with panic at finding themselves attacked both before and behind.

It was soon plain that the battle was lost. Rallying the remnant of his cavalry, King Philip put spurs to his horse and fled from the fatal hills of Cynoscephalæ.

The king foresaw that this defeat would strike a great blow at the influence of Macedonia in Greece. Henceforth Greece would be more likely to appeal to Rome than to Macedonia when she was in need of help against her foes.

He therefore saw little good in prolonging a struggle which he felt to be useless. So, collecting the remnant of his army, Philip withdrew to his own dominions.

When Rome heard of the victory of Cynoscephalæ she was greatly pleased, but perhaps her people were even more delighted that after the victory peace was proclaimed. They were growing weary of incessant war.

Flamininus stayed in Greece during 196 B.C., to arrange terms of peace, with the aid of commissioners sent from Rome. It was determined that his decision should be announced at the Isthmian games, which were held at Corinth in the month of July.

Crowds always flocked to see the games, but this year the number of people was greater than ever, for the decree of Rome was awaited with anxiety.

On the appointed day, while the people stood idly talking to one another in the Stadium or racecourse, the herald's trumpet suddenly rang out. When silence was secured this is what he read:—

"The Senate of Rome and Quinctius Flamininus, pro-Consul and Imperator, having conquered King Philip and the Macedonians, declare the following peoples free, without garrison or tribute, in full enjoyment of their respective countries."

The list of names which followed was drowned, for the people, hearing that freedom was

FLAMININUS IS COVERED WITH GARLANDS

to be granted to many of their towns, burst into loud shouts of joy, which could not be controlled.

At length there was a pause, and the herald again read the names of the favoured towns.

Then in their gratitude the people pressed around Flamininus, until he was in danger of being crushed to death. Garlands and flowers were showered upon him, so that he was forced to beg the people not to smother him in their wild delight. But it was long before the Roman could escape from the expressions of their joy.

Two years later Flamininus, having finished his work in Greece, prepared to return to Rome. Before he left he summoned the free states of Greece to meet him at Corinth, that he might bid them farewell.

Wisely he spoke, telling them to live in "harmony and moderation." Then, as a farewell gift, he promised to remove the Roman garrisons from three other towns.

As at the Isthmian games in 196 B.C., so now again, the easily moved people overwhelmed Flamininus with their gratitude. But when at length the tumult grew less, the Roman said that there was a practical proof of their goodwill which he would like them to give to him.

Many Romans had been taken prisoners and sold as slaves in Greece during the wars with Hannibal. These he begged them to set free.

The Greeks were eager to show that their gratitude was sincere. So when Flamininus reached the coast of Epirus, where his fleet was lying, he found a great band of Roman captives awaiting him. They had been ransomed by the grateful citizens.

In Rome, when Flamininus celebrated his triumph, he had in his procession no more splendid trophies than these prisoners, who had been redeemed by his unselfish thought.

CHAPTER LXXIV

THE DEATH OF HANNIBAL

THE Ætolians were once a wild and savage race who lived among the mountains of Greece and ate raw food. After long years, when they had left many of their more savage customs behind them, they became one of the most powerful peoples in Greece.

In the wars with Macedonia, of which you have just read, the Ætolians, believing that they were used unfairly by King Philip, fought on the side of the Romans. After the battle of Cynoscephalæ, they haughtily said that the victory was due to them.

They disliked Flamininus, and grumbled that they had gained nothing by helping him against the Macedonians. They had, so they said, but changed one master for another, when Flamininus conquered Philip.

In their foolish discontent they resolved to free themselves from Roman influence, but to be able to do this they must, they knew, seek the aid of a foreign prince. So they turned to Antiochus III., King of Syria, and begged him to liberate Greece from Roman influence.

Antiochus had already, in Egypt, had his ambitions frustrated by Rome, and knowing her strength, he hesitated to respond to the appeal of the Ætolians.

But as he hesitated, the great Carthaginian general Hannibal arrived at the court of Ephesus, and placed his sword at the service of the king.

It was now seven years since Rome had made peace with Carthage, and during that time Hannibal had been working for the welfare of his country. In spite of the terms by which Rome had crippled her, his genius had succeeded in making the city once again both wealthy and prosperous.

Rome began to grow jealous of the restored fortunes of the city she chose to consider her rival. Influenced by Cato, of whom I will tell you in another chapter, she began to think that until Carthage was destroyed, Rome herself would never be safe.

Certainly Hannibal was a menace to Rome, so an embassy was sent to Carthage to demand that he should be given up.

Like other reformers, Hannibal had many enemies, and he knew that he must escape from Carthage if he would not fall into the hands of Rome. So he fled from his own country, and after some adventures by the way, he at length reached Ephesus, where he offered his services, as I told you, to Antiochus.

THE DEATH OF HANNIBAL

It was perhaps the arrival of the Carthaginian that determined the king to join the Ætolians in their defiance of Rome. But although Antiochus welcomed Hannibal, it was soon evident that he did not care to follow the great general's advice.

Hannibal, when he saw the troops of the king, knew that they were not fitted to cope with the well-trained legions of Rome. In his blunt soldier fashion he told Antiochus so, and advised him to attack Italy by sea, offering to command the fleet himself.

But the king was quite sure that his soldiers were able to meet the Roman forces. Nor, in any case, did he wish to place Hannibal at the head of his fleet, lest, should a victory be won, the glory of it should be given to the Carthaginian.

It seemed as though Antiochus was jealous of his new officer.

Hannibal saw that the king had not cared to adopt his first plan, so he proposed another.

"Make Philip of Macedon your ally," he said, "or the Romans will certainly do so."

Antiochus was not inclined to follow this suggestion either, and, as Hannibal had foreseen, the Romans secured the help of King Philip.

Meanwhile, in 193 B.C., envoys from Rome arrived at the court of Antiochus. The king was absent, mourning the loss of a son whom, so ran the report, he had himself poisoned from jealousy. But Hannibal was there, and he and the Romans appeared to be so friendly that the courtiers grew suspicious, and by their tales made the king also suspect the good faith of the Carthaginian.

When Antiochus returned to his court Hannibal did all he could to allay his suspicions, telling him of the vow he had taken when a child—the vow of undying hatred to Rome.

It is said that one of the Roman ambassadors was Scipio Africanus, and that one day as he chatted with Hannibal he asked him who he thought was the greatest general that had ever lived.

"Alexander," said Hannibal, meaning Alexander the Great, who died in 323 B.C.

"Who next?" asked Scipio.

"Pyrrhus," was the answer.

"Who third?" then demanded the Roman.

"Myself," answered Hannibal.

"What should you have said, then," asked Scipio, "if you had conquered me?"

"I should have said that I was greater than either Alexander or Pyrrhus," was the quick retort.

Early in the spring of 192 B.C. the ambassadors had an interview with the king. He, however, refused to listen to their demands, which were, that he should not molest the Greek towns which had appealed to Rome to save them from the interference of the King of Syria.

War was now inevitable, but before it actually began his officers had persuaded the king not only to ignore any advice Hannibal might give, but to offer him no responsible command in the campaign that was before them.

"If you follow Hannibal's advice," said one of the king's officers, "the glory will all be his, and not the king's, while if he fails, the fleet and the army will be fatally weakened. Hannibal is but a soldier of fortune, and may usefully be employed as a subordinate, but in a position of supremacy he would be intolerable."

To such foolish words Antiochus listened, and was so influenced by them that he gave the general who had led so many armies to victory only a subordinate naval command.

I need not tell you of all the battles that were fought in this war, but in the end the King of Syria was defeated. Peace was made, and one of the conditions of the Roman Senate was, that "above all, Hannibal the Carthaginian should be given up."

So once again the great soldier was forced to flee, or fall into the hands of his lifelong enemies.

He reached Crete in 190 B.C., and before long he was at the court of Prusias, King of Bithynia. Here he won a great victory for the king, with whom he had taken service. Unfortunately his victory happened to be over one of the allies of Rome, and she at once demanded that Prusias should deliver the Carthaginian into her hands.

Prusias may have been grateful to Hannibal, but he was too weak to defy Rome, and he promised that the general should be surrendered.

Escape was impossible, for the king had ordered his guards to watch Hannibal's house before he was aware of his doom.

But death was better than to be dragged to Rome, to take part as a prisoner in a triumph. How the Romans would gloat over such a captive! The Carthaginian determined that they should never have such a chance, so he took poison, which he is said to have carried about with him—ever since his fortunes began to fail—concealed in a ring.

Thus, in 183 B.C., at the age of sixty-four, died the great warrior whose name had made Rome tremble for so long.

Twelve years later Antiochus was stirring up strife in Egypt, whereupon the Ptolemies (Ptolemy was the name of the Macedonian Kings of Egypt) asked Rome to protect them from the King of Syria.

So in 168 B.C. Popilius was sent from Rome to remonstrate with Antiochus.

Four miles from Alexandria the Roman met the king. Antiochus hoped to disarm the ambassador by his courtesy, so he greeted him with his royal hand outstretched.

But the Roman did not seem greatly affected by such condescension. He took no notice of the king, save to offer him a tablet, on which the Senate of Rome had engraved an order, forbidding Antiochus to threaten or to attack Egypt.

The king read the tablet, and although he knew that he would be forced to obey the mandate, pride dictated his words to Popilius.

"It is necessary that I should consult my council," said the king, "before I can send an answer to the Senate."

Then Popilius quietly stooped, and with a staff which he carried he drew a circle in the dust, in which the king stood enclosed.

"Before you step out of the circle I have drawn I must have your answer, O King," said the Roman.

Antiochus seems to have been fascinated by the boldness of Popilius, for without more ado he gave up the struggle.

He was rewarded by being greeted by Popilius with as great ceremony as though he had just arrived, and been granted an audience with the king. He was then politely asked to arrange a time to withdraw his troops to his own dominions.

CHAPTER LXXV

THE HATRED OF CATO FOR CARTHAGE

When Scipio sailed with his fleet from Lilybæum, Cato was on board one of the ships, as quæstor, under Lælius.

It may be that his hatred of Carthage began at this time. But in any case, in years to come his dislike to the city was bitter, and it grew to be his one desire that it should be destroyed.

Cato had served his country as prætor in Sardinia, and when he was Consul Spain was his province. Wherever he went he was known as a just and honest Roman, who had a contempt for luxury, and himself lived frugally.

In 184 B.C. he was appointed Censor, and in that position he came to be dreaded, so severe was he in his judgments. His speech, too, was often bitter, and stung his hearers into indignation.

Scipio, the Censor disliked. For he encouraged Greek culture, and by his advice many Roman youths were taught by Greek tutors, and for this new learning Cato had little care.

THE HATRED OF CATO FOR CARTHAGE

He loved the quiet, old-fashioned ways in which his countrymen had been used to live. Cincinnatus was his ideal of a Roman citizen, and he would fain have the nobles still live on their farms, plough their lands, and leave them only when the State demanded their service. The service rendered, Cato would have liked to see them hasten back to their homes, to plough, to sow, to reap.

This was the man who, often as he spoke in the Senate, never failed to refer to Carthage before he ended. "Every speech which I shall make in this house," he sternly announced, "shall finish with these words, 'Carthage must be destroyed.'"

One day as he spoke in the Senate he plucked some fresh figs from the folds of his toga. Holding them out that all might see, he said: "This fruit has been brought from Carthage. It grows but three days' sail from Rome. I say that it is not well to have so prosperous and so strong a city near to us. Carthage must be destroyed." The reiteration of these words had its effect.

But a reason for proclaiming war on the Carthaginians was necessary before Rome could send her armies to destroy their city. In 149 B.C. she found the pretext she wished.

By the treaty made after the battle of Zama the Carthaginians had been bound not to take up arms against any ally of Rome. Yet Masinissa was left to harass them as he pleased, and he proved as troublesome a neighbour as the Carthaginians had foreseen.

For half a century Carthage was true to her bond and raised no army even for her own defence.

In spite of Masinissa's raids upon her territory, the city had again become rich and populous. So it was now a simple matter to form an army and send it against their troublesome and greedy neighbour. Their army was led by a general named Hasdrubal. Rome knew all that was going on in Carthage, but for the time she did not interfere. She was watching for the time when the city would be worn out by her struggle with Masinissa.

In 151 B.C. the army of Carthage took the field against her foe, and a great battle was fought. It lasted for the whole of one day, yet neither side gained a decisive victory.

Masinissa, although now an old man of about ninety years of age, was still a clever general. Soon after the battle he succeeded in enticing the enemy into a tract of desert country.

Here he surrounded it with his troops, who watched so closely, that it was impossible for a soldier to go out to search for succour or for provisions. Hunger and sickness soon compelled the Carthaginians to surrender at discretion.

Hasdrubal and those of his men who had not perished were allowed to return to Carthage, Masinissa promising that they should go in safety.

But he did not scruple to break faith with the soldiers, who were weak for want of food and unarmed, after having passed beneath the yoke. His

THE HATRED OF CATO FOR CARTHAGE

son Gulussa was allowed to surprise the miserable men as they crept along toward Carthage, and scarcely one escaped to tell what had befallen.

Masinissa was triumphant, for now he believed that he had gained all Africa for himself. The Carthaginians would certainly not be able to dispute his sway. He would join Numidia and Carthage, and become a great king.

But, although he might well have known better, he forgot to wonder what the Romans would have to say to his plans. He was soon to learn.

Rome sent a peremptory order to her former ally, just when he was at the zenith of his happiness. Carthage was not to be joined to Numidia; she was to be left alone, for the Senate itself would now see that she was destroyed.

CHAPTER LXXVI

THE STERN DECREE

CARTHAGE soon learned that it was with Rome, and no longer with Masinissa, that she had now to deal.

That she would be punished for having taken up arms against her troublesome neighbour she knew. So she determined if possible to disarm the anger of Rome.

She therefore condemned Hasdrubal and the leaders of the war party to death, and sent ambassadors to Rome to say that they only were guilty of breaking the treaty. We do not know if Hasdrubal and his fellows were content to be made the scapegoat of their people.

In Rome, the ambassadors were coldly treated, and told that not only the leaders, but Carthage herself, must atone for the broken treaty.

Meanwhile, to the dismay of Carthage, Utica, which was strongly fortified and almost as rich and powerful as the capital, surrendered to Rome.

With Utica in their hands, the Romans had a convenient port at which to land their forces, and

THE STERN DECREE

they at once declared war. The two Consuls for the year 149 B.C. were sent to Sicily with a large force, and ordered to sail from Lilybæum to Africa, nor were they to think that their work was ended until Carthage was destroyed.

When the Carthaginians received the declaration of war, they decided to send another embassy to Rome, with an offer to surrender.

If the offer was accepted, Carthage could be treated as a town conquered in war. But this right was often put aside when a town surrendered of its own free will. It was in the hope that Rome would prove merciful that Carthage now offered to submit.

The Roman Senate accepted the surrender of Carthage, demanding that the city should send three hundred hostages to Sicily within thirty days. Then these ominous words were added: "Carthage must also obey the further commands of the Consuls." When they had obeyed these "further commands," Rome promised that the Carthaginians should be granted liberty, and that their possessions should not be taken away.

It was with a sinking heart that Carthage complied with the first condition. Three hundred hostages were sent to Sicily within thirty days. Many of them were but children, whose mothers were in despair at being separated from them.

When the ships which were to carry the hostages away were ready to sail, the miserable parents gathered at the water's edge. In their agony, scarce knowing what they did, some of the mothers ran

THE STORY OF ROME

into the sea and held on to the ropes which tied the ships to the harbour. Others, as the ropes were loosened and the ships began to move off, swam after the vessels, weeping and uttering pitiful cries that their children might be restored to them. But the ships sailed relentlessly on their course.

In spite of the arrival of the hostages, the Consuls sailed from Lilybæum and landed at Utica.

Here ambassadors from Carthage came to learn the meaning of the words that had sounded ominous in their ears. What were the further commands to which they must bow?

"The Carthaginians must disarm," was the sentence that fell like lead on the hearts of the ambassadors.

But the Romans had their reason for this demand, and saw no hardship in it.

"How," said the Consuls, "could those want arms who were resolved to live in peace, who were protected from their enemies by the strong arm of Rome, and had their liberty, independence, and possessions guaranteed them?"

It was a hard decree. Yet to appease the wrath of Rome the ambassadors agreed that this condition also should be fulfilled. They did not dream that worse could be in store.

So one day a long procession of wagons set out from Carthage, laden with suits of armour and catapults. Not catapults as you think of them, small and easily handled, but great heavy slings for hurling

THE STERN DECREE

stones at the walls of besieged cities. Two hundred thousand suits of armour were carried away and two thousand catapults, and the walls of Carthage were left defenceless.

The procession was a solemn one. Ambassadors, priests, members of the Senate, most noble citizens, all went with the wagons to the Roman camp to deliver their contents to those who claimed this mighty sacrifice. "Surely now," they said to one another, "Rome will be content, and we shall be able to go back with glad tidings of certain peace to our defenceless town."

But a still more bitter blow was to fall upon the ambassadors, a blow bitter as death itself. The "further demands" had not yet been exhausted.

Rome now decreed that the Carthaginians should leave their town, nor would they be allowed to settle within ten miles of the sea. Carthage herself must be destroyed.

When the ambassadors heard this last terrible sentence, their distress was profound. No humiliation was too great could they but obtain mercy.

They threw themselves at the feet of the Consuls, with tears streaming down their cheeks, and with cries of anguish pleaded that they might be spared this last bitter ordeal.

But no cries, no tears could change the stern decree. Nor was Carthage even allowed again to send messengers to Rome to plead her cause before the Senate.

CHAPTER LXXVII

THE CARTHAGINIANS DEFEND THEIR CITY

THE ambassadors of Carthage had a hard task before them, a task it needed all their courage to perform.

Some of them, indeed, were not brave enough to face their countrymen with the dire tidings of the city's doom, and these did not go back to Carthage.

Others begged the Consuls to send a squadron to the mouth of their harbour, that the citizens might see how impossible it was to defy Rome. This the Consuls agreed to do.

Then the ambassadors who had not shirked their mournful task went back to the city with downcast and gloomy faces. They knew that the fury of the inhabitants would be roused when they heard the last cruel demand of Rome.

Even as they entered the gates, the people thronged around them, and seeing their stricken faces, they clamoured to be told what had happened. But the ambassadors pushed their way in silence through the crowds until they reached the Senate-

THE CARTHAGINIANS DEFEND THEIR CITY

house. Here, in faltering tones, they told the cruel sentence that had been pronounced upon their city.

As they listened, a great cry burst from the lips of the assembly, and was heard by the people without. Then silence, desperate, despairing silence, settled down upon the senators, until, unable longer to bear the suspense, the crowd thrust open the door, rushed into the Senate-house, and demanded to be told the truth.

It was told. Then the citizens in their anger abused the senators who had first advised the city to submit to Rome, while many of them rushed into the streets and ill-treated every Italian whom they could find. An outlet for their passion they needs must find.

Some hastened to close the city gates, as though the Roman legions were already marching upon them, others crowded into the temples to pray, or to curse the gods who had failed to save them from this great disaster.

Little by little the frenzy of the rabble died away, and then senators and people met, and with one voice declared that they would die in defence of their city, rather than give her into the hands of their enemy.

It is true that they had no allies to help them, no arms, no ships. Yet it was better far to die within the walls of Carthage than to live in exile.

No sooner was their decision made than the people, knowing that there was not a moment to spare, set to work.

Day and night men and women toiled without ceasing, until the whole city seemed turned into a huge workshop.

One hundred shields, three hundred swords, five hundred missiles, and a large number of catapults were made each day by the untiring labours of the citizens. It is said that the women in their zeal cut off their hair and twisted it into cords for the catapults.

The slaves in the city were all set free, that they might fight the more whole-heartedly in the struggle that had now begun in grim earnest.

Hasdrubal, who had been condemned to death in an attempt to pacify the Romans, but whose sentence had not been carried out, was now reinstated in favour, and given the chief command of the army.

Although he had been so harshly treated by the Senate, Hasdrubal had been, all this time, working for his country, and had raised an army of twenty thousand men.

Meanwhile, the Consuls had yet to learn that Rome, by the severity of her conditions, had passed the limits of Carthaginian endurance.

They made no haste to march to the capital, deeming that it was already theirs. The last thing they expected was that the citizens, who had no arms,

THE CARTHAGINIANS DEFEND THEIR CITY

would offer any resistance when they appeared before her gates.

But when at length they reached the town they were speedily undeceived.

Arms the Carthaginians seemed to have in plenty, and as missiles were hurled at the Roman troops, and a heavy rain of arrows descended upon them, the Consuls were forced to attack the town which they had imagined was defenceless, and ready to receive them.

Twice the Roman army was repulsed. It was plain that the city would have to be besieged.

For a whole year the Consuls did their utmost to take the town, but it defied all their efforts. Even on the battlefield the Roman arms had no greater success than before the walls of Carthage.

Cato died while the city was still being bravely defended by its inhabitants. Masinissa who, like Cato, had been a bitter enemy of Carthage and the source of much of the evil that had befallen her, was also dead, and still the Romans remained without the walls of the city.

The year 148 B.C. passed, and the Senate at Rome began to grow impatient. It was plain that the Consuls would never be able to take the city, and it determined to find a general who could, and place him at the head of the army.

There was, indeed, even then, a soldier serving under the Consuls who was fitted to command.

This was Scipio, the adopted grandson of the great Scipio Africanus.

Already the army was devoted to him, for he had shown his courage and skill more than once in helping the Roman legions out of difficult positions in which they had been placed by their incompetent leaders.

Before his death Cato had heard of the exploits of the young soldier, and while he scorned his commanders, he admired Scipio.

"He alone has the breath of life in him, the rest are but flitting phantoms," said the old man, who had begun to learn Greek and to love Homer, from whom he was now quoting, only when he was about seventy years of age.

According to Roman law, Scipio was still too young to be elected Consul. Nevertheless he returned to Rome in 147 B.C., and in spite of his youth was chosen Consul, and given the command of the army in Africa.

CHAPTER LXXVIII

THE DESTRUCTION OF CARTHAGE

UNDER the rule of the previous Consuls the discipline of the army had been slack. When Scipio returned to Africa, his first work was to restore strict discipline.

The soldiers were no longer allowed to stray out of the camp when they chose in search of plunder; while bands of traders and a crowd of idle folk who had followed the army, also in hope of plunder, were banished. Luxuries which had abounded in the camp were forbidden by the young commander. Plain fare and regular drill soon made the army more anxious to meet the enemy than to plunder and waste its days in idleness.

Now Carthage stood on a peninsula, a narrow isthmus joining it to the mainland. Beyond this isthmus lay Megara, a suburb from which Carthage procured most of her provisions.

When his army was ready for work, Scipio determined to cut Carthage off from Megara, so that she might no longer be able to get food for the city.

Across the narrow isthmus the Consul therefore ordered trenches to be dug, three miles in length. Along the trenches, fortifications and towns were speedily built, and when these were finished it was impossible to get a morsel of food into the city by land.

Megara was then taken, and Hasdrubal was forced to retire with his army into Carthage itself, of which he was at once made governor.

The Carthaginians could now only bring food into the city by sea, and this was no easy task.

But with a strong wind blowing, there were many brave sailors daring enough to risk being able to run past the Roman cruisers, and thus to carry food into the harbour. So, although Megara was taken, the city was able to still hold out against the enemy without being starved.

Scipio saw that he must now block the sea passage as he had already blocked the land, if he meant to starve the city into submission, and he ordered a strong barricade to be built across the mouth of the harbour.

The Carthaginians mocked at the Roman soldiers as they watched them bringing great stones to the harbour, for they thought that the enemy had undertaken a task it would never be able to complete.

But as they saw that the Romans worked night and day, and as the huge embankment rose before their eyes, they mocked no more. Perhaps

THE DESTRUCTION OF CARTHAGE

after all the Romans would succeed in blocking the harbour, and if that were done they must starve.

So they, too, set to work, but in secret, to make a new opening from the harbour to the sea.

Men and women, and even children, joined in the work, and at the same time workmen in the city built a new fleet. It is true the ships had to be built of old timber, or any wood that could be found, but this was not enough to daunt the indomitable courage of the besieged.

Noiselessly the work was done, so that Scipio knew nothing about what was going on, until one day when his barricade was almost finished.

Then, to his astonishment, he saw a fleet of fifty ships, which was plainly but just built, sail out of a newly-cut passage from the harbour.

The Roman was ill-pleased to be thus outwitted by his foe, yet perhaps he also felt that here was a people worthy of his skill.

Three days later a great battle was fought at sea. From morning until evening the battle raged, but neither side could claim the victory.

At length the Carthaginian fleet attempted to sail back to its harbour. But the smaller vessels blocked the passage so that the large ships were forced to stay without.

The Romans seized their chance, and attacked the enemy in this position.

A desperate struggle followed, and the Carthaginians, who were as used to the sea as to the land, fought with unfailing courage. But at length they were beaten, and the greater part of the new fleet was destroyed.

Winter was approaching, and Scipio had at length succeeded in closing every approach to the city. Neither by sea nor by land could the wretched people now get food.

As the weeks dragged slowly by, the misery in the besieged city grew terrible. Many of the citizens killed themselves rather than endure a day longer the pangs of hunger, while others in their desperate need even ate the dead bodies of their fellows. Some gave themselves up to the Romans, and were then sold as slaves.

In the early spring of 146 B.C. the Carthaginians were so exhausted that they had little strength left to withstand the attack which Scipio now made upon the town. Yet still they would not yield.

Hasdrubal, seeing that the enemy could not be repulsed, ordered the outer harbour to be set on fire.

But as the flames leaped up, Lælius succeeded in scaling the wall, and entered the city with his men, unnoticed in the confusion caused by the fire. They soon reached the gates, and opened them to their comrades, and in a short time the Forum was in the hands of the Romans.

From the Forum, three narrow streets led up to the Byrsa or Castle of Carthage. The houses on

THE DESTRUCTION OF CARTHAGE

either side of these streets were six storeys high, and to these the inhabitants of the city rushed.

As the Romans pushed their way along the narrow streets, the Carthaginians flung down upon them from windows and roofs every missile or weapon on which they could lay their hands.

At length Scipio ordered his men to storm the houses. Then a terrible hand-to-hand fight began with the starving citizens.

Clambering on to the roofs, which were flat, the soldiers stretched boards or beams across from one house to another, and hurled out of the way those citizens who still tried to hinder their progress.

For six days and nights the desperate townsfolk continued to baffle the efforts of the Romans to reach their last stronghold, the Byrsa.

During this awful struggle, Scipio himself sent forward continually new companies of men, and in his anxiety he scarcely found time to sleep or to eat.

At length, however, the foot of the citadel was reached, and Scipio ordered the narrow streets to be set on fire.

Then the Carthaginians knew that they could do no more, and those who had taken refuge in the Byrsa surrendered, on being promised that their lives should be safe.

Fifty thousand men, women, and children, pale and haggard with all that they had gone through during the long drawn out siege, left the castle and were carried off as prisoners.

Hasdrubal, who had defended the city so bravely, was still untaken. He, with his wife and children, as well as about nine hundred Romans who had deserted their own camp, now took refuge in the temple of Æsculapius, and set fire to it themselves.

But Hasdrubal, feeling, it may be, that he could not help his country by his death, resolved to save his life.

He escaped from the burning temple, and, with an olive branch in his hand, threw himself at the feet of Scipio, begging for life. And the Roman commander granted his request.

It is told that the wife of Hasdrubal stood on the roof of the temple and cursed her husband as she saw him crouching at the feet of the conqueror.

Calling aloud to him that he was a traitor and a coward, she flung first her two sons and then herself into the flames before the eyes of her horror-stricken husband.

Meanwhile, with all speed a ship was sent to Rome, laden with the spoils of Carthage.

Great was the rejoicing in the city when it was known that her ancient rival was in ruins. Orders were at once sent to Scipio, bidding him complete his work by destroying the town.

So Carthage was given to the flames, and for seventeen days the fire blazed untiringly. Scipio, as he watched the doomed city, thought of other great countries that had been destroyed by their enemies—Assyria, Persia, Macedonia. In the unknown

THE DESTRUCTION OF CARTHAGE

The City was given to the flames.

future would Rome fall even as these?

Thinking thus, Scipio murmured the lines of Homer:

> "The day shall come when holy Troy shall fall,
> And Priam, lord of spears and Priam's folk."

When the flames had at last died out, a plough, drawn by oxen, was driven over the site of the town, and Scipio uttered a solemn curse against any one who should venture to build a new city on the ancient site of Carthage.

CHAPTER LXXIX

CORNELIA, THE MOTHER OF THE GRACCHI

CORNELIA and her two sons, Tiberius and Gaius, are famous in the annals of Roman history.

The mother of the Gracchi was the daughter of the first Scipio Africanus. With her father's consent, Cornelia married a young plebeian, named Tiberius Gracchus.

Her husband died while her children were still young, and from that time Cornelia lived to train and educate her boys.

Princes in foreign countries heard of the wisdom and goodness of the noble matron, and journeyed to Rome to beseech her to bestow her hand upon them. Even King Ptolemy of Egypt wished to make her his queen.

But Cornelia steadfastly refused each suitor, that she might be free to watch over her sons. From their childhood she taught them to love their country, telling them tales of those who had served Rome well, and had even given their lives for love of her.

And so the lads grew up longing that they too, like the heroes of old, might live and die for their country. But their mother taught them lessons the heroes of old had never learned, and one of these lessons was to care for the poor and oppressed.

One day, while her children were still young, a lady came to visit Cornelia. She was a rich lady, and proud of her jewels and her wealth.

Cornelia listened quietly as her guest told her of the precious stones and ornaments she possessed. When at length she grew tired of talking of her own beautiful things, she said she would like to see the treasures of her hostess.

So Cornelia led the lady to another room. There, in bed, fast asleep, lay her children. Pointing to the little ones, she said to the bewildered visitor, "These are my jewels; the only ones of which I am proud."

Tiberius was nine years older than his brother Gaius. The elder boy was gentle and deliberate, both in his ways and in his speech, the younger was vehement and impetuous. As they grew up, the differences between them grew more marked.

Both were great orators, but Tiberius spoke without gestures, and seldom stirred from one spot while he addressed his audience.

Gaius, on the other hand, was never still for a moment. His quick, passionate words were emphasised by his gestures, and as he talked he would walk

CORNELIA, THE MOTHER OF THE GRACCHI

up and down, sometimes in his excitement throwing his gown off his shoulders.

The two brothers were known as "The Gracchi." They had a sister who was named Sempronia, and she had married the younger Scipio. Tiberius served under his brother-in-law in Africa, and he was the first to mount the wall when the suburb of Megara was attacked.

In 137 B.C., soon after he returned to Italy, he was sent to Spain to serve with the army there.

On his way he passed through Etruria, where the land was divided into large estates. These estates belonged to rich people, who employed gangs of slaves to cultivate their fields.

Tiberius saw the slaves at work as he journeyed through the country. He noticed that they were loaded with chains and bent with the hard tasks that their masters forced them to do.

The young man looked at these poor creatures with pity, for Cornelia had taught her boys that slaves were human beings, and should be treated justly and kindly.

Why should the land belong only to the rich? Tiberius wondered. Had these very fields and estates not been won for Rome by her citizen soldiers? Yet many of the soldiers were now struggling with poverty, instead of owning part of the soil for which they had fought.

As he thought of the slaves, and of the unfair division of land, Tiberius remembered that the old

Licinian laws forbade any one man to own large tracts of land.

So he determined that when he went back to Rome he would plead with the Senate to enforce these old laws, that the poor might share the land with the rich.

After he had made this resolution, Gracchus went on his way with happy thoughts.

Soon no chained slaves would be seen toiling in the fields, but citizen farmers, like Cincinnatus of old, would live on their own land and till their own fields. And he, Tiberius Gracchus, would have freed his country from a great evil.

The dreams of the young Roman that night were happy dreams.

When the time came for Tiberius to return to Rome, his mind was still full of reform. No sooner did he reach home, than he told to his noble mother his plans for helping the slaves and the poorer citizens of Rome, and begged for her advice.

Cornelia was full of interest in all that her son had to tell. She was pleased that he should wish to help the oppressed, and she knew that it was she herself who had taught him to be thus pitiful.

"I have been called the daughter of Scipio, but in days to come I shall be known as the mother of the Gracchi," she told Tiberius, for Cornelia believed that both her boys would be honoured by the country they sought to serve.

So in 133 B.C. Tiberius offered himself as one of the people's tribunes. He was young, it was true, but already the citizens knew that he was their friend, and he was elected without difficulty.

CHAPTER LXXX

TIBERIUS AND HIS FRIEND OCTAVIUS

THE Senate and the wealthy landowners were displeased that Gracchus had been chosen as one of the tribunes. They knew that he was eager for reforms, which they had no wish to see carried out.

But Tiberius was too wise not to try to please those in authority. So his first measure was not so sweeping as his opponents had expected it to be. The young reformer even said, that those who would lose great estates, if the old Licinian laws were enforced, should have compensation.

But although the landowners had not expected this concession, they were very angry with Tiberius, and they did all that they could to make the people misunderstand him. If his wishes were made laws, the lot of the poor would only become more difficult, they told the plebeians, who did not know what to believe.

Then, lest the people should begin to think that the landowners knew better than he what was for their good, Tiberius determined to tell them

TIBERIUS AND HIS FRIEND OCTAVIUS

plainly what he thought about their struggles and their poverty.

In the Assembly of the people his fervent words rang out.

"The wild beasts of Italy," he said, "have their caves and lairs, but to the men who fought and bled for Italy nothing remains except the open air and the light of heaven. Bereft of home and shelter, they wander about with their wives and families. It is a mere mockery and a delusion in a general to exhort his warriors before a battle by bidding them fight for the graves of their ancestors and for their household altars, for not one of them owns an altar bequeathed him by his father, nor the ground where his fathers are laid. They fight and fall that others may enjoy affluence and luxury; they are called lords of the earth, and have not a single clod which is their own."

These words, so full of pity for the treatment that they suffered, touched the hearts of the people, and they would no longer listen to a word against their tribune.

Among his fellow-tribunes, Tiberius scarcely looked for support, save, perhaps, from his friend Octavius.

At first, indeed, Octavius refused to oppose the bill Gracchus now brought forward, but in the end he yielded to the enemies of Gracchus, and promised to do so.

This was fatal to the success of the bill, for it was the rule that if one tribune disapproved of a measure, the others were powerless to do any more in the matter. It was allowed to drop out of sight. Tiberius was too much in earnest to be willing that this should happen. He met his friend and begged him not to persist in opposing the bill.

Octavius himself was a landowner, and Gracchus, careless, as it seemed, of his friend's feelings, even offered to compensate him for what he would lose if the law was passed.

But Octavius was neither to be persuaded nor bribed. He refused to do as Tiberius wished, and so it was still impossible to pass the bill.

Then Tiberius, who as tribune had exactly the same power as his friend, resolved to use it.

He opposed every measure brought before the State, just as Octavius had opposed his bill. He also put his seal on the treasury, so that no money could be obtained, and thus it was soon impossible to carry on public business.

The landowners knew that Tiberius would not rest until he had gained his end. To show their distress they put on mourning, and walked up and down the streets with a melancholy mien, for their estates were dear to them.

But they did more than parade their grief; they called together their followers that they might be ready to resist Gracchus by force, if it became necessary. Plots, too, were laid against his life, but Tiberius heard of these, and from that time he carried a dagger beneath his robe.

TIBERIUS AND HIS FRIEND OCTAVIUS

The landowners were right in believing that Gracchus would never be content until his bill had been voted either for or against by the people.

Not only did the tribune intend to have the vote taken, but he was resolved that it should be taken without delay. For the people had crowded into the city from all parts of the country to support him, and he feared lest they should have to go back to their homes before their vote had been given.

So he made another attempt to bring his bill before the popular Assembly, but again Octavius interfered, while some haughty nobles led their followers into the Assembly and overturned the urns in which the votes were placed.

Again Gracchus appealed to his friend, this time in the presence of the Senate, but once again his friend refused to yield to his entreaty.

Tiberius felt that he had done his utmost to win Octavius by kindness. He now determined to appeal to the people to remove his friend from the tribuneship.

This was to go in the face of law and justice, for a magistrate when appointed by the people was free to do as he thought right during his year of office, without interference from those who had given him authority.

But the influence of Gracchus was so great that seventeen out of thirty-five tribes had already voted that Octavius should be deposed, when Gracchus stopped the proceedings.

He saw that he was going to win, and he wished to give Octavius the chance to resign of his own free will.

But when Octavius disdained to accept this suggestion, the voting was continued, and Octavius was soon declared to be no longer tribune.

The unfortunate man was then dragged from his seat by the servants of Tiberius, and it was not without trouble that he escaped with his life from the fury of the people.

Now that the obstinate tribune was out of the way, Gracchus had no difficulty in passing his bill. But he was so angry with the landowners for the opposition with which they had treated it, that he dropped the clause saying they should have compensation for their loss.

Tiberius, his father-in-law Appius Claudius, and his brother Gaius were now appointed to survey and divide the land in accordance with the bill.

Summer passed, and soon Tiberius would no longer be tribune, and his enemies rejoiced. For when he was once more a private citizen they hoped to punish him for deposing Octavius.

But Tiberius did not mean to become a private citizen at the end of his year of office, if it was possible to avoid doing so.

It was true that it was against the law for a tribune to be re-elected for a second year. But the people had before now ignored this law, and Tiberius hoped that they would do so again for his

TIBERIUS AND HIS FRIEND OCTAVIUS

sake. It may be that Tiberius was anxious to retain his authority, lest the new land law should suffer were he not able to see that it was enforced.

But the country folk had got what they wished, and would not flock to the city for the coming elections in such crowds as they had done when the passing of the law had depended on their presence.

Gracchus would have to depend, for the most part, on the city populace to vote for him. It was influenced, he was well aware, by the Optimates, that is, by the party that supported the Senate, so that Gracchus knew that the chance of re-election was small.

On the day of the election two tribes had, however, already voted for Gracchus, when the Optimates broke in upon the Assembly, saying that the proceedings were illegal.

The other tribunes sided with the Optimates, or at least they opposed the re-election of Gracchus, and, much against his will, Tiberius saw the election put off until the following day.

CHAPTER LXXXI
THE DEATH OF TIBERIUS GRACCHUS

TIBERIUS did all that was possible to influence the people in the short time that was his before the votes were to be taken. He appeared before them clad in mourning, and bade them guard his young son should he not escape from the coming contest with his life.

The citizens were easily moved, and his eloquent words and sombre garb appealed to their imagination. They flocked to his side, escorted him to his home, and promised to give him their support on the morrow.

That night Tiberius arranged to give his friends a sign—to raise his hand to his head—should he think it necessary to use force.

Early the next morning the people assembled on the Capitol, and Gracchus left his house to join them, although he was warned that danger would overtake him.

Omens of ill were rife. As he left his house, Tiberius stumbled and wounded his great toe so

THE DEATH OF TIBERIUS GRACCHUS

severely that the blood dripped from his shoe. In spite of this accident he went on, and before long he noticed two ravens fighting on the top of a house. Gracchus was at the moment surrounded by people, yet a stone struck from the building by one of the ravens fell at his feet.

Even the boldest of his friends was daunted by such occurrences. It was plain that it would be wise for him to return to his home after such distinct warnings of disaster.

But Gracchus went on toward the Capitol, where he was joyfully greeted by his friends.

The voting began almost immediately, but again and again it was interrupted by the enemies of Gracchus, until at length he determined to settle the matter by force.

He gave the signal he had arranged with his followers, and they flew to his aid. Before long a riot had begun, and the opponents of Gracchus were driven away by a fierce attack of stones and cudgels.

The Optimates were enraged by this rebuff. They declared in their anger that Gracchus wished to overthrow the nobles that he might become king.

They had seen him raise his hand to his head. It was the signal he had arranged to give his friends, but they said that it was a sign to the people that he hoped to wear a crown. Some even asserted that he had already been presented with a royal diadem and a purple robe.

The Consul, they agreed, ought to employ force to scatter the followers of Gracchus.

But Mucius Scævola was a wise Consul, and refused to kill a single citizen without a trial.

"Since the Consul betrays the republic," cried Scipio Nasica, "I call upon those men to follow me who desire to preserve the laws of our country." Then, drawing his toga over his head, Nasica marched against the followers of Gracchus at the head of a band of senators and knights.

The people saw the officers of state marching towards them, and stricken with fear they fled, leaving Gracchus, whom they had promised to defend, alone and unprotected.

Tiberius hastened toward the temple of Jupiter, thinking that he would find shelter there, but the priest had closed the door.

As he turned away he stumbled for the second time that day. But he quickly raised himself, only, however, to be struck brutally on the head by one of his enemies. Before he could recover from the blow, a second stroke ended the life of the unfortunate man. Three hundred of his followers were slain before the tumult ended, and the bodies of the victims were thrown into the Tiber.

Gaius begged that he might be allowed to bury his brother, but his request was refused, and the body of Tiberius was also dragged to the river and flung into the tide.

THE DEATH OF TIBERIUS GRACCHUS

Tiberius had paid with his life for his reforms, but he had been successful in wresting the land laws from the patricians, and in shaking the power of the Senate by his appeal to the people. Nor was the law repealed after his death.

The place left empty on the committee by the murder of Tiberius was filled by Publius Crassus, the father-in-law of Gaius, and the division of land for the good of the people was slowly carried on.

CHAPTER LXXXII

THE DEATH OF GAIUS GRACCHUS

THERE were some citizens who did not fear to show their regret for the death of Tiberius Gracchus, and one of these was named Carbo.

That the populace was sorry that it had forsaken Gracchus at the critical moment was proved by the sympathy it gave to Carbo, and by its choice of him as their tribune in 131 B.C.

Carbo determined to carry on the reforms of Tiberius Gracchus, and his first measure was to try to make it legal for a tribune to be elected for two years in succession.

In the Assembly of the people Scipio Africanus opposed this, and also declared that Tiberius was put to death justly for trying to be elected tribune a second time.

Ominous mutterings were heard among the crowd at these words.

But Scipio was always masterful, and, annoyed at the interruption, he sternly said: "Let no man speak to whom Italy is but a stepmother."

He said this to remind the people that many of them had been conquered by the Romans, and had not even the full rights of citizens.

Not to have the full rights of citizenship was a sore point with the Italians, and at so bitter a taunt they grew the more threatening.

"Do you think," added Scipio scornfully, as he noticed their attitude, "do you think I fear the men whom I brought here in chains now that they are set free?"

The influence of Scipio was so great that Carbo's bill was rejected.

In 129 B.C. Scipio was at the height of his power, and more popular than ever before. Crowds gathered to watch and admire him as he went to and fro from his house to the Senate.

One day as he left the Forum his progress was like a triumph. He left his admirers early that evening, and took his writing tablets to his room to prepare a speech which he intended to give the next day. But when morning came he was found dead in bed. At his funeral it was plain that he had been respected not only by his friends but by those too who did not agree with his views. His great success at Carthage was never forgotten, and in him Rome knew that she had lost one of her truest and noblest citizens.

Meanwhile, after the murder of his brother, Gaius Gracchus lived quietly in his own home.

The enemies of Tiberius began to hope that Gaius would prove unlike his brother, and be willing to leave the laws of his country alone. But they forgot that Cornelia had trained Gaius even as she had trained her elder son. Gaius never dreamed of letting his brother's fate keep him from serving his country. He was but waiting for the best opportunity to follow in his footsteps.

In 123 B.C. Gaius was elected tribune. The Optimates, it is true, did their utmost to defeat him. But, as in the time of Tiberius, the people flocked from all parts of Italy to vote for him.

In the place of Assembly many could find no room. But, rather than be thwarted, the excited people climbed on the roofs of the neighbouring buildings, and raised their voices in favour of Gaius.

The younger Gracchus was even more eloquent than his brother, and his quick, passionate words swayed the people this way or that, as he willed.

Sometimes in his earnestness he lost control of his voice, and spoke more loudly than was pleasant, and he had invented a curious way to check this habit.

When he spoke in public a slave always stood near to him, a flute in his hand. Should his master's voice rise, the slave would strike a few soft notes on

THE DEATH OF GAIUS GRACCHUS

his flute, and Gaius hearing, would remember, and strive to regain control of his voice.

After his election Gaius reminded the people of his brother's cruel death, and they wept. He told them that he meant to carry on the reforms for which Tiberius had died, and they applauded.

The first effort of the young tribune was to try to punish Octavius for having opposed his brother.

He brought forward a bill proposing that any man who had been deposed from one office should henceforth be incapable of being elected to another.

Octavius had been deposed, and if this bill became law he could no longer hope to serve his country in a public position.

But Cornelia was wiser than her son, and knowing that such a law would only anger the people, she persuaded Gaius to withdraw his bill.

In many ways Gaius tried to keep the affections of the people. He built bridges, and ordered milestones to be erected for their benefit. He brought in laws making grain cheaper for the poor, and this greatly increased his popularity. Above all, he was eager to give the full rights of citizenship to all Italians.

The laws passed for these and other measures were called the Sempronian laws, as Sempronius was the name of the family to which the Gracchi belonged.

Meanwhile the Senate was growing alarmed. Gaius Gracchus promised to give more trouble even than his brother had done. Reforms were being carried out too rapidly to please either the Senate or the patricians. His enemies resolved not to kill him as they had killed his brother, for they believed that they could injure him in a more subtle way.

From that time, if Gaius proposed a measure for the good of the people, one of the Optimates would suggest another, that would be sure to please them more than that of Gaius.

Drusus was the man employed by the enemies of Gracchus to undermine his influence in this way. He was rich, and eloquent as Gaius himself, and little by little he wormed his way into the favour of the people. The more Drusus grew in favour with the plebeians, the less popular became Gaius.

Now Gracchus believed that if the poor people in Italy were sent out to settle in the new lands which the Romans had conquered they would soon grow more prosperous than was possible at home.

His colleague had proposed to make Carthage, in Africa, one of these new colonies, for a city was being built on the old site, in spite of the curse that had been pronounced over it by Scipio.

The Senate agreed to make Carthage one of the new colonies, and gladly sent Gaius out to take charge of the scheme. He would be forgotten by the people while he was away.

THE DEATH OF GAIUS GRACCHUS

During his absence, which, after all, only lasted for sixty days, Drusus introduced a much greater scheme for the settling of the people in colonies. His colonies were not to be far away, as were those of Gracchus and his colleague, but in Italy herself. Besides, Drusus promised that there should be no taxes to pay in his colonies, while Gracchus had made no such concession.

It did not matter to the people that it was unlikely, if not impossible, that Drusus's plan could be carried out. That he had proposed it was enough. When Gracchus came back from Africa he at once saw how coldly the people welcomed him, how little they trusted him.

But he determined not to be disheartened. He would yet win back the confidence of the people. So he left his house on the Palatine, where the nobles lived, and dwelt near the Forum, in the midst of the poorer citizens of Rome.

But Gaius was too impetuous to be wise, and his next move did not win the favour of the citizens, although it may have pleased the rabble.

One day he noticed that stands were being put up round the ground where public games were to be held. These stands were for the rich, who could afford to pay for them. As they took up a great deal of room, and would spoil the view of many of the poorer folk, Gaius begged that they might be removed. But his request was refused, and he himself was ridiculed by his enemies.

Then Gaius took the matter into his own rash hands.

The evening before the games were to take place he ordered workmen to pull down the stands and level the ground, so that on the morrow rich and poor would be forced to stand side by side if they were to see the games.

Soon after this the election of tribunes took place, and although Gaius had done much for the sake of the people's welfare, they showed no gratitude. In 121 B.C. he was not again chosen as their tribune.

What was even more serious was that the Consuls for the year, Fabius Maximus and Opimius, were leaders of the Optimates, so that the enemies of Gaius were now powerful enough to attack him publicly.

First they worked upon the superstitious fears of the populace. They reminded the people that the site of Carthage had been cursed, yet here were Gracchus and his friends venturing to build a new city on the very spot.

Omens, too, had been ignored. His enemies told how the boundary stones of the new city and the measuring poles had been torn out of the ground by wild beasts and carried away. Such things, they said, must portend the wrath of gods.

Thus they paved the way for the blow which they hoped to inflict upon Gracchus. For they now called the tribes together and asked them to repeal

THE DEATH OF GAIUS GRACCHUS

the law permitting the building and colonising of Carthage. The people themselves had passed the law only the year before.

Gracchus and his friends determined to fight against the repeal of this law. But while Gracchus hoped to avoid violence, his friends were ready to use force to gain their ends.

The anger of both parties was roused, and lest one side should take advantage of the other, both took up their position on the Capitol, meaning to spend the night on the hill. But it was unlikely to be a quiet night. Any moment a spark might set the flames of anger alight.

As Gracchus walked up and down, speaking to one and another, the servant of the Consul came from the temple carrying away part of the sacrifice that had just been offered, and shouting in a rude manner to the people to leave room for him to pass.

When he drew near to Gracchus the people imagined that he threatened their leader.

At once the mob was in a panic. Some one cried that the life of Gaius was in danger, and in a moment the insolent servant was killed.

Gracchus was deeply grieved that one of his party should have been so rash. It gave to his enemies the very opportunity which they wished.

The Senate, indeed, showed great horror at such a deed of violence, and ordered the body of the dead man to be held up to the people. "This is how Gracchus and his friends treat the poor," was what

THE STORY OF ROME

the Senate wished the people to think. It then denounced Gaius and his party as enemies of the republic.

After this both the parties left the Capitol, Gracchus and his friends taking up their position on the Aventine hill early the following morning.

Before he left home Gaius refused to wear armour, but put on his gown as though he were simply going to an Assembly of the people. He did, however, wear a short dagger beneath his tunic.

As he reached the threshold his wife rushed after him and caught him with one hand, while with the other she clasped one of her children.

"You go now," she said to her husband, "to expose your body to the murderers of Tiberius, unarmed, indeed, and rightly so, choosing rather to suffer the worst of injuries than do the least yourself."

But Gaius would listen to no more. Gently he withdrew himself from her hold, and stricken with grief, his wife fell to the ground.

When Opimius, the Consul, heard of the gathering on the Aventine, he declared that it was an act of war to seize a position within the city and hold it against the Senate. He ordered it to be proclaimed that he would give its weight in gold to any one who brought him the head of Gaius Gracchus. Then, with a troop of soldiers and archers, Opimius prepared to march against those whom he had declared rebels.

THE DEATH OF GAIUS GRACCHUS

The leader of the mob, for indeed it was little else, was Fulvius, who had been both tribune and Consul.

He now sent his young son, of eighteen years of age, to propose to the Senate that peace should be arranged without having recourse to arms.

The lad was sent back to say that the rebels must disperse, and Gracchus and Fulvius appear before the Senate to answer for what they had done, before it was possible to think of terms.

Gracchus would have agreed to do this, but Fulvius refused to give way, and sent his son back to the Senate with other proposals.

This time the messenger was not sent back, but was kept prisoner by Opimius, who without further delay went forward toward the Aventine hill.

Fulvius had not courage to face the troops of the Consul, and he fled and hid himself in a bath, from which he was soon dragged ignominiously, and put to death.

Gracchus did not attempt to lead his followers against the soldiers. He may have felt it was hopeless to do so.

His friends urged him to escape, but he, it is said, first fell upon his knees, and in the bitterness of his heart besought the goddess Diana to punish the fickle, ungrateful people of Rome by sending them into unending slavery.

Here it would be possible, he thought, to hold the enemy at bay.

THE DEATH OF GAIUS GRACCHUS

Then he fled down the hill toward the river Tiber, followed by two of his most faithful friends and a slave.

One of his friends fell and sprained his foot. He quickly rose and faced the pursuers, resolved to hinder them as long as might be. But he was soon put to death.

At the bridge that crossed the Tiber the other friend stopped. Here it would be possible, he thought, to hold the enemy at bay for a time. Perhaps as he stood at his post he thought of the old Roman hero, Horatius Cocles, who had so nobly held the bridge against the foes of Rome. But ere long he too was slain.

Then Gaius, knowing that all hope was at an end, called for a horse. But his enemies were watching, and no one dared to answer his request.

Yet taken alive he would never be! So with desperate speed he ran on until he reached a little grove, which was consecrated to the Furies, and here for a few brief moments he was hidden from his pursuers. Then in a stern voice he bade his slave, who was now alone with him, to kill him before he was discovered by his enemies.

His slave obeyed, and, faithful to the end, slew himself as well as his master.

Here in the grove his enemies found the body of Gaius Gracchus, covered by that of his devoted slave.

The head of the dead man was cut off, and to increase its weight was filled with lead. This was done, it is told, by one who was once his friend. But this we cannot easily believe. It was, however, taken to the Consul, who gave for it the promised reward—its weight in gold.

The body of Gaius was then dragged through the streets, and thrown into the Tiber.

And Cornelia, the mother of the Gracchi?

She bore the loss of her two sons as she had borne all the disasters of her life, with an undaunted spirit.

Her friends marvelled to hear her speak of her sons with no outward sign of grief, but Cornelia was too proud of the service they had done for Rome to weep. Yet she left the city and lived in retirement, for, with all her fortitude, she could not bear to meet those who had approved of the murder of her sons.

In after years the Romans learned to be ashamed of their treatment of the Gracchi, and in reverence for the noble matron who had borne them they erected a bronze statue in the Forum. On it were inscribed these simple words: "To Cornelia, the mother of the Gracchi."

CHAPTER LXXXIII

THE GOLD OF JUGURTHA

Jugurtha was king, King of Numidia. It is true that he had stolen his kingdom, or at least the greater part of it, from his two young cousins, the grandsons of Masinissa, yet he was safely seated on the throne.

One of the princes Jugurtha had murdered, the other had escaped to Rome and claimed her help.

But Jugurtha was rich, and he knew that at Rome gold could purchase what he wished. So now he sent large sums of money to some of the senators, and these could not resist the wealth that was offered to them.

In this way justice went awry, to the bewilderment of Adherbal the prince, for the senators who were bribed, voted that Jugurtha should keep the wealthiest and strongest part of Numidia, while Adherbal might claim what was left.

But even this was not enough to satisfy the ambition of the king. He now wished to wrest from the prince even the small dominion that had been allotted to him.

Again and again Adherbal appealed to Rome, but her hands were filled with the gold of the tyrant, and she would do nothing to help his victim.

At length Jugurtha besieged his cousin in his capital town of Cirta.

The prince was not strong enough to defy his enemy, and there was no choice but to surrender, and this Adherbal did, on condition that his life and that of the inhabitants should be spared.

But it was vain to trust Jugurtha. He cared little for the promise he had given, and no sooner had the prince left the city than his cousin ordered that he should be put to death, while the inhabitants, Italians as well as Numidians, were also slain.

The treachery of Jugurtha was known in Rome, but it was ignored. How could it be otherwise when those who should have rebuked and punished him were spending his money.

But among the tribunes there was one man, whose hands were clean, and he, in the Assembly of the people, denounced the nobles for taking bribes and allowing Jugurtha to go on his treacherous way unchecked.

So earnest were the words of Memmius that the people were roused, and the Senate dared no longer refuse to call the tyrant to account. War was therefore declared against the King of Numidia in 112 B.C.

But it was useless to send an army to Africa unless the officers were honourable men.

THE GOLD OF JUGURTHA

Bestia, the Consul, when he reached the enemy's country, did at first attack and capture several towns, as well as take many of Jugurtha's men prisoners.

Then, all at once, the activities of the Consul came to an end. He fought no more against the enemy. For Bestia had been offered the gold of Jugurtha and had accepted it, and the tyrant was again left to use his power as he chose.

At home, however, Memmius did not scruple to expose the conduct of Bestia, and to denounce it as unworthy of a Roman. His persistence won the day.

In 110 B.C. Jugurtha was brought to Rome under a safe conduct, that he might give evidence against those who had accepted his gold.

But even now the king still found some willing to handle his money, and justice was delayed, if it was not altogether turned aside.

One of the Consuls meanwhile wished to depose Jugurtha and make a young prince King of Numidia.

When Jugurtha heard this he did not hesitate to order his slave to go at once to put his rival to death.

Such a deed was more than Rome could tolerate, and Jugurtha found it necessary to escape from the city.

The Senate saw that the war in Africa must be carried on. But to do so with any hope of success it was necessary to find a general who would scorn to take a bribe.

In the summer of 109 B.C. such a man was found in the Consul Metellus, who was now sent to Numidia as commander of the army. With him, as his lieutenant or legate, he took Gaius Marius, of whose boyhood I must tell you.

CHAPTER LXXXIV

GAIUS MARIUS WINS THE NOTICE OF SCIPIO AFRICANUS

Gaius Marius was born in 157 B.C. His parents were humble folk, who had to work for their daily bread.

Marius grew up knowing nothing of the indolence and luxury that surrounded so many Roman youths of noble birth.

His boyhood was lived in a mountain village, where, if his training made him rough and uncouth, it also taught him to endure hardness, and to eat and drink only what was needful for his health. It was many long years before Marius knew anything of the polished manners and indulgent ways of the city.

From his youth Gaius Marius was bold and active. As he grew older, his temper would often flash out in ungovernable passion when there was little to provoke it.

The lad first served as a soldier under the younger Scipio Africanus. He was used to frugal fare, and to him the simple manner in which Scipio insisted that his soldiers should live seemed only natural.

The young soldier's bravery gained the attention of his commander more than once, and it is easy to believe that such notice awoke his pride and roused his ambition.

One evening, as he sat at supper, Scipio was asked where the Romans would find another leader when he was no longer with them.

"Perhaps here," answered Scipio, and as he spoke he touched Marius lightly on the shoulder.

At these words the ambition of Marius leaped to greater heights than ever before.

When he was thirty-eight years of age he became a tribune, and he at once set himself to win the favour of the people by bringing forward a measure to keep the election of magistrates free from bribery, but the Senate refused to allow the bill to be put to the vote.

Marius, nothing daunted, threatened that the Consuls should be imprisoned if they did not compel the Senate to let the bill take its course. So determined was he that he gained his end. The bill came before the people, and they, well pleased that Marius had compelled the Senate to yield, voted for it, and the bill became law.

In 115 B.C. he became a prætor, and was sent to service in Spain. Here he showed that he was a leader of men, for under him the Roman army

GAIUS MARIUS WINS NOTICE OF SCIPIO AFRICANUS

speedily cleared the land of the robbers that had for long infested it.

At this time those who rose to fame in Rome were almost always either rich or eloquent.

But Marius was poor, and he had no gift of speech, yet these things did not prevent him from looking forward to the days when he, too, would be famous.

And already the people believed in him. He worked so hard and lived so simply that they looked on the uncouth soldier with goodwill.

A little later he married into the family of the illustrious Cæsars, and this improved his position, and added to his growing influence in the State. His wife Julia was the aunt of the great Roman, Julius Cæsar.

This was the lieutenant Metellus took with him to the war against Jugurtha.

CHAPTER LXXXV

GAIUS MARIUS BECOMES COMMANDER OF THE ARMY

WHEN Metellus reached Africa, he found that the discipline of the army was so lax that it was unfitted to fight with any hope of success.

So he drilled and trained his men with great strictness and persistency, until he believed that they were again worthy to fight for their country.

Meanwhile Jugurtha found that here at length was a Roman who scorned to touch his gold. This same Roman, too, had so disciplined his troops that Jugurtha now distrusted his power to meet them. He therefore offered to submit, if Metellus would promise to spare his life and the lives of his children.

But the general paid no attention to this offer, and led his army into Numidia. Gaius Marius was with the Consul, in command of the cavalry.

Now Marius did not love his general, and he cared less that Metellus should be successful in battle than that he himself should win glory by his deeds.

GAIUS MARIUS BECOMES COMMANDER OF THE ARMY

But already the soldiers adored Marius, for he shared their life, giving up his own comfortable quarters to sleep, as did they, on a rough camp bed; often, too, eating their hard bread. When they found him even digging in the trenches their enthusiasm knew no bounds.

Jugurtha, meanwhile, had encamped in a strong position, but Metellus dislodged him, and at length defeated him, so that he was forced to flee.

The king determined that he would not risk another battle, so for a time he took refuge among the hills of his native land.

But even as he had bribed the Romans, so now he found that Metellus had won some of his officers from their allegiance, either with gold or with promises. This made him gradually suspicious of all who surrounded him.

Growing more and more uneasy, Jugurtha at length marched across the desert to a town named Thala. Metellus, however, hastened after him and besieged the town, which after forty days was in his hands. But the Roman general was not satisfied, for it was Jugurtha himself whom he wished to capture, and the king and his children had escaped from the town by night.

Jugurtha knew that Metellus was more than a match for him alone, but if he could secure a powerful ally the Romans might yet be driven from his land.

So, in 108 B.C., Jugurtha persuaded his father-in-law, Bocchus, King of Upper Numidia, to join him, and together they marched upon Cirta, near which town the Romans were encamped.

It was here that Metellus learned that he had not been elected Consul for the following year.

Meanwhile, Marius had begun to show his dislike of his commander.

The general had entrusted the care of an important town in Numidia to a friend of his own named Turpulius.

Turpulius was honest and kind, but he was not clever, and he did not see that the inhabitants of the town were taking advantage of his kindness.

Before he was aware, they had succeeded in betraying the town into the hands of Jugurtha, while he, owing to the goodwill of the townsfolk, was allowed to escape uninjured.

Among the Roman officers there were some ready to blame Turpulius, not only for negligence, but for actually giving the town up to Jugurtha.

A council of war was held, and on this council was Marius. He attacked Turpulius more fiercely than any other officer, and this he did knowing that he was the trusted friend of Metellus.

It was due to the influence of Marius that the other members condemned Turpulius, and Metellus was forced to sentence his friend to death.

GAIUS MARIUS BECOMES COMMANDER OF THE ARMY

Soon after the unfortunate man was executed it was clearly proved that he was innocent.

Metellus was overpowered with grief, and his officers did what they could to comfort him, all save Marius. He was heard to boast that he had caused the catastrophe, and he showed no sympathy for the distress of his general.

It was natural that from this time Metellus should look on Marius with aversion, and the two men were soon open enemies. Marius did not disguise that he hoped some day to supplant the general in his command.

During the winter of 108 B.C., Marius applied for leave, that he might go home to stand for election as Consul.

Metellus was indignant at what seemed to him the presumption of his officer, and he refused to let him go.

Marius was not disturbed by the refusal. He knew that in due time he would go to Italy, and meanwhile he wrote home unfavourable reports of his general, hinting, too, that if he had been in command of the army, Jugurtha would have been captured long ago.

The soldiers, he knew well, adored him, and when they sent messages home would say nothing but good of him.

After some time had passed, Marius again asked for leave to go to Rome.

Then Metellus scoffed at his desire, saying: "Will you not be content to wait and be Consul with this little son of mine?"

As the son of the general was a lad of about twenty, and as Marius was already forty-nine years of age, the taunt was not easy to bear.

But at length, as Marius persisted in asking leave, Metellus was forced to let him go. Only a short time was now left before those who intended to stand for the Consulships must be in Rome.

The journey from the camp to the coast was a long one, but Marius accomplished it in two days and a night.

In spite of the need for haste, he waited to offer a sacrifice before he sailed. And it seemed to him well that he had done so, for the priest bade him go his way, assured that success, greater than he had dreamed, would be his.

So in great good temper Marius went on board ship, and in four days landed on Italian soil.

In Rome he was received with favour, and before long his ambition was satisfied. He was elected Consul, and given the command of the army of Africa.

When Marius returned to take up his new position in Africa, Metellus had already left the army in charge of an officer. His pride would not let him stay to receive his erstwhile subordinate, who, as he said in anger, had now usurped his command.

GAIUS MARIUS BECOMES COMMANDER OF THE ARMY

Soon after this Metellus sailed for Rome, with the miserable feeling that he had been disgraced. He was, however, surprised by the welcome the people gave to him. They had not forgotten that he had refused to touch the gold of Jugurtha.

CHAPTER LXXXVI

THE CAPTURE OF JUGURTHA'S TREASURE TOWNS

Jugurtha and Bocchus knew that they had cause to dread the new Roman General. Certainly he would move swiftly, so the king and his ally resolved to march in different directions, in the hope that one of them would be able to fall upon Marius when he was least expecting an attack.

But it was Marius who in the end surprised Jugurtha, near the town of Cirta, and after a skirmish forced him to fly, hearing that he was defeated, determined to forsake him and make peace with Rome. But Marius was too anxious to capture Jugurtha to pay much attention to the advances of King Bocchus.

As the kings had foreseen, Marius moved swiftly. He marched first to Capsa, a city in which Jugurtha kept many of his royal treasures.

It was taken without much difficulty and burned, while the inhabitants were either killed or sold into slavery.

THE CAPTURE OF JUGURTHA'S TREASURE TOWNS

City after city, fort after fort, fell into the hands of the untiring general, until at length he reached another of the king's treasure forts.

The name of the fort is unknown. It was not a town, but a mere border citadel in the far west of Numidia, and was built on the top of a high rock, which looked impossible to scale. The one way of approach to the fort was by a steep and narrow path.

Marius besieged the fort, but it was strongly defended, and had a large store of arms, as well as of food and water.

It was here that a reinforcement of Italian cavalry joined him, under the command of Cornelius Sulla. As Marius had proved a thorn in the flesh to Metellus, so Sulla was to prove to his commander. In days to come he was his rival and his most bitter enemy.

Marius had at length decided to give up the siege of the border fort, when a way was found to take it.

A soldier from the Roman camp was one day looking at the steep rock which sloped down from the fort, when he noticed a ledge on which there were a number of snails.

As snails happened to be his favourite food, he climbed up to gather them, then clambered farther in search of more.

Higher and higher he mounted, until at length he found himself near the top of the cliff.

He now saw that he was close to an oak tree, the root of which was embedded deep in a crevice.

The soldier mounted to the topmost branch, and looking over into the fort he saw that no sentinels were near. He had made a great discovery.

Down the rock he clambered as quickly as he dared, and hastening back to the camp, told Marius that it was possible to scale the cliff at a point where the citadel was not guarded.

Marius promptly ordered some soldiers to follow the mountaineer up the face of the cliff.

It was no easy task, for the soldiers were cumbered with weapons, but by the help of their guide they reached the top in safety. Not a sentinel was to be seen.

Marius waited until he thought the soldiers had had time to accomplish their hazardous climb, then he ordered an attack to be made at the front of the fort.

The garrison rushed to the walls to repel the assault, but in the midst of their struggle they were startled to hear behind them the noise of trumpets, the clash of arms.

The soldiers who had scaled the rock had entered the fort, and the garrison and the wretched inhabitants were seized with sudden panic at their appearance and fled.

Then the Romans pursued the fugitives, cutting down all who resisted, and soon the citadel, which had so nearly defied them, was in their hands.

THE CAPTURE OF JUGURTHA'S TREASURE TOWNS

But Marius was not yet satisfied, for Jugurtha was still free, and he had promised the Roman people that he would speedily capture or kill the king.

CHAPTER LXXXVII

THE CAPTURE OF JUGURTHA

SULLA, who joined Marius in Numidia, was nineteen years younger than his commander.

The young officer was a patrician, while Marius was a plebeian, and he had had many advantages which had been denied to Marius.

But if the Consul was envious of his subordinate's accomplishments, he successfully hid it, and even scoffed at the attainments he did not possess.

As Sulla had ridden into the Roman camp the soldiers had looked at him with sudden interest. He was so unlike a soldier, and indeed he had not then been on a battlefield. But although he had looked to the troops like a man who had spent his days in pleasure, they had noticed that his blue eyes were keen, and gazed at them with fierce mastery.

That he was clever and quick was soon evident to all, and Marius speedily found that he could count on Sulla's brains and on Sulla's strength. As for the soldiers, they learned to respect him, although he was so unlike their own rough, uneducated hero.

THE CAPTURE OF JUGURTHA

Jugurtha had meanwhile again persuaded Bocchus to join him, although to do so he had been forced to promise him a large part of his kingdom.

The Roman army soon knew that Jugurtha was again supported by an ally, for the two kings, each with his army, followed and harassed it as it marched away from the border-fort towards Cirta.

Twice, indeed, the enemy had been in front, and the Romans had found their road blocked, and twice, before they could go forward, they had been forced to fight with their foes.

The latter time it was Sulla, who, by a skilful movement, saved the army from a disastrous defeat. He had proved an apt pupil in the art of war.

At length, after a tedious and difficult march, Marius reached Cirta, where he meant to remain during the winter.

But the campaign of 106 B.C. had convinced him that it would be well to treat with King Bocchus, if he was to redeem his promise to Rome and capture or kill Jugurtha.

So when Bocchus again sent to ask Marius to enter into negotiations with him, the Consul agreed to do so, and sent Sulla and his legate Manlius to treat with him.

But Bocchus himself was so treacherous that he distrusted other people, and after hearing from the Consul's officers what he was willing to do, he dismissed them. For he had determined to send an embassy to the Senate at Rome, lest it should refuse to confirm the promises of the Consul.

The ambassadors returned with a reassuring answer, at least King Bocchus seemed to think it was such, although the annalists couch it in Rome's most arrogant manner. "The Senate and the people of Rome are wont to remember kindness and wrong. They pardon the offence of Bocchus because he repents it, and will grant him alliance and friendship when he shall have deserved them."

This sounds as though it were a reproof as well as a pardon offered to a wilful child, and historians tell us it is not the answer that was actually sent to the king.

However, that may be, Bocchus now determined to cast in his fortune with Rome, and to betray Jugurtha to his enemies.

To do this would be no easy task, for Jugurtha was sure to be on his guard, knowing that his father-in-law had been negotiating with Marius.

So Bocchus asked the Roman general to send Sulla again to his tent, that he might ask Jugurtha to meet him. He intended to tell his victim that Sulla wished to discuss with him the terms offered by Rome.

Sulla set off for the camp of Bocchus, escorted by a body of the best Italian soldiers.

On his way he was met by the son of Bocchus, with a large troop of cavalry. As Jugurtha and his Numidian army were not far off, Sulla knew that

THE CAPTURE OF JUGURTHA

it would be easy to take him prisoner, should Jugurtha play him false. However, the Numidians allowed him to pass unharmed, and Sulla was soon seated in the tent of Bocchus.

Even here he was in greater danger than he knew. For the king hesitated whether, after all, he would not give Sulla to Jugurtha, rather than Jugurtha to the Roman.

But it would have been no easy matter to play fast and loose with Rome, and Bocchus determined to keep to his first plan.

So he invited Jugurtha to meet Sulla in his tent, and made the king believe that Sulla was to be given into his hands.

Jugurtha's suspicions had been laid to rest entirely, and he came to the tent of his father-in-law unarmed, with only a few servants.

But almost at once he found himself surrounded by troops, and before he had recovered from his surprise, he and his son were secured. Sulla then ordered them to be taken to the Roman camp and delivered to Marius.

Jugurtha was at last in chains, but the joy of Marius in his capture was spoiled.

It was he, he said to himself, who had made it possible to secure the dangerous enemy of Rome, yet Sulla seemed to claim the glory as his own. Marius felt bitter as he thought of it. And as the days passed his anger against Sulla grew.

Jugurtha came to the tent of his father-in-law unarmed.

THE CAPTURE OF JUGURTHA

He, Sulla, had dared to have a seal made, with a picture of Jugurtha being delivered into his hands stamped upon it. Nor did he scruple to use the seal to stamp his letters, so that all the world might see.

Moreover, those who were jealous of Marius tried to take away from his renown, muttering to one another: "The chief battles of the war were fought by Metellus, and its end is achieved by Sulla."

These things chafed the pride and ambition of Marius.

CHAPTER LXXXVIII

JUGURTHA IS BROUGHT TO ROME IN CHAINS

In 106 B.C., the same year that Jugurtha was captured, Rome was disturbed by the rumour that a great army of barbarians was approaching Italy.

They were tall and blue-eyed, these hordes of barbarians, and were believed to come from the shores of the North Sea, where the German races had their home.

The Senate sent brave generals and strong armies against these terrible foes, but the barbarians scattered the Roman legions and shamed the brave generals.

Their victories made the Teutones and Cimbri insolent and proud.

"We can destroy the Roman legions," they said, "so it will be an easy task to plunder Italy, and destroy even Rome herself."

The Senate and the people grew more and more alarmed, while those who had sought to belit-

JUGURTHA IS BROUGHT TO ROME IN CHAINS

tle the fame of Marius repented. For was he not the only general who could save them now?

So Marius, although he was still in Africa, was elected Consul a second time.

It is true that the law forbade the election of any one who was absent from Rome. But necessity knows no law, said the Romans, and Marius was elected.

When Marius was told of the honour that had been conferred upon him he was well pleased. It was another step in the ambitious path he was ascending. He at once sailed for Italy, that he might be ready to defend his country from the barbarians.

By the 1st January 104 B.C., Marius had reached the gates of Rome and celebrated a splendid triumph, Jugurtha and two of his sons being led in his procession loaded with chains.

Jugurtha had been a dangerous foe, and the people of Rome could scarcely believe, until they saw, that he was actually a captive and in chains.

When the triumph was over, many of them ventured to approach him, to put out their hand to touch the broken-spirited king. In wanton cruelty they snatched the clothing off his body, and even wrenched the gold rings from off his ears.

But soon he was led away and thrust into the prison at the foot of the Capitoline hill. His misery had confused his mind, and as he was left alone his foolish laughter echoed through his prison, while he cried, "O Hercules, how cold your bath is."

For six days he endured the pangs of hunger, for his gaolers gave him no food, and so at last the king, shorn of his strength and power, died.

After his triumph Marius at once set out with his army to fight against the barbarians. But the Teutones and the Cimbri had turned away from Rome, and it was a long time before Marius encountered them.

He was not, however, the kind of general to let his troops be idle. He kept them at work, and the discipline of the camp was strict.

If the soldiers marched, each was made to carry his own baggage, and each had also to cook his own food.

Soon the men, if they carried their loads without grumbling, were nicknamed "Marian mules."

Another story tells that this nickname arose in quite a different way.

When Marius first joined the army under Scipio, the general on a certain day inspected not only the arms and horses of his men, but their mules and wagons as well.

Both the horse and mule belonging to Marius were in perfect condition, and had evidently received more care than those of his comrades.

Scipio commended the beasts, and often reminded the soldiers of their well-groomed appearance, until at length, half in scorn and half in mirth, any man in Marius's army who worked harder and more persistently than his neighbour was called by his comrades "a Marian mule."

A year passed, and the barbarians had not yet appeared.

Marius was elected Consul for the third time, for the Senate still dreaded the appearance of the enemy, and wished him to be in command when it did descend into Italy.

Another year passed, and still they did not come.

At the end of 103 B.C. Marius went back to Rome. It was time for the new elections, and Marius pretended that he did not wish to be Consul again.

But Saturninus, one of the tribunes, said that if he refused office when his country was in danger he would be a traitor.

This was strong language, but it did not displease Marius, who in reality would have been greatly disappointed had he not been elected.

So now he promised to accept the office if it was the wish of the people that he should do so. Then for the fourth time Marius was chosen Consul, with Catulus as his colleague.

CHAPTER LXXXIX

MARIUS CONQUERS THE TEUTONES

Soon after Marius had been chosen Consul for the fourth time, the Teutones, and the Ambrones, another of the fierce barbarian tribes which Rome had feared, did actually approach Italy.

So Marius marched toward the Rhone, and here, not far from the river, he set up his camp. His first work was to secure a safe passage to the sea, so that he could be sure of getting provisions for his army.

As the mouth of the Rhone was choked with huge banks of sand and mud, Marius ordered his soldiers to clear the bank away, and then set them to work to dig a great canal.

Now soldiers would usually rather fight than dig, and as the summer passed, and still their general did not lead them to battle, they began to grumble.

"Has Marius found us cowards," they cried, "that he should thus like women lock us up from encountering our enemies? Come on, let us show ourselves men, and ask him if he expects others to

MARIUS CONQUERS THE TEUTONES

fight for Italy. Does he mean merely to employ us to dig trenches and cleanse places of mud . . . and turn the course of the river?"

These complaints reached the ear of Marius, but they did not at all displease him. He wished that his soldiers should be eager to fight, and bade them wait but a little longer and he would lead them against the enemy.

The Teutones were encamped not far off, and they, seeing that the Romans did not attack them, began to wonder if these legions, of which they had heard so much, were, after all, as brave as they had been told. They would at least find out what the enemy was worth, and they determined themselves to attack the Roman camp.

But their attempt was discouraging. Many of them were killed and wounded, and this although the Romans were restrained by the orders of their general from rushing out upon the foe, and could only hurl upon them any missile on which they were able to lay their hands.

The barbarians now resolved to take no more notice of the Romans. Since the enemy would not fight, they determined to break up their camp, cross the Alps, and invade Italy, as had been their intention before Marius placed his army in their path.

So the vast hordes of Teutones and Ambrones began to march slowly past the Roman camp. For six days, it is said, Marius refused to let his men stir, while the great procession filed past their tents.

The Roman soldiers were like caged lions, and when some of the barbarians jeered at them as they passed, asking if they had any message for their wives in Rome, they all but broke loose.

At length the long line of the barbarian hosts came to an end, and then Marius broke up his camp, and to the undisguised relief of his soldiers marched after the enemy.

The barbarians had encamped a few days' march from the pass into Italy, at a place called Aquæ Sextiæ.

Marius set up his camp near to the enemy, but while he had not enough water for his army, the barbarians were close to a river, and had a plentiful supply.

When the Roman soldiers complained that they were thirsty, Marius pointed to the river which flowed past the camp of the enemy.

"There," said he, "you may have drink if you will buy it with your blood."

"Why, then," answered the soldiers, "do you not lead us to it before our blood is dried up in us?"

"Let us first fortify our camp," replied the general, and reluctantly the men began to obey.

But the servants and slaves belonging to the Roman army determined to get water at once for themselves and for the horses. So, carrying pitchers in one hand, and swords and axes in the other, they went boldly down to the edge of the river.

On the bank sat a band of the enemy. It had been bathing, and was now carelessly eating and drinking.

But seeing the Roman servants, the barbarians sprang to their feet, and with loud shouts fell upon them.

Their cries and the clash of their weapons were heard in both camps, and, hastily arming, Romans and barbarians alike rushed to the river. Soon the Ambrones and the Romans were engaged in a fierce battle.

But the Ambrones were not a match for the strictly-trained soldiers of Marius. Numbers of them were cut to pieces, while others turned and fled to the wagons which surrounded their camp, hotly pursued by the enemy.

When the Ambrones reached the wagons, they met with neither welcome nor help.

The women, in anger that their men had turned their back upon the foe, had climbed into the wagons, carrying with them the first weapon which they had been able to find. And now, shouting the wild war-cry of their peoples, they attacked with sword or hatchet all who came within their reach, were they friends or foes.

The arms of the women were bare, and as they fought they received many wounds. Then they tried to pull from the Romans the shields with which they protected themselves.

Still the battle raged, and only when night fell did the Romans retire, leaving the field strewn with the dead bodies of the Ambrones.

But there was no rest for the Roman soldiers that night, nor did they dare to rejoice as though the barbarians were vanquished. For the Teutones were not yet beaten. Even then their wild cries and lamentations over the dead, mingled with threats against their enemy, reached the ears of the Romans. In the darkness the strong soldiers trembled, lest they should be attacked that night, while their camp was defended by neither trench nor rampart.

But although the terrible cries never ceased, the Teutones did not attempt to attack their enemy.

Next morning Marius saw that it would be easy to set an ambush beyond the camp of the Teutones.

So he ordered Marcellus, one of his officers, to take three thousand men and hide them in the thickly wooded hills behind the camp of the enemy. His orders were strict, that Marcellus should not stir from the hill until the Teutones were in the thick of the battle with the main body of the Romans.

The Roman camp was on a hill, and Marius now ordered his cavalry to ride down to the plain.

But when the Teutones saw the horsemen coming toward them, they threw prudence to the winds, and dashed up the side of the hill to meet the enemy.

MARIUS CONQUERS THE TEUTONES

Marius, who had followed his cavalry with the main body of his army, saw that the steepness of the ground would make the foothold of the Teutones uncertain and their blows less strong than they would have been on the plain.

So he bade his troops to stand and await the attack of the barbarians, and then, after hurling their javelins into the midst of the foe, to force them steadily backward with sword and shield.

Marius himself stood by the side of his men, ready to fight where the danger was greatest.

Against the solid front of the Roman army the Teutones threw themselves in vain. They could not break its ranks. Slowly and in disorder they found themselves being pushed back toward the plain.

At length they were once more on level ground, and immediately they attempted to form their front ranks anew, meaning again to attack the enemy.

Suddenly those in front heard behind them wild cries of despair. Swords flashed in the air, javelins seemed to fall among their ranks as thickly as a storm of hail.

Marcellus, with his three thousand men, had dashed out of his ambush, and had fallen upon the rear of the Teutones.

This was more than the barbarians could bear. With the terrible enemy before and behind, they yielded to panic, broke their ranks, and fled.

The Romans followed, determined that the enemy should not escape, and cut down more than one hundred thousand men.

For long months the bones of the barbarians were left in the field, until at length, bleached clean, they were used by the neighbouring folk to fence their vineyards.

After this great victory, Marius chose the most splendid treasures from the spoil and laid them aside, to grace his triumph when he returned to Rome.

He then ordered the rest to be gathered into one great heap, to be sacrificed to the gods.

Around the huge pile the soldiers were presently gathered, their arms in their hands, their clothes decked with garlands. In their midst stood Marius, wearing a robe with the purple border, and holding aloft a lighted torch with which to set fire to the sacrifice.

But at that moment horsemen were seen in the distance spurring their horses toward the assembled army.

What tidings did they bear? No one in the great gathering stirred until the horsemen rode up, and crying that Marius had been elected Consul for the fifth time, handed him letters from the Senate to tell him of this new honour.

The soldiers were well pleased that their general should be so distinguished, and clashed their shields to show their delight, while the officers crowned him with a wreath of laurel.

Marius then touched the pile of treasures with his lighted torch. The flames leaped up, crackled, and soon the sacrifice was consumed.

CHAPTER XC

MARIUS MOCKS THE AMBASSADORS OF THE CIMBRI

WHILE Marius was carrying all before him, his colleague Catulus was in a sorry plight.

He had found it impossible to hold the passes of the Alps against the Cimbri, and had been forced to descend into the plain of Northern Italy. Here he crossed the river Adige, and encamped on its bank.

The Cimbri never doubted that they would be able to conquer the Romans. Already they were elated to find that the passes were not guarded. No tidings of the terrible battle of Aquæ Sextiæ had yet come to daunt their courage.

And so, in the sheer pride of their strength, they flung aside their clothing, and naked, climbed through falling snow and over ice-clad rocks to the top of the mountain passes. Then, turning their broad shields into sledges, they boldly shot down the slopes on the other side.

MARIUS MOCKS THE AMBASSADORS OF THE CIMBRI

When they reached the Adige they saw the Roman camp across the river. Before attacking it they determined to dam the stream.

The Roman soldiers, as they watched the barbarians at work, were amazed at their strength.

Giant trees were uprooted and flung into the river as though they were saplings. Huge rocks, too, that seemed beyond the strength of man to move, were hurled into the bed of the Adige as though they were stones. Who could fight with such men as these barbarians seemed to be?

To the dismay of Catulus, his army decided that they could not face such foes, and they began to steal out of the camp. It was evident that soon the whole army would take to flight before it was attacked.

But the Consul could not let the soldiers so disgrace their fame. Rather would he take upon himself the blame of having ordered a retreat. So, seizing the Roman eagle, he hastened with it to the front of his men, and himself led them away.

When the Cimbri saw that most of the Romans had left their camp they crossed the river and captured it, in spite of the brave defence of those who had scorned to turn their backs upon an enemy.

The barbarians showed that they could respect courage, for they spared the lives of these brave soldiers. But before they let them go they made them swear upon their brazen bull to observe certain conditions. Now the brazen bull was to these barbarians sacred as a god.

When, a short time after this, the Cimbri were defeated, the bull was carried away with other spoil, and treasured by Catulus in memory of his victory.

After taking the Roman camp, the barbarians wandered through the plains of Lombardy, burning and plundering wherever they went.

Marius, meanwhile, after his victory over the Teutones and Ambrones, was recalled to Rome, and voted a triumph.

Hearing, however, that Catulus was in danger from the barbarians, he would not stay to celebrate it, but hastened to join his colleague.

The two Consuls met near the river Po, and crossing the river they found the Cimbri at Vercellæ.

Here the barbarians expected each day to be joined by the Teutones and Ambrones.

As they did not wish to fight until their allies arrived, they pretended that they were anxious to make terms with Marius, and sent to ask him to give them land for themselves and their brethren.

"Who are your brethren?" the Consul asked the ambassadors who stood before him.

"The Teutones," answered they.

Those who surrounded Marius laughed, for well they knew what had befallen the Teutones.

MARIUS MOCKS THE AMBASSADORS OF THE CIMBRI

"Do not trouble yourselves for your brethren," replied Marius, taunting them, "for we have already provided land for them, which they shall possess for ever."

Then the ambassadors understood that their brethren lay slain upon the ground, and their anger rose. Fearless of danger, they hurled threats at the Consul, saying that the Cimbri and those Teutones who were still left alive would avenge the death of their fellows.

"Their rulers are not far off," cried Marius. "It will be unkindly done of you to go away before greeting your brethren."

Then the kings of the Teutones, who had been captured, were brought before the ambassadors, loaded with chains.

Seeing how these mighty chiefs had been humbled, the ambassadors were silent, and soon after they went back to the Cimbri to tell them what they had heard and seen in the Roman camp.

The Cimbri could not restrain their rage when they knew what had befallen their allies. Three days later they were on the plains of Vercellæ, impatient to avenge their defeat.

Marius, too, was eager for battle. His cavalry, strong as ever, wore that day strange helmets. Each one looked like the head of some strange beast, while above the head waved a lofty plume, that added to the height of the soldier. Their white shields gleamed in the sun, and their breastplates were of iron.

The day began in discomfort for the Cimbri. Cold and frost they could endure, as they had shown when they crossed the Alps, but heat soon made them weak and stupid.

In vain they tried to shelter their faces with their shields. The sun shone in their eyes, beat upon their heads. Clouds of dust, too, were blowing, and hiding them from the Romans, who, not seeing the great numbers arrayed against them, fought the more fearlessly.

To help them to keep their ranks unbroken, the front rows of the Cimbri were fastened together by long chains, which were slipped through their belts. But when the battle went against them these chains were a source of danger.

On this day the Cimbri were worsted, and when the Romans began to cut them down, the chains made it impossible for those in the front to escape.

Those in the rear fled to their camp. But here, as in the camp of the Ambrones, the women, clad in black, mounted upon the wagons and slew their own husbands, brothers, sons, if they ventured to seek refuge from the enemy.

Rather than fall into the hands of the Romans, many of the men and women hanged themselves, after first killing their little children. Although many

MARIUS MOCKS THE AMBASSADORS OF THE CIMBRI

of the Cimbri died in this terrible way, more than sixty thousand were taken prisoners.

Catulus claimed the victory of Vercellæ as his, and was dissatisfied with Marius, who, he said, did not wish to share the honour with any one.

However that may be, when the Consuls returned to Rome, Marius was offered two triumphs, but he would only accept one, and that one he shared with Catulus.

CHAPTER XCI

METELLUS IS DRIVEN FROM ROME

Marius had been Consul five times already, but he was not yet content. He wished to be elected for the sixth time, and he determined to do all he could to gain his end.

But it was no easy task, for now that no enemy threatened Rome, she was ready to cast Marius aside.

Moreover, although on the battlefield Marius was brave above all others, in the Senate or the Assembly of the people his courage deserted him. He knew that he was not eloquent, and he no sooner stood up to speak than he grew timid and ill at ease.

Yet he did his best, and to the people he tried to behave more pleasantly than he felt, and that is at no time an easy thing to do, nor even, it may be, a right thing to attempt. But Marius smiled when he would much rather have frowned, and spoke kindly when a cross answer was hidden in his heart.

Metellus, from whom he had wrested the command of the army, was the man he feared most,

METELLUS IS DRIVEN FROM ROME

and he thought if only he could have him banished from Rome all would be well. Although Marius at once began to plot and plan, it took a long time to get rid of Metellus. But this is how in the end he succeeded.

First, Marius joined Glaucia and Saturninus, who were popular with the people, but too daring not to be hated by the Optimates.

Saturninus had been tribune in 101 B.C., and wished to be re-elected for the following year. When he found that the people had not voted for him, he was so angry that he did not scruple to order his successful rival to be put to death.

The people, subdued by the violence of Saturninus, then gave him the post he coveted without more ado.

Glaucia became prætor for the same year, while Marius achieved his ambition, and was made Consul for the sixth time.

Saturninus now brought forward a bill regarding the division of land. The people would, as usual, be asked to vote for or against this bill, but the tribune added an important clause to his measure, saying that whatever the people voted, to that the senators must take an oath to agree.

Marius, as Consul, pretended to be very angry with Saturninus for adding this clause to his bill, and he said that he, for one, would never take such an oath. The senators, he added, needed to take no oath

THE STORY OF ROME

to make them agree to anything that was for the good of the State.

The other members, among whom was Metellus, were equally indignant, and swore that they would never take the oath demanded by Saturninus. Marius was now satisfied that he had entrapped Metellus.

He himself had promised Saturninus secretly that he would take the oath, and as soon as the people had voted in favour of the bill he did so. Nor did he make any worthy excuse for breaking his word, but, as Consul, advised the other members of the Senate also to agree to the clause which before they had sworn to reject.

When Marius took the oath the people could not control their delight, but broke out into loud applause. But the nobles were angry with the Consul for saying one thing and doing another, yet, because they were afraid of the people, they took the oath, all save Metellus, who refused to break his word.

This was just what Marius had hoped would happen, for he knew that Metellus was too upright a man to stoop to act as he and the other senators had done.

Saturninus now demanded that the Consul should punish Metellus for refusing to confirm the vote of the people. He wished that the senator should be forbidden to stay under the shelter of any roof in the city, that he should be refused the use of fire or water.

METELLUS IS DRIVEN FROM ROME

The mob went even further, and would have killed Metellus had his friends not defended him.

But Metellus would not allow his friends to fight, telling them that he would leave the city rather than cause strife. "For," said he, "either, when the position of affairs is mended and the people repent, I shall be recalled, or if things remain in their present position it will be best to be absent."

Thus Marius, with the help of Saturninus, succeeded in driving Metellus from the city. But the price he had to pay for his success was heavy.

For Saturninus and Glaucia were determined that the bills which they brought forward, for the good of the people as they believed, should be passed. If any one ventured to oppose their measures or to become their rivals, they speedily perished. Saturninus hired assassins to slay such insolent folk.

At length even the people grew angry with the tribune and with Glaucia, and threatened to put them to death, so that the two men were forced to flee for refuge to the Capitol.

The Senate at once condemned them and their followers as public enemies, and called upon the Consuls to punish them.

Marius was now in a difficult position. He did not wish to punish those who had helped him to banish Metellus, yet as Consul he could not ignore the crimes that these men had committed. So at length he ordered them to be arrested, but he still hoped to save their lives.

Saturninus and Glaucia, however, continued to defy the Senate, until Marius was forced to order the water-pipes on the Capitol to be cut, and their thirst soon compelled the rebels to surrender.

Marius sent them for safety to the Senate-house. But it was useless to try to protect such evil-doers. The Consul found that he was but turning the people's rage against himself, without doing his friends any good. For the mob broke in the door and took the tiles off the roof of the Senate-house, and rushing in, killed Saturninus and his friends.

The Senate not only did not punish the people for this deed, it approved of it.

Marius had now made himself hated by the nobles, because he had taken the oath he had declared he would never take, and by the people, because he had been the friend of Saturninus, and had tried to protect him from the just punishment of his cruel deeds.

When the Consul found that the people were clamouring for the return of Metellus, of whose honesty they had had proof, he left Rome. He could not bear to see the return of his rival.

He journeyed to Asia, and here he tried to rouse Mithridates, King of Pontus, to fight against an ally of Rome. For he thought that if war broke out he would once more be called upon to deliver his country from her foes.

CHAPTER XCII

SULLA ENTERS ROME WITH HIS TROOPS

During the absence of Marius the influence of Sulla grew by leaps and bounds. It was this, it may be, that drew Marius back to Rome.

He came, hoping once again to win the goodwill of the people, and he even took a house near the Forum so as to be in their midst.

But the people paid little attention to the general whom in time of war they had courted and admired. In time of peace they had no use for one who was above all else a soldier.

Sulla, too, had proved himself a great general, but he, unlike Marius, was an educated man and an Optimate, and was useful in time of peace as in time of war.

The ever-ready jealousy of Marius was roused when he noticed that Sulla was now much more powerful in Rome than was he.

Nor were his feelings soothed when he saw on the Capitol a new statue of victory, which had been erected by Bocchus, King of Numidia. By the side of the chief figure were others in gold, representing Bocchus delivering Jugurtha to Sulla.

To Sulla! Marius was very angry when he saw that. Jugurtha would never have been captured but for him. It was he, Marius, who should have stood in the place Sulla had been given!

The old general determined to pull down the statue. But Sulla heard what Marius meant to do, and refused to allow it, so that a struggle between them was inevitable. But at this very time a new war broke out, and all private quarrels were laid aside.

The war that began in 89 B.C. was called the Social War. It was caused by the discontent of the Italian people, to whom the full rights of Roman citizens had not been given. Marius and Sulla both fought in this war.

As of old, Marius was never to be enticed to fight against his will. So slow, indeed, was he to lead his men to battle, that one of the generals on the other side doubted his courage. "If you are indeed a great general, Marius," he said, "leave your camp and fight a battle."

But all Marius answered was: "If you are one, make me do so against my will."

Although Marius was now sixty-six years of age, he was as good a commander as ever, and won a great battle, in which six thousand of the enemy was slain. But at the end of a year, although the war was

SULLA ENTERS ROME WITH HIS TROOPS

not yet over, Marius resigned his command, saying that his health was not good.

Sulla also gained many victories in this Social War, which came to an end in 88 B.C., for the Senate then granted the Italians the rights of citizens, and to obtain this had been the object of the war. But while all the Italian cities enjoyed new privileges, Rome was still to continue the centre of the Republic, where magistrates were elected and laws were ratified.

Sulla returned to Rome in time to be elected Consul for the year 88 B.C. He was also appointed by the Senate to take command of the army which was now to go to Asia. For war had broken out against Mithridates, King of Pontus.

Now one of the tribunes, named Sulpicius, was not satisfied that Sulla should have this honour, and he proposed that Marius should be made proConsul and general of the war.

Marius, you remember, had laid down his command in the Social War on account of his health. So now those who wished Sulla to be commander of the army jeered at Marius, bidding him stay at home to tend his worn-out frame.

Marius was too eager to oust his rival to give heed to these taunts. He laid himself, indeed, open to more. For now he was to be seen out each day taking exercises with the youths of the city.

He had grown stout and heavy, but he soon showed that, in spite of this and of his infirmities, he could vault lightly enough into his saddle, and could claim still to be "nimble," even when he wore his armour.

Sulpicius now brought forward a series of laws, bribed, so said some, by Marius. It is certain that one of the laws proposed that Marius should be commander of the war.

As these laws, if they were passed, would make the Populares, or party of the people, powerful, the Optimates determined to overthrow them. But Sulpicius was not a man to yield without a struggle. He sent armed men to attack the Consuls, for they were on the side of the Optimates.

Rufus, the colleague of Sulla, escaped from the city, but in the riot raised by the people his son was killed.

Sulla saved his life only by hiding in the house of Marius, where no one dreamed of looking for him. When the riot was over, he escaped to the camp at Nola.

With the Consuls absent, and the Optimates for the time cowed, the laws which had caused all this trouble were passed, and became known as the Sulpician Laws.

By one of these laws Marius became commander of the army, and he at once sent two tribunes to Nola to warn Sulla that he would soon arrive at the camp to take over the command.

But, as Marius might have foreseen, Sulla did not mean to submit to such a defeat.

SULLA ENTERS ROME WITH HIS TROOPS

He, Sulla, had been appointed by the Senate, while it was by violence that Marius had been proclaimed commander.

Sulla knew that the army was devoted to him, and would do anything to win his favour. So he assembled the troops, and told them the story of his defeat, and how Marius was coming to lead them to Asia.

They at once broke out into loud shouts of protest, crying that none but he should be their leader. If it was his will they would follow him to Rome and overcome his enemies. In the meantime, they would put to death the two tribunes who had been sent by Marius to the camp.

Thus it was that before long Sulla was marching toward Rome, at the head of his troops, being joined on the way by Rufus.

Marius and Sulpicius, when they heard that Sulla had appealed to the army, had at once tried to raise a force to oppose him, even offering freedom to the slaves if they would fight faithfully.

But their efforts were vain, and they fled from the city before Sulla entered it.

From the people Sulla received but a sorry welcome, for so angry were they with him for bringing his army within the walls of the city, that they climbed to the roofs of the houses and flung stones and every missile that they could find upon the troops. But the Senate welcomed the Consuls with open arms.

Marius, Sulpicius, and twelve of their followers were at once declared public enemies. This meant that it was not only the right, but the duty, of every one to kill them.

Sulpicius, who had found shelter in a house in the country, was put to death by a slave.

Sulla gave the slave his freedom, and then, in dislike of his treachery, he ordered him to be hurled from the Tarpeian Rock.

CHAPTER XCIII

THE FLIGHT OF MARIUS

When Marius fled from Rome, he hastened to Ostia, a seaport at the mouth of the Tiber. So eager was he to escape that he sailed without waiting for his son, young Marius, whom he had sent to procure provisions.

Young Marius, meanwhile, had reached the farm where his father-in-law lived, and had spent the night there undisturbed.

But when morning dawned a servant rushed into the house, saying that he had seen soldiers riding in the direction of the farm. The steward at once ran to his barn, dragged out a wagon full of beans, and hid young Marius under them. Then, without any apparent haste, he yoked his oxen to the wagon and drove off toward the city.

Before he had driven far he passed the search party, which, unconscious that it had missed its prey, went on at a sharp trot toward the farm. In this way Marius reached the coast safely, and sailed to Africa.

THE STORY OF ROME

But Marius, the father, was no sooner on board the ship, in which he had so hurriedly embarked, than difficulty after difficulty beset him.

Before he had sailed far along the coast of Italy a violent storm arose and blew the vessel to the shore.

Here Marius and his few followers were forced to land, and to wander about in a desolate country in search of food and shelter.

At length they met some herdsmen, but they had neither roof nor bread which they could share with the fugitives.

The herdsmen warned them, however, that horsemen were scouring the country; so, almost fainting with hunger, they struggled on, until they came to a wood, and here they hid themselves for the night.

In the morning, weak as he was, and still famished for want of food, Marius dragged himself along in the direction of the sea, for there lay his one hope of escape.

The old soldier still carried with him a brave spirit, and he believed that he would yet overcome his misfortunes. He begged his companions not to forsake him, telling them that he would reward their faithfulness. Had not the diviners assured him that he would be Consul a seventh time?

The poor little company struggled on, encouraged, it may be, by the promises of Marius. They were now only about two miles from the sea, and

THE FLIGHT OF MARIUS

not far off the coast, ships under sail were visible. Surely now they would soon be safe on board one of these vessels!

But just as their hopes began to rise, the sound of horses' feet struck upon their ears. The sound grew nearer and nearer.

In desperate fear the wanderers, feeble as they were, began to run, and at length actually reached the shore, and plunging into the water, swam toward the ships.

Marius had to be helped by two of his followers, for he was too heavy to swim with ease. He was only just safe on board when a troop of soldiers on horseback reached the edge of the water.

The soldiers shouted to the crew of the vessel on which Marius had found refuge, bidding them either to send the fugitive back to the shore, or to throw him into the water.

With tears streaming down his cheeks Marius implored the sailors to save him from his enemies.

At length, after thinking now that it would send the unfortunate man to shore, now that it would sail away with him, the crew made up its mind to put off to sea.

But even then the troubles of Marius were not ended.

In a very short time the sailors again changed their minds. They were, after all, afraid to keep the man whom Rome had banned, so, although they had not given him up to the enemy, they now determined to desert him.

They therefore put in to land near a town called Minturnæ, and bidding Marius go on shore, they told him to rest until a more favourable wind arose.

Marius had no suspicion that the sailors intended to desert him. Perhaps he was too bewildered with the hardships he had already endured to think of others that might yet befall him.

But the sailors had no sooner got rid of their unwelcome guest than they sailed away, leaving Marius alone. His companions had, it seems, gone on board another ship.

When at length Marius realised that the sailors had played him false, he struggled to his feet and looked around. The ground was full of bogs and marsh, but he stumbled on, for shelter he must find. In time he reached the hut of an old man who worked in the fens.

Marius begged the old man to hide him, and he appeared willing to do so, for he led the stranger to a secret place in the fens and covered him with rushes.

Even here, however, Marius was not safe. The horsemen succeeded in tracing him to the hut, and Marius could hear their loud voices as they threatened to punish the old man for concealing an enemy of Rome.

THE FLIGHT OF MARIUS

He must escape, and that without delay! So, hastily stripping off his clothes, Marius plunged deep into the thick and muddy bog, hoping to find a ditch into which he might slip and yet baffle his pursuers. But his hope was vain.

The horsemen had dismounted, and were searching everywhere for their prey. At last one of them caught sight of the desperate man, and darting into the bog, pulled Marius out, covered with mire.

Thus, naked and begrimed, he was carried to the magistrates of Minturnæ.

CHAPTER XCIV

THE GAUL DARES NOT KILL GAIUS MARIUS

As you know, Marius had been proclaimed a public enemy, and it was the duty of any one who captured him to put him to death. The magistrates of Minturnæ resolved to do their duty.

But no citizen was to be found who would undertake to put Marius to death, for his fame made him still terrible in their eyes.

At length a Gaul, who had seen him as he fought with the Cimbri, was sent, sword in hand, to kill the prisoner.

Marius had been thrust into a dimly-lighted room. As the Gaul opened the door he saw nothing save two eyes which gleamed like fire. As he advanced the eyes seemed to follow his every movement, until he was conscious of nothing save the terror of that burning gaze.

The next moment a loud voice cried: "Fellow, darest thou kill Gaius Marius?" and in a flash the Gaul knew that in truth he dared not. Throwing down his sword, he rushed from the room in a

THE GAUL DARES NOT KILL GAIUS MARIUS

frenzy of terror, crying: "I cannot kill Gaius Marius." So the magistrates and citizens of Minturnæ had the prisoner once more on their hands.

It may be that something of the same awe that had overpowered the Gaul took possession of them, for now they determined to help their prisoner escape.

Marius was brought out of his gloomy prison and taken once more to the seashore and placed on board a ship.

A favourable wind carried the vessel swiftly to Africa, where Marius landed, to find his son already there and awaiting him.

After young Marius had listened to the tale of his father's adventures, he was sent to Hiempsal, King of Numidia, to beg for protection for his father and himself.

Marius, meanwhile, went to Carthage. But scarcely had he reached it when Sextilius, the Roman governor, sent an officer to bid him leave the province.

"Sextilius forbids you to stay in this province," said the officer. "If you do, he declares he will put the decree of the Senate in execution, and treat you as an enemy to the Romans."

After all he had gone through, must he be persecuted still? In grief as well as in anger Marius sat silent and dismayed.

Gaius Marius sitting in exile among the ruins of Carthage.

THE GAUL DARES NOT KILL GAIUS MARIUS

At length the officer asked what answer he should take back to Sextilius. "Go tell him," answered he, "that you have seen Gaius Marius sitting in exile among the ruins of Carthage."

Meanwhile, young Marius had reached the King of Numidia, and was treated by him with kindness.

But each time that he proposed to go back to his father, Hiempsal had some polite reason for not allowing him to leave his court.

The king, indeed, was hesitating as to whether or not he would send the exiles back to Sulla, and so win the favour of Rome.

But young Marius grew impatient of these delays, and one day he made his escape and went back to his father.

It was plain that the King of Numidia could not be trusted, and that there was no safety for the exiles in Africa. So father and son hastened to the coast, and hiring a little fishing-boat, they sailed to an island named Cercina, which was not far from the continent.

It was well that they had not lingered in Carthage, for soon after they had embarked in their little boat, horsemen, sent by the King of Numidia, reached the shore, expecting to capture both Marius and his son.

CHAPTER XCV

MARIUS RETURNS TO ROME

SULLA, you remember, entered the city with his troops as Marius fled from Rome. He at once revoked the laws of Sulpicius, and ruled in his own way.

But he was impatient to go to war against Mithridates, and so, in the summer of 87 B.C., he set out with his army for Greece.

No sooner was he gone than Cinna, one of the Consuls, proposed that Marius and his friends should be recalled. But Octavius, his colleague, was greatly opposed to this, and determined to frustrate Cinna's schemes.

The Consul soon gave Octavius the opportunity he wished. For when the citizens assembled to vote for or against the return of the exile, Cinna led a band of armed men to the Forum, that they might be too frightened to vote save as he wished. He drove away, too, the tribunes who attempted to speak against him.

MARIUS RETURNS TO ROME

This was against all laws of justice, and Octavius did not hesitate to go to the Forum at the head of an armed force to punish Cinna's men.

In the struggle many of the rioters were killed, while Cinna himself was forced to flee. The Senate then declared that he was no longer Consul, but had become a public enemy.

When Cinna heard of the Senate's decree he was very angry, and determined to gather together troops to fight against Octavius. He was speedily joined by Marius, who was no sooner told what had happened in Rome than he hastened back to the city.

When he arrived Cinna received the exile with great honour, and urged him to wear the robes of a pro-Consul.

But Marius pretended to be too humble to don such garments, and he persisted in wearing old and shabby clothes.

His hair, which had not been cut since his banishment, he left still untouched, although it now reached to his shoulders, while he walked as though bent with the weight of his seventy years. It did not seem, to judge from his pitiable appearance, as if the old man could be of much use to Cinna.

But his enemies muttered that Marius was only trying in these ways to make the people sorry for all he had suffered. They needed only to look in his face to see that he was harbouring grim thoughts of revenge on those who had ever shown themselves to be his enemies.

Soon Cinna had four armies ready to march on Rome. One was under Marius, another Cinna himself intended to lead, while two more were under his legates, Sertorius and Carbo.

The city walls were in no fit state to stand an attack, for in many places they were even broken down. Octavius ordered these weak places to be repaired and strengthened by fortifications, while at the same time he sent messengers to the lieutenants of Sulla, bidding them hasten to the aid of the city.

Two of these officers, Metellus and Strabo, hastened to obey Octavius. But they did, perhaps, more harm than good, so many of their troops deserted and joined Cinna's army.

Metellus did not stay in the city long, and refused to take the command of the troops, as Octavius wished.

Strabo did his best, for although his men were suffering from fever he attacked Sertorius. But the battle was undecided, and soon after this Strabo was killed by lightning. Octavius was thus left without the officers on whose help he had relied.

Marius, meanwhile, had, as it seemed, thrown off the weight of his years. He was as active and as successful as in his earlier battles.

Ostia, the port of Rome, was taken by his troops, and this, as he meant it to do, kept the corn supply from reaching the city, and Rome began to fear that famine was before her.

MARIUS RETURNS TO ROME

Before long Cinna and Marius were able to meet on the Janiculum. Large numbers of the troops under Octavius continued to desert and to join their army.

Then the Senate saw that they would gain nothing by continuing to defy the successful generals. So they bent their pride, and invited Cinna and Marius to meet them within the city.

When the generals arrived, the Senate begged that they would spare the lives of the citizens, even if they saw fit to punish them.

Cinna did not scruple to promise that all should be as the Senate wished. Marius, who stood close to the chair of Octavius, said not a word, but his face was stern and forbidding. And again those who looked at him foresaw that dire punishment would overtake his enemies.

Marius and his followers were still under the ban of exile, so the first thing Cinna demanded was that the sentence should be withdrawn.

But Marius was now within sight of his revenge, and he was too impatient to begin his cruel work to wait for the decision of the people.

When only a few tribes had voted, he dashed into the Forum, closely followed by a band of slaves, which band he called his bodyguard.

The slaves were ruffians hired to do his bidding, and now, at a word or sign from their master, they began to murder the citizens. The glance of Marius was enough to show them whom to slay.

Soon they did not even look to him for a sign, but simply fell upon all whose greetings Marius did not return.

Octavius was cut down as he sat in his consular chair, and his head was taken to Cinna.

Catulus, too, who had fought side by side with Marius against the Cimbri, was doomed, although his friends begged that his life might be spared. Marius answered their petitions roughly, saying only, "He must die."

But Catulus did not wait for the cruel sentence to be carried out. He shut himself up in a room, and making a huge fire, he suffocated himself.

These were days of terror in Rome, for no man knew if his life was safe.

At length even Cinna grew ashamed of the cruelty of Marius's slaves, and he and Sertorius put a number of the ruffians to death. After this the citizens' lives were in less danger.

The time had now come to elect Consuls for the year 86 B.C. As usual the people assembled, but they had no choice save to vote for Marius and Cinna. To do otherwise would have been to court death.

Thus, as Marius had believed would happen, even during the miserable days of his flight, he became Consul for the seventh time. But he did not live many days to enjoy the new honour, if honour it could be called, when fear alone had bestowed it upon him. Worn out with the passion of revenge to which he had yielded, and attacked by fever, he died on the 13th of January 86 B.C.

Cinna was now the most powerful man in Rome. He had no difficulty in making the people elect himself and Carbo Consuls for the years 85 and 84 B.C.

There was but one name Cinna dreaded, and that was the name of Sulla. But he thought that, if he proclaimed that the great general who was fighting for Rome in the East was a public enemy, he soon would have no reason to fear him. So he did this, and at the same time ordered Sulla's house in the city to be pulled down.

Cinna, however, had now gone too far. Many of the Optimates, who belonged to the best families in Rome, at once left the city and fled to Greece to the camp of Sulla. So many senators also joined the general, that Sulla could act in the name of the Senate more truly than could his rival in Rome herself. He therefore proclaimed that when the war was over he would come back to Rome with his army and overthrow Cinna and his government.

The Consuls, when they heard this, at once began to enrol troops, that they might be prepared to hold the city against Sulla when he came.

But Cinna, after all, was not alive to meet his dreaded enemy. For in 84 B.C. the soldiers of the Consul mutinied and murdered him. Sulla did not return to Italy until the spring of 83 B.C.

CHAPTER XCVI

THE ORATOR ARISTION

MITHRIDATES, the king against whom Sulla went to fight in 87 B.C., was a brave and skilful commander. His kingdom, Cappadocia Pontica, was a district on the south shore of the Black Sea.

The king who ruled before Mithridates came to the throne had tried to enlarge his kingdom, but more than once the Romans had thwarted his ambitious plans.

When Mithridates began to reign in 111 B.C., he knew that no one save the Romans would be strong enough to keep him from adding to his kingdom.

The king proved himself so strong and so good a general that the Greek towns in Asia Minor resolved to throw aside the friendship of Rome and ally themselves with the King of Pontus. It was this revolt that Sulla, with his five legions, went to Greece to subdue.

It was ungrateful of Athens to forsake Rome, for she had been treated most honourably by her in

THE ORATOR ARISTION

the past, and still was enjoying many privileges when she rebelled.

But the Athenians wished their city to be more glorious in the future than she had been even in the past, and they believed that Mithridates would help them to achieve this better than Rome. So an ambassador named Aristion was sent to the King of Pontus to offer him the friendship of Athens.

The king received Aristion with great respect, and gave to him gifts of gold. Above all, when he took leave of Mithridates, he was presented with a ring, on which was engraved a portrait of the king himself.

When the ambassador returned to Athens and showed the gifts which he had received, the enthusiasm of the people knew no bounds. He was escorted by crowds to the Peiræus, the port of Athens. Here, in the citadel, he was asked to tell what had taken place at the court of the king.

Now Aristion was a great orator, and he knew that his words would influence the people to do as he wished.

So first he reminded them of all the wrongs that Athens had suffered from the Romans, and if these wrongs were not all real, Aristion made them seem so by his eloquence.

Then he spoke of Mithridates, and of the king he had nothing but good to tell, while the magnificence of his court, Aristion modestly declared, baffled even his powers of description.

Before Aristion had finished his oration, the magistrates of Athens had determined to proclaim their republic restored, and to form an alliance with Mithridates. Aristion was appointed chief minister of war, and you shall hear how sadly he failed to do his duty when trouble befell the city.

Sulla having landed with his army at Epirus, at once marched to Athens, for by this time both the city and the Peiræus were strongly fortified, and held by Archelaus, the general of Mithridates.

The Roman commander determined to besiege the citadel, and to surround Athens with soldiers, to prevent the citizens from escaping, or provisions from being sent to their relief.

As he had neither money nor material for the siege, Sulla robbed the temples of Greece of their treasures.

Timber was brought from far and near in carts drawn by mules, ten thousand, it is said, in number. When even this was found not to be enough, Sulla ordered the sacred groves to be cut down, as well as the trees which surrounded the famous academy of Athens.

But, in spite of the forts he built and the trenches he dug, Sulla could not take the Peiræus.

As they worked, the Roman soldiers were often interrupted by Archelaus, who with his troops would sally out of the citadel to attack them.

At length Sulla was convinced that without a fleet he need not hope to take the citadel, for the harbour was commanded by the ships of Mithridates.

CHAPTER XCVII

SULLA BESIEGES ATHENS

THE Peiræus could not, indeed, be starved into submission as long as the king held the harbour, but Athens was already suffering from famine.

Now the Athenians were a gay and careless people, little accustomed to endure hardships, yet no one grumbled at the lack of food, but each bore his hunger manfully, or tried to stay its pangs as best he could.

Some fed on herbs, which they gathered painfully, for they had grown feeble with long fasting. Others hunted for old leather shoes or pieces of oil-skin, and when they found them, soaked them in oil, and so made a sorry meal.

But while the inhabitants of Athens starved, Aristion, the orator and minister of war, who was largely responsible for the misery of the people, lived at his ease, and ate and drank as much as he pleased. Nor did he feast in secret, but before the eyes of the famished folk, for he was as careless of their sufferings as of his own responsibilities.

At length the senators and priests went to the tyrant, for such had Aristion proved, and begged him to make terms with Sulla before the citizens died of hunger. But Aristion did not wish his pleasures interrupted by such solemn messengers. He drove them from his presence, bidding his servants to send a flight of arrows after the procession as it turned sadly away.

A little later, however, he appeared to yield to the wishes of the senators, and sent two or three of his gay companions to meet the Roman general.

But they had no serious terms to propose, and were not commissioned to accept any. All they seemed able to do, was to talk eloquently about their ancient towns and games, until at length Sulla grew impatient and said: "My good friends . . . begone. I was sent by the Romans to Athens, not to take lessons, but to reduce rebels to obedience."

Soon after this, Sulla, by chance, found out how the city might be taken.

Two old men were talking to each other of Aristion's follies, and Sulla overheard them blame him for leaving a certain weak part of the city walls unguarded.

The Romans at once set to work to find out the weak spot in the defences, and when it was found an attack was made at that point.

Only a few sentinels were on duty, and they fled at the approach of the enemy, so a breach was soon made, through which Sulla marched into the city at the head of his troops.

In their triumph at having taken the city the soldiers ran wild, plundering and slaying the wretched inhabitants, many of whom killed themselves rather than fall into the hands of their cruel conquerors.

Sulla looked on, heedless of the fate of the citizens, careless, too, of the destruction of the beautiful city. Only when two citizens, who had refused to give up their friendship with Rome, flung themselves at his feet and begged him to spare the city for the sake of her ancient renown and her famous Athenians, did he yield.

Even then it was with ungracious voice and sullen face that he bade his soldiers desist from further plunder. Then, turning to those who had pleaded with him to save the city, he said: "I forgive the many for the sake of the few, the living for the dead."

Soon after this the Peiræus also fell, and Sulla ordered it to be destroyed, and the docks and magazines to be burnt.

In the same year as Athens and the Peiræus fell, Sulla met the troops of Mithridates at Chæronea, where a great battle was fought. Archelaus was defeated, although he had nearly four times as large a force as Sulla.

Greece now began to repent of her folly in having rebelled against Rome. Mithridates seemed

SULLA BESIEGES ATHENS

unable to help them as much as Aristion and their own hopes had led them to expect. So, many of the Greek cities in Asia Minor left the king and submitted to the Romans.

But Mithridates determined to make one more great effort to regain his power. He met the Romans at Orchomenus, and here another great battle was fought in the autumn of 86 B.C.

At first the Romans began to give way before the fierce attack of the king's troops. But Sulla saw the danger, and leaping from his horse he seized a standard and rushed into the thick of the fight, shouting: "To me, O Romans, it will be glorious to fall here. As for you, when they ask you where you betrayed your general, remember to say at Orchomenus."

Stung by their general's words his men rallied, and after a desperate struggle the battle was won, and the power of Mithridates broken.

In 84 B.C. the king was forced to make terms with the Romans, while those cities which had fought by his side had to pay enormous sums of money to Sulla.

The victorious general was now anxious to go back to Rome, to punish those who had declared him a public enemy. So, in the spring of 83 B.C., he set out for Italy with his army.

CHAPTER XCVIII

SULLA SAVES ROME FROM THE SAMNITES

SULLA returned to Italy three years after the death of Marius. During that time the popular party had been in power. But now it feared that its reign was nearly at an end, for Sulla was in Italy, and was coming to Rome, and coming not alone, but with his army.

Carbo was the leader of Sulla's enemies. He had gathered together a large army, but it was scattered over Italy, under his lieutenants. Pompey, who was soon to be known as Pompey the Great, was fighting for Sulla, and he, with three legions, kept Carbo's forces from uniting. This made Sulla's victory the easier.

But while Romans fought with Romans, a new danger threatened the city. An army of Samnites, under a leader named Pontius, slipped past both the army of Sulla and the scattered troops of Carbo, and marched straight toward Rome.

The citizens were in despair. They remembered the Samnites who long ago had entrapped their army at the pass of the Caudine Forks, and

SULLA SAVES ROME FROM THE SAMNITES

their leader Pontius, who had made Roman officers and soldiers pass beneath the yoke, and they trembled. What if the enemy proved as powerful as of old?

Private quarrels were forgotten, while all those of military age in the city armed for her defence.

In their walls the people had no confidence, for here and there they were broken down and unfit to stand a siege.

So out of the city to meet the terrible foe marched the valiant band of Romans, only to find the enemy too strong for it.

When it was known in the city that the army so hastily enrolled had been defeated, the despair was profound. Women ran about the streets crying aloud to their gods and shrieking in terror. At any moment, they believed, the Samnites might enter their city.

Then, just when hope of relief was faintest, a large company of cavalry was seen approaching the gates. It was the vanguard of Sulla's army, and he himself was close behind with the main body of his troops.

For the time a feeling of immense relief was felt in the city. At least the Samnites would not enter Rome now unopposed.

Sulla's officers begged him to allow his troops to rest before attacking the enemy. But he refused, ordering the trumpets at once to sound for battle.

Crassus commanded Sulla's right wing, and, unknown to the general, beat the enemy. The left wing of the Romans was all but repulsed, when Sulla rode to its help, mounted on a swift white steed.

He was recognised by the Samnites, and two of them prepared to fling their darts at the great Roman general. They thought that if he were slain the battle would soon be at an end.

But Sulla's servant saw his master's danger, and gave his steed a touch that made him start suddenly forward. The darts fell harmless to the ground close to the horse's tail, so that the servant had just succeeded in saving his master's life.

Darkness fell, and the battle was still undecided. But during the night messengers from Crassus stole into Sulla's camp for provisions, and the general heard that the enemy had been driven to Antemnæ, three miles away, and that Pontius, the Samnite leader, had been slain. He at once resolved to join Crassus. In the morning the Samnites were surprised to find a large army ready to attack them. But their leader was dead, so they were afraid to fight, and three thousand offered to submit to Sulla.

The general promised these their lives on one condition—that they should attack their own comrades. This the Samnites actually agreed to do, and a large number were killed in the unnatural struggle.

Six thousand who survived were taken to Rome, and by Sulla's orders cut to pieces. The cruelty of the Roman commander seemed to increase the nearer he drew to Rome.

CHAPTER XCIX

THE PROSCRIPTIONS OF SULLA

AFTER his victory over the Samnites, Sulla met the Senate in the temple of Bellona, without the walls of the city.

Ominous thoughts stole into the minds of the senators and distracted them, as the general's speech was suddenly interrupted by terrible shrieks as of those in agony.

Sulla alone remained undisturbed. But seeing that the senators were not listening to his speech, he sternly bade them "not to busy themselves with what was doing out of doors."

The cries were those of the six thousand Samnite prisoners, who were being ruthlessly slain by Sulla's orders.

At this time, too, young Marius, who had fought against Sulla, killed himself rather than fall into the hands of his father's enemy.

His head was brought to Sulla at Rome. "One should be rower before one takes the helm," said the tyrant, looking with unconcern at the hideous trophy. For he was angry that young Marius had been chosen Consul when he was only twenty-seven years of age.

The forebodings of many were now justified, for Rome became as a city of the dead. Sulla had determined to kill all who had been his enemies while he was absent in Greece.

Day after day the cruel slaughter went on. Forty senators and sixteen hundred of the citizens were condemned, and to add to the consternation among those who had escaped, there were others yet to be punished. Sulla said that he could not remember their names. The suspense in the city was terrible.

One senator, bolder than the others, said to Sulla: "We do not ask you to pardon any whom you have resolved to destroy, but to free from doubt those whom you are pleased to spare."

"I know not as yet whom I will spare," grimly answered the general.

"Why, then," persisted the senator, "tell us whom you will punish."

Sulla promised to do this, and henceforth lists of those who were doomed were hung up in the Forum. These lists were called the "Proscriptions of Sulla."

In the first list eighty persons were proscribed, and for a moment Rome dreamed that there would

THE PROSCRIPTIONS OF SULLA

Lists of those who were doomed were hung up in the Forum.

be no more dread uncertainty, that the end of the death sentences had at least come in sight.

But the horror in the city was but heightened by the proscriptions, when the first list was followed by another, and yet another.

Moreover, an edict was published, saying that if any one dared to give shelter or food to a proscribed person he would be punished with death. While, if any one killed a person whose name was on the list of the condemned, he would be rewarded. The property of those who perished was forfeited, and in this way Sulla and his friends soon grew rich. These cruel proscriptions remain for ever a blot on Sulla's fame.

For one hundred and twenty years there had been no Dictator. But now Sulla determined to become the ruler of Rome under that name.

In other times a Dictator was elected only for six months, but Sulla had no intention of abdicating in so short a time. He meant to remain Dictator as long as he wished.

The tyrant was of course elected, for no one dared to resist his will. He took the title toward the end of 82 B.C., and held it for about three years.

But there was one man in Rome whose influence was fast increasing, and he was not afraid of Sulla. This was Pompey.

Pompey had been sent to Africa by Sulla, and in forty days had defeated the enemies of Rome, and restored the King of Numidia to his throne.

THE PROSCRIPTIONS OF SULLA

When the successful general returned Sulla went out to meet him at the head of a great procession, and welcomed him as Magnus, or the Great. And the name clung to him, for from that time he was known as Pompey the Great.

But when Pompey claimed a triumph, Sulla was not pleased, and refused to grant it.

Pompey knew that he was liked by the people, while Sulla ruled only because he had inspired them with terror. It would not be long in the Dictator's power to refuse his claim.

"More worship the rising than the setting sun," he murmured, and those around him who heard these bold words were startled. Sulla, seeing their amazement, demanded what Pompey had said.

On being told, he cried out testily: "Let him triumph, let him triumph."

In 79 B.C. Sulla, to the surprise and relief of Rome, laid down his Dictatorship, and retired to a beautiful villa he had built near Cumæ.

Here he employed his time in entertaining men of letters and artists, and in writing his memoirs. He died in 78 B.C., while his memoirs were still unfinished.

CHAPTER C

THE GLADIATORS' REVOLT

Six years after the death of Sulla, while Pompey was in Spain, putting down an insurrection, the gladiators revolted.

The gladiators were first heard of in 264 B.C., when their shows were given only at funerals. Usually they were criminals or prisoners of war, who, in any case, were condemned to death. To give them arms and make them fight until one or other was killed in the arena of some great building, for the amusement of a crowd of spectators, was cruel, but not so cruel as what was done in later years.

For the shows of the gladiators came to please the people so well that they forsook for them theatres and other places of amusement. And then rich citizens who wished to win the favour of the people began to keep bands of gladiators and train them as in a school.

Each citizen who kept one of these schools vied with one another to find the most powerful and muscular barbarians, for the stronger and better trained the gladiator the more exciting and pleasing to the people was the show. So the unfortunate men who were forced now to slaughter one another for the amusement of the people were no longer criminals already condemned to death.

In one of these large schools at Capua there was a great number of Gauls and Thracians. Two hundred of these men resolved to escape, but their plot was discovered, and only about eighty succeeded in getting away. They first rushed into a cookshop and frightened the owner, until he let them take his knives as weapons, so only that they would depart. Then, seizing a wagon-load of arms, they made Spartacus, a Thracian, their leader, and encamped on a spur of Mount Vesuvius.

Other gladiators and slaves soon joined the camp, and Rome, in fear of what these trained barbarians might do, sent out two armies against them.

But Spartacus was a skilful general, and the Romans were defeated, while the army of the gladiators still increased each day.

Again the Romans sent troops against these rebels, and one of their leaders was slain. But Spartacus speedily avenged his comrade's death, defeating the Roman army, and forcing three hundred prisoners to fight as gladiators at the funeral of the barbarian whom they had slain. This is the one cruel deed of which we are told Spartacus was guilty.

After this the rebels moved across Italy unmolested. Spartacus wished to cross the Alps and go back to his native land, but his followers for the most part wished to stay in Italy to fight and plunder.

During the winter of 72 B.C. Spartacus led his troops near to the town of Thurii. Here his followers busied themselves forging weapons for the great adventures they meant to achieve in spring.

But before spring came, Crassus, the richest man in Rome, determined to subdue the rebels. He himself trained and disciplined the soldiers Spartacus had beaten, until they were fit to face the foe.

The rebels were now driven to the Bruttian peninsula, in the extreme south of Italy, and here Spartacus shut himself up with his followers in the town of Rhegium. Yet he managed to send messengers to the pirates, who at that time roamed the seas, and often sailed along the coast of Italy. With heavy bribes he tried to persuade them to take his army in their vessels to Sicily.

The pirates accepted the money, but proved faithless, and sailed away from the coast without taking the gladiators on board.

Crassus thought that Spartacus could not now escape. He dug trenches and built fortifications across the narrow neck of land that shut off the Bruttian peninsula from the rest of Italy. But in spite of all that Crassus could do, the rebel leader, with a third part of his army, succeeded in crossing the trenches and climbing the fortifications, and so escaping from the trap in which the Roman had hoped to capture him.

THE GLADIATORS' REVOLT

Then Crassus, finding that his prey had escaped, had a moment of panic, lest the gladiators should march on Rome, and he asked the Senate to recall Pompey from Spain, that he might be ready to help should his fears be realised.

Soon after this, however, Crassus won a great victory over the rebels, killing, it is said, twelve thousand. Out of this great number only two had wounds in their back.

Spartacus was still undaunted. He had withdrawn to the mountains, but dashed down unexpectedly upon the Roman forces, and in his turn defeated them.

His followers were so proud of this victory that they longed to face the foe again, and bade their captain lead them once more to battle.

Spartacus believed it would be wiser to keep to the hills and woods, yet he yielded to the wishes of his followers. But as he advanced towards Crassus at the head of his troops, he found that another army, under Lucullus, had cut him off from the sea.

Victory or death was now before the rebels. Spartacus killed his horse as a sign that he would scorn to fly.

Then, leading a desperate charge, he attempted to cut his way through the Roman soldiers. But his followers proved less brave than was their wont, and deserted him. In this desperate plight he was struck by a javelin.

Even then his courage did not fail. Though the pain of his wound forced him to his knees, he still went on fighting, until at length he fell and was covered by the slain.

Thousands of his followers fled to the mountains. But Pompey, who was on his way home from Spain, followed the fugitives, and killed them in great numbers. He boasted indeed, that although Crassus had beaten the gladiators in battle, it was he who had brought the rebellion to an end.

Six thousand slaves were captured and put to a cruel death, being crucified along the Appian Way.

Spartacus, the barbarian, had been more merciful than the Romans showed themselves to be. For in his camp were thousands of prisoners, none of whom had been unkindly treated.

CHAPTER CI

THE PIRATES

POMPEY THE GREAT returned to Rome in 71 B.C., to celebrate his second triumph, and to be elected Consul for the following year.

The people were eager to see the great general return, yet they were afraid as well.

Suppose Pompey should do as Sulla had done, and bring his army to Rome! Suppose he should make himself Dictator, and destroy his enemies!

But these fears proved groundless, for no sooner had Pompey reached Italy than he disbanded his army, bidding his soldiers to go home until he recalled them to grace his triumph.

He was at once elected Consul, while his colleague was the wealthy Crassus. The two Consuls did not agree well, for Pompey's sympathies were, in these days, with the people, while Crassus was anxious to please the Optimates.

The general who had just returned victorious endeared himself to the populace in many ways, but in none, perhaps, more than by his respect for their ancient customs.

It was usual for each Roman knight, after having served his appointed time in the wars, to lead his horse to the Forum, and there, in the presence of two Censors, tell under what generals he had served and in what battles he had taken part. According to his achievements he was then discharged, either with praise or blame.

Pompey, as Consul, might easily have ignored this custom. But to the delight of the people he was one day seen among the other knights, clad in his Consul's robes, indeed, but leading his horse to the Forum.

As he drew near to the Censors, Pompey bade his lictors go aside, while he went to stand before the judges.

The Censors were well pleased to be thus honoured by the Consul, but they behaved as though he were like any other knight.

"Pompeius Magnus, I demand of you," said one of the Censors, "whether you have served the full time in the wars that is prescribed by the law?"

"Yes," answered Pompey, and his voice rang out clear in the Forum, "Yes, I have served all, and all under myself as general."

The citizens clapped their hands and shouted with pleasure at the answer of their favourite, while the Censors rose to accompany him to his house.

THE PIRATES

When his Consulship came to an end, Pompey spent two years quietly in his own home, and during this time he was seldom seen in the Forum. Those who admired him went often to his house, where he entertained his guests hospitably.

But at the end of two years Pompey was again called upon to serve his country.

The pirates, who for long years had ravaged the Mediterranean, were troublesome foes. Of late these sea-robbers had seemed more numerous than ever, and there was no doubt of their increasing boldness.

No vessel, unless its crew was armed, need hope to escape these desperate men. The coasts of Asia, Greece, Epirus, and Italy had all suffered from the attack of the pirates; no temple, no property was safe from their raids.

Two Roman prætors had been carried off by these same bold robbers, and even Roman ladies of high rank had been captured, and kept until a heavy ransom had been paid for their release. In recent days they had even been seen at the mouth of the Tiber, and in the harbour at Ostia Roman ships had been set on fire.

King Mithridates had sometimes employed these men, and encouraged them by gifts to plunder his enemies.

The pirates' ships were adorned with the spoils which they had stolen. Their sails were of costly silk, the colour of which was a rare purple which in time to come was used only for royal robes. Their oars as they dipped in the water shone as silver, their masts were gilded with gold. At their banquets the rough sailors sat down before dishes of silver.

To thus flaunt their booty before the eyes of those they had plundered was foolish, for it roused the Italian cities, at last, to demand revenge.

Besides, there was cause for alarm lest the supply of grain from Africa and Sicily should be captured, unless the pirates were banished, and if the grain supply were stopped, famine would stare Rome in the face.

One day a tribune proposed to the Senate that some one should be sent to the Mediterranean with absolute power to deal as he thought fit with the pirates. That the pirates might be finally banished, the appointment was to be made for three years, and be not only over the sea, but fifty miles inland as well.

The Romans would give such great powers to no one but to Pompey, who had already shown that he knew how to use them without crushing the people.

So, amid the cheers of the citizens, Pompey was appointed to this great trust. Julius Cæsar, of whom you are soon to hear, voted for the favourite, perhaps to gain the goodwill of the people.

THE PIRATES

With a large fleet Pompey set out to perform the task entrusted to him, and his success was speedy.

He divided the sea coast into separate districts, and sent his officers to sweep the pirates from these regions, while he himself went in pursuit of them to the shores of Sicily and Africa. Within the short space of forty days the pirates were scattered, and west of Greece their dreaded sails were no longer to be seen.

But in the Archipelago there were many useful inlets in which the pirates could seek shelter, and thither Pompey hastened and thoroughly searched and emptied these natural hiding-places.

Then the pirates assembled all that was left of their fleet at Cilicia, to make one last stand against the enemy. But there they were finally defeated by the great Roman general.

Those who were left alive after the battle surrendered, with their strongholds and islands. These had been so well fortified that Pompey would have found them difficult, if not impossible, to storm.

Many prisoners had been taken, and these the Romans did not kill. Pompey, indeed, spent the winter in Cilicia to look after their welfare. For he founded cities in which the pirates could settle, and, if so they willed, work honestly to earn their livelihood.

CHAPTER CII

POMPEY GOES TO WAR WITH MITHRIDATES

WHEN the Romans heard that the pirates had been scattered and forced to submit to Pompey their joy knew no bounds.

No longer need they live in dread of the sudden appearance of the ships with scarlet sails and silver oars along the Italian coasts, no longer need they fear the sudden capture of their corn. And this was due to Pompey! In Rome at this time no one was so popular as he.

His success determined the Senate to send him to take command of the war that was going on in the East, against Mithridates.

Lucullus had been in the East at the head of the army for some time. But the Senate refused to send him money to pay or to clothe his men, and they had grown rebellious, and had begun to grumble at his strict discipline. They wished Pompey the Great to come to take command of them, and then they would do great deeds. So in 66 B.C. Pompey was

POMPEY GOES TO WAR WITH MITHRIDATES

appointed commander of both army and navy in the East, to the delight of soldiers and sailors alike.

Pompey himself seemed none too pleased at the honour conferred on him.

"Alas, what a series of labours upon labours," he cried, frowning as he spoke. "If I am never to end my services as a soldier ... and live at home in the country with my wife, I had better have been an unknown man."

These were unsoldierly words, but his friends paid little attention to them, believing that he did not mean them seriously. And his deeds were proof that he longed to win glory for himself and his country, although he never risked any great adventure on the battlefield.

Mithridates had little hope of withstanding Pompey, when he had barely been able to hold his own against Lucullus. However, he encamped in a strong position on a hill, and hoped that this would make an attack difficult, perhaps even impossible.

Pompey, leaving his fleet to guard the seas, marched into Pontus, but not before the king had been driven from the hill on which he had entrenched himself, by lack of water for his army.

The Roman general had more discerning eyes than the old king. For he, noticing that the plants were green and healthy, encamped on this same hill, and when his soldiers complained of thirst he bade them dig wells. As he expected, there was soon abundance of water in the camp.

But Pompey did not linger long on the hill, for he was eager to follow Mithridates, and soon after this the king found his camp besieged so closely by the Romans that it was impossible to get supplies for his army. It was plain that he and his soldiers must either starve or escape.

So one night Mithridates ordered the sick and wounded to be killed, for they would have hampered the army in its fight. The king did not hesitate to give such a cruel order, for he and his followers had not been taught to pity the weak and helpless.

The watch-fires were lighted at the usual time, that the suspicions of the Romans might not be roused. Then when the camp seemed quiet for the night, Mithridates and the main body of the army slipped out into the dark, and somehow succeeded in passing unnoticed through the Roman lines.

In dread of pursuit, they hid themselves by day in forests, at night they marched as quickly as possible toward the river Euphrates.

When Pompey found that Mithridates had escaped, he blamed his own carelessness and followed swiftly in pursuit. As he marched by day as well as by night, he was soon in advance of the king. So it happened that when Mithridates encamped by the banks of the river Euphrates, the Romans were already there, and determined that the enemy should not again escape.

But the very first evening as it grew dark Pompey became restless. He had set a strict watch, it was true, yet Mithridates had already shown himself skilful in evading sentinels. It would be safer to attack the camp without delay. Pompey summoned his officers, and arranged that the assault should take place at midnight.

Meanwhile, Mithridates lay asleep in his tent, worn out with fatigue and anxiety. As he slept, his troubles slipped from his mind, and the old king dreamed pleasant dreams. He thought that he had reached the sea, and was in a ship. The winds blew soft and fair, wafting the vessel quietly along toward a harbour where no foes could touch him.

In his dream the king began to tell his friends how pleased he was to have reached so safe a haven, when suddenly the wind rose, lashing the sea into fury. The king grasped a spar, but his strength failed, and he was beginning to sink, when he awoke, and lo! it was a dream.

At that moment his officers rushed into his tent, to tell him that the Romans were preparing to attack them.

Swiftly the king shook off the effects of his dream, and ordered his troops to defend their camp to the last.

Now, as the Romans approached the enemy, the moon rose behind them and cast their shadows on the ground.

The soldiers of Mithridates saw the black flitting forms and grew bewildered. In the indistinct light they thought the shadows were the real soldiers and they flung their darts at these imaginary foes.

Then with a great shout the Romans rushed in upon the puzzled enemy, fear was at once added to their confusion, and in sheer panic they turned and fled. But more than ten thousand were killed, and their camp was taken.

Mithridates himself once more escaped. At the head of about eight hundred horse he made a desperate charge through the enemy's lines, and then in the darkness of the night he was seen no more.

Pompey did not follow the king further. But he stayed in the East to fight, and by his skill he won many new territories for Rome.

He even marched to Palestine, where the city of Jerusalem soon surrendered to the powerful enemy that had surrounded her walls. But the Jews refused to give up their temple, and for two or three months they defended their holy place bravely against every attack.

In December 63 B.C., however, it was taken, and Pompey, who had entered many temples and seen many pagan gods, now entered the temple of the Jews.

Nor would he be content until he had penetrated into the Holy of Holies, where the High Priest alone might enter once every year. Here he saw the golden table and the golden candlesticks, of which you have read in Old Testament stories. But the Roman, although he felt a Presence there, looked in vain for the God of the Jews, for His dwelling is in a house "not made with hands."

POMPEY GOES TO WAR WITH MITHRIDATES

While Pompey was still in Palestine, he heard that the king whose rebellion had brought him to the East was dead.

Forsaken by his allies, deserted by the one son who was still alive, Mithridates had cared to live no longer, and had taken poison, which he had carried with him in the hilt of his sword.

After his death there was no one to lead an army against the Romans. So the rebellion in Asia came to an end, and Pompey the Great was free to return to Italy.

Once again the Roman citizens wondered what would happen when he came. Would his many victories have changed the conqueror into a tyrant? But once again the people found that their fears were groundless. For as soon as he landed in Italy Pompey disbanded his army and set out for Rome, attended only by a few friends.

When the Italian cities saw Pompey the Great journeying in this simple guise they determined to send him to Rome in more suitable fashion.

So, in happy, careless mood, the citizens crowded around him, and themselves became his escort. In such multitudes did they follow him that they were more in number than the troops which he had disbanded.

Never was such a triumph as Pompey held! Although, indeed, he had to wait more than nine months before he was allowed to hold it.

His long list of victories was written on tablets that all might read. Kings, princes, chiefs were led in chains in his procession, while the temples of Rome were enriched by the treasures that he had brought from the East.

Plutarch, who writes the life of Pompey, says, that he seemed to have led the whole world captive, for his first triumph was over "Africa, his second over Europe, and his third over Asia."

CHAPTER CIII

CICERO DISCOVERS THE CATILINARIAN CONSPIRACY

THE excitement caused by Pompey's return to Rome was soon over. Then the great general found that, in spite of all that he had done for his country, and in spite of the splendour of his triumph, there were many in the city who did not welcome his return.

His very first request to the Senate was refused, and it may be that Pompey thought half regretfully of his disbanded army. To it his slightest wish had been law. The Optimates, too, had grown used to his absence, and were ready to thwart or ignore him.

So Pompey determined to join the two most powerful men in Rome at that time. One of these was the wealthy Crassus, the other was Julius Cæsar, who was destined to become the greatest man Rome had ever known.

Pompey did not like Crassus, and he soon became jealous of Julius Cæsar. But in the meantime these three men formed a secret union, for they thought that then they alone would govern Rome.

This union was afterwards called The First Triumvirate. When Pompey married Julia, the beautiful daughter of Cæsar, it seemed probable that the father and husband would share many interests.

For a time another great man named Cicero threw in his lot with the three leaders. It is of him that I wish to tell you now.

Cicero was a great orator and man of letters. In 63 B.C. he was chosen Consul. During the lifetime of Sulla, Cicero's influence was used on behalf of the plebeians. But before long his reverence for the Rome of the past made him ready to denounce any side which threatened to disregard the ancient laws.

In the end he joined the Optimates, because he believed that if they would cease to live only for pleasure, and would learn to govern the provinces with justice, the old order of things might be restored.

By eloquent speeches he tried to rouse the nobles to live more useful and upright lives. But they paid little heed to his words, partly, perhaps, because they did not find that his teaching rang true. For they knew that he did not always act justly although he bade them do so, that he often used his eloquence to defend his friend or his party, when it was plain that the cause of neither was just. And so his words had not the power which true words always have.

Two years before Cicero became Consul, Rome had been greatly disturbed by the discovery of a plot to kill the Consuls, to seize the government, and even to burn Rome.

CICERO DISCOVERS THE CATILINARIAN CONSPIRACY

This plot, which was never proved, was known as The First Catilinarian Conspiracy, for Catiline, who had belonged to Sulla's party, was said to have planned it.

In 63 B.C. Cicero declared that a new plot was being prepared by the same leader.

Catiline had gathered around him a band of the wildest of the popular party. His followers hoped that Catiline would be elected Consul, and that then he would reward them. One of the ways in which he could do this would be by passing a law for the abolition of debts.

But Catiline was not chosen Consul, while Cicero was. It was then, in his rage and disappointment, that Catiline was said to have made a deliberate plot to assassinate Cicero, to attack the houses of the senators, and to burn the city. While this was being done, an invading army was to march into Rome.

Now there seemed reason to be alarmed, for it was known that troops were assembling near Fæsulæ, a small town about three miles from Florence. And not only so, but their captain was Manlius, an old officer of Sulla. Since the terrible proscriptions, it was natural that any one who had been connected with Sulla was feared as well as hated.

Although Cicero had no doubt that a plot was on foot, he could not find proof enough to arrest the conspirators. Yet at a meeting of Senate, early in November, the Consul rose, and in a vehement

The following morning Cicero made another speech against Catiline.

CICERO DISCOVERS THE CATILINARIAN CONSPIRACY

speech denounced Catiline, who was present. The conspirator sat apart from the other senators, for he knew that they were suspicious of him.

When Cicero's speech ended, Catiline begged the Senate not to judge him hastily, and then he left the Assembly.

That same night the conspirator left Rome apparently for Marseilles, where, if a Roman chose to live in exile, he could escape being impeached by his fellow-citizens.

On his journey, Catiline wrote a letter to a friend, begging him to protect his wife, and at the same time he assured him that he, Catiline, was innocent, "save only that he wished to help his countrymen who were poor and downtrodden."

The following morning Cicero made another speech against Catiline, and as the people clamoured to know why the conspirator had been allowed to escape, the Consul confessed that he had not proof sufficient to arrest him.

Before long the city was startled to hear that the fugitive had not gone to Marseilles, but to the camp at Fæsulæ, where he was now in command of the army.

CHAPTER CIV

THE DEATH OF THE CONSPIRATORS

THE Senate no sooner knew that Catiline was with the army than it proclaimed both him and Manlius public enemies.

A messenger was sent to the camp to offer pardon to any who should leave it within a certain time. But no one took advantage of this offer, while many soldiers continued to crowd into it. Rome grew more and more alarmed.

Antonius, the colleague of Cicero, was sent at the head of an army to Fæsulæ. As he was a friend of Catiline he pretended to be ill, and his army did the conspirators no harm. Cicero himself stayed to guard the city, for it was suspected that there was treachery within her walls.

Soon after this the Consul unexpectedly received the proof of the conspirators' guilt.

A Gallic tribe that had been forced to pay a heavy tax to the Romans now sent envoys to Rome to beg that the tax might be removed.

THE DEATH OF THE CONSPIRATORS

As it chanced, the conspirators in the city saw the envoys, and tried to persuade them to hasten back to their tribe and send a troop of cavalry to the help of the camp at Fæsulæ. They were assured that if they would do this Catiline would see that the money tax was removed.

The envoys promised to aid the conspirators, but they had scarcely left the city when they changed their minds.

Catiline's plot might fail, they said to one another, and then what would happen to their tribe for sending soldiers to his aid, while, if they told Cicero all that they knew, the Consul would certainly reward them well? So they went back into the city and told Cicero what they had been asked to do.

The Consul knew that he now possessed the proof he had so long sought in vain. Moreover, the whole city would rise in fury when she heard that the conspirators had wished to invade Rome with the aid of Gallic troops. So he promised to reward the envoys well if they would do as he bade them.

They were again to leave Rome, and to appear to be faithful to Catiline. But when they had gone a little distance they would be arrested. Now were they to resist overmuch, while the letters they carried were to be given up after a mere show of reluctance.

The envoys agreed to do as the Consul wished, and soon the letters which betrayed the four conspirators within the city were in the hands of the Consul. They were at once arrested and put under guard, while one of them, being a prætor, was forced to resign his office.

Cicero then assembled the people, and delivered his third speech against Catiline and his fellow-conspirators.

When the people heard of the attempted league with Gaul they were roused to a frenzy. Their own leaders had betrayed them, and they were loud in their praise of Cicero for detecting the traitors' schemes.

The Consul had power to pronounce sentence of death on evil-doers, if it seemed necessary for the good of the State. But he did not use his power, begging the Senate rather to counsel him as to what sentence they should suffer.

Many of the senators urged that the four guilty men should be put to death, but Julius Cæsar was more merciful.

"Their crimes," he said, "deserve the severest punishment, but when the excitement is over, severity beyond the laws will be remembered, the crimes forgotten."

He then proposed that the four men should be imprisoned for life, and that their property should be confiscated.

Cæsar's words almost won the day. But Cato, the great-grandson of the Censor, spoke violently against mercy being shown to the conspirators.

Cato was one of the sternest of the Optimates, and his influence was great enough to sway

THE DEATH OF THE CONSPIRATORS

the Senate. It now voted by a majority for the death of the prisoners, and the Consul at once ordered the four men to be strangled.

As Cicero left the Senate-house and hastened through the crowd in the Forum, he said to the people: "They are dead." The citizens seemed satisfied that their city would now be safe, while Cato and Catulus commended Cicero as the "Father of his country."

Early in 62 B.C. Catiline tried to march into Gaul with the troops that had remained faithful to him. But the Roman army was watching for him. He was forced to fight, and nearly all his men were slain.

CHAPTER CV

JULIUS CÆSAR IS CAPTURED BY PIRATES

JULIUS CAESAR was born in 100 or 101 B.C., and belonged to one of the most illustrious patrician families of Rome.

From his boyhood, Cæsar was a favourite with the people. They liked his frank, bright ways, and then he spent money lavishly, and that was what they thought the young nobles ought to do.

But they never dreamed that this youth was different from the other pleasure-loving youths of Rome, that in his heart he hid great ambitions, and had already, in his own way, begun to pave the way toward their fulfilment.

That he was fearless and not easily turned away from his purpose he soon showed. Even of Sulla in his most powerful day he felt no dread.

When Sulla commanded that all those who were connected with the party of Marius by marriage should send their wives away, Cæsar, who was then only nineteen years of age, refused to obey. So Cornelia stayed with her husband in spite of the danger

JULIUS CÆSAR IS CAPTURED BY PIRATES

they both knew they would incur by defying one of Sulla's commands.

Cæsar would indeed have lost his life, had not powerful friends begged Sulla to be merciful, adding that it was surely not necessary to put a mere boy to death.

But Sulla was a reader of character, and he believed that Cæsar was too clever not to be dangerous to the State.

To those who begged for his life, he said, "You know little if you do not see more than one Marius in that boy."

When Cæsar heard what Sulla had said, he escaped to the Sabine hills and hid himself, until Rome should become a safer city.

Some time after this the young patrician was on his way to Rhodes to study rhetoric, when he was captured by pirates. For this was before Pompey had cleared the seas of the terrible sea robbers.

The pirates did not know how great a prize they had captured when they took Julius Cæsar prisoner, and they demanded merely twenty talents for his ransom.

Cæsar laughed, for he valued himself at more than that modest sum, and offered them fifty talents.

He then sent his followers away to raise the money, while he stayed alone with the pirates, save for one friend and two attendants. And this he did, although he knew that they often put their prisoners to death.

For thirty-eight days he lived with them, sometimes amusing himself by joining in their sports, sometimes reading to them poems he had written, or rehearsing speeches he had prepared.

To these they would listen, indeed, but without giving any applause. Then Cæsar would grow angry with them, calling them names, saying that when he was free he would crucify them.

At other times, if he wished to sleep and the pirates were making a noise, he would send to bid them be quiet.

The pirates laughed at the strange ways and words of their captive, and paid no heed to his threats. But Cæsar was in earnest when he was angry, and no sooner was his ransom paid and he set free, than the first thing he did was to hire ships to go in search of these very same pirates.

He soon found and captured them, and in the end he crucified them, as he had more than once threatened to do when he was their prisoner.

Cæsar then went to Rhodes to study rhetoric. And he profited by his studies, for on his return to Rome his eloquence won him fame.

As for the citizens they still loved him, for he was kind to them and feasted and spent money as before. But that he would prove a great soldier, one who would astonish not only Rome, but the whole world, there was nothing yet to tell.

Cicero, indeed, as Sulla had done before, saw that Cæsar was ambitious. Beneath his pleasant smiles and ways, Cicero sometimes thought that the young patrician had a hidden purpose, which he would not easily lay aside. At other times the orator thought that, after all, Cæsar was a trifler and nothing more. "When I see his hair so carefully arranged," says this wise man, "and observe him adjusting it with one finger, I cannot imagine it should enter into such a man's thoughts to subvert the Roman State."

But whatever others thought, there was no doubt that to the people Cæsar had become an idol. And he was pleased that this should be so, for he liked well to be popular and beloved.

About the year 67 B.C., Cæsar was appointed to superintend the repairs of the Appian Way. On these repairs he spent large sums of his own, and the people whispered to one another that this was done for their welfare, and they smiled more warmly than ever on the young noble.

But he looked after their pleasures as well as after their more practical welfare. For he held a show of gladiators in which six hundred and forty took part, to the delight of the citizens, while the games he celebrated were more magnificent than those usually seen in Rome.

The height of his popularity in these early days was reached, however, when he restored the statues of Marius and of his triumph over Jugurtha and the Cimbri. These had been banished from the Capitol during the time that Sulla ruled the city.

In 63 B.C. Cæsar determined to put his popularity to the test. The high priest had died, and Cæsar wished to succeed him. It was true that Catulus and another Roman of influence were known to expect that the appointment would be given to one of them. But in spite of this Caesar insisted on letting the people know that he too was a candidate.

Catulus, dreading a contest with one who was so popular, offered Caesar a large sum of money if he would withdraw.

But Caesar, although he had spent all his money and was deep in debt, scornfully refused the offer of Catulus. "I would borrow a larger sum to carry on the contest," he said, with proud defiance.

On the day that the votes were to be taken, his mother accompanied him to the door of their house, her tears betraying her anxiety. But he, as he embraced her, said, "To-day you will see me either high priest or an exile."

The excitement ran high as the different tribes gave their votes, but it was Cæsar, the idol of the people, who won the day.

It was what, in his proud confidence he had expected, but he was pleased, while the people were elated.

But the nobles were exceedingly annoyed. What would the citizens do next? Would they not be content until Julius Cæsar reigned supreme in Rome?

CHAPTER CVI
CÆSAR GIVES UP HIS TRIUMPH

THE Senate and the nobles now began to fear the ambition of Cæsar. And they were glad to give him the command of the army in Spain, so that he might, for a time at least, be away from Rome. They hoped that the people, who were always fickle, would find a new favourite in his absence, one whom they might be able to influence. Already they knew that they could not move Cæsar to do their will.

So in 61 B.C. Cæsar went to Spain. With new duties he quickly developed new powers. There was now no time spent in idle pleasures, or even on the more serious joy of composing poems. His whole energy was devoted to his soldiers. Soon he had added to the numbers of his army, and marched into districts as yet unconquered by Rome.

Everywhere he went he was victorious, and when he returned to Rome it was to claim a triumph.

Now he had arrived before the city gates just in time for the election of Consuls. To stand for the Consulship it was necessary to enter the city and proclaim oneself a candidate. To enjoy a triumph it was necessary to stay outside the walls until the Senate has decreed that a triumph was deserved.

Cæsar was thus in a strait, and of this his enemies were not slow to take advantage. For when he asked the Senate to allow him to stand for the Consulship without entering the city, it refused. And more than that, it would not decide that he should enjoy a triumph until it was too late to have it and stand for the Consulship as well.

Which should he give up? Cæsar himself, being wise, had no doubt. But the Senate and the nobles hoped that he would choose the triumph. That was a glory that would soon be forgotten, while if he became Consul he would be more powerful than they cared to think.

But Cæsar gave up the triumph and proclaimed himself a candidate for the Consulship. And his enemies were forced to look on as he walked to the assembly of the people between Pompey and Crassus, the two most powerful men in Rome. With their support he was elected Consul with unusual honours.

It was now that Pompey, Crassus, and Cæsar formed the secret union which became known as the First Triumvirate.

The laws the Triumvirate brought forward were framed chiefly to please the people and to win their support. One was regarding the vexed question of allotments of land for Pompey's veterans, another was about the distribution of corn.

CÆSAR GIVES UP HIS TRIUMPH

When some of the senators and the Optimates tried to hinder these measures from becoming law, Pompey took an armed force to the Campus, to keep order it was said. But every one knew that the real reason was to make the voters afraid to oppose the Triumvirate.

A year passed and Cæsar's Consulship came to an end. He then demanded that the Senate should give him Gaul as his province. As a rule a province was allotted to an officer for a year, but Cæsar insisted that he should have Gaul for five years.

The Senate, again thinking it would be well that he should be absent from Rome, granted his request. And so in 58 B.C. Cæsar left Rome to begin his new duties in Gaul.

But before he left the city he arranged that the chief offices of the State should be held by friends of his own, so that his enemies might not grow too powerful during his absence.

Cicero had shown himself no friend to Cæsar, and he was now forced either to leave Rome or be brought to trial for executing the four Catilinarian conspirators.

Rather than be brought to trial Cicero went into exile. But in sixteen months he was again in Rome, trying to win Pompey from his secret agreement with Cæsar.

CHAPTER CVII

CÆSAR PRAISES HIS TENTH LEGION

THE years which Cæsar spent in Gaul were so full of hard-fought battles and well-earned victories, that even his love of adventure and glory must surely have been satisfied.

Gaul at this time was divided into two parts, Cisalpine and Transalpine Gaul.

Cisalpine Gaul was the name given to the Gallic settlements in northern Italy, and here Cæsar spent only a short time.

It was in Transalpine Gaul, or Gaul beyond the Alps, that Cæsar's great work lay, and the countries that we now call France and Switzerland were included in this part of Gaul.

When the Roman army reached Transalpine Gaul it found that two tribes, the Helvetians and the Ligurini, had burnt their villages and towns because the land around their dwellings was covered with marsh and forest.

CÆSAR PRAISES HIS TENTH LEGION

They were now going to journey in search of a better country, even thinking that they might invade Italy and settle there.

The tribes were fierce and brave, but Cæsar determined to meet them and keep them from setting foot in Italy. So he sent his chief officer against the Ligurini and they were defeated. But the Helvetians succeeded in surprising Cæsar as he was marching, and fell upon him before he had time to arrange his men in a good position.

As the Romans prepared to repulse the Gauls, Cæsar's horse was brought to him, but he refused to mount, saying, "When I have won the battle I will use my horse for the chase." He then led the charge on foot.

The struggle was fierce, for the Helvetians were fighting for all that they counted most dear. But at length the Romans drove them from the field and pursued them to their wagons.

Here, not men alone, but women and children joined in the fight, and fiercely the battle raged once more. It was only after a desperate onslaught that the Gauls resolved to submit.

Many of the Helvetians had fallen in the battle, but Cæsar sent for those who had escaped, and bade them go back to the country from which they had come, and rebuild their towns and villages.

The conquered people had expected to be cut to pieces or to be made slaves for the rest of their lives, and they could scarcely believe what they heard.

Cæsar saw that they were bewildered, so again he told them to go and live peacefully in their old homes. And this he did because he did not wish the Germans, who were a powerful people, to seize the district the Helvetians had forsaken and make it theirs.

This victory over the Helvetians made the other Gallic tribes afraid of Cæsar. Yet perhaps, they thought, as he was so brave and strong, he would be willing to protect them from Ariovistus, king of the Germans, who was their most terrible foe. So some of the tribes sent messengers to Cæsar to beg for his protection.

This Cæsar promised to give them, but when he had conquered Ariovistus, he determined that he would next subdue the tribes that had just appealed to him and make their land a province of Rome.

Some of the Roman officers were very angry when they heard that Cæsar meant to march against the German king. They were young nobles who had been brought up in luxury and had joined the army, dreaming of the riches that they would gain, and the victories which would make their names famous. Of the long terrible marches that would be necessary, of the hardships of the camp, they had not thought, and so now they grumbled.

And what was worse, they not only grumbled themselves, but they tried to make the soldiers dis-

CÆSAR PRAISES HIS TENTH LEGION

satisfied. The example of their brave commander should have shamed these cowards.

Cæsar was not strong, yet he was always to be found where the danger seemed the greatest. Nor was he ever heard to say that because his health was poor he must have more comfort than his men enjoyed.

Indeed when his soldiers marched, he marched at their side, if they ate coarse food, he made the same his daily fare, and often he would share their rough camp bed. He was much more than the commander of his men, he was their friend. It was he who taught them too to care for the wounded and the sick.

Once a fierce storm drove him to seek shelter in the cottage of a poor man. When he saw that there was only one room, he ordered it to be given to an officer who was ill, while he and the troops slept in a shed.

For deeds like this, the soldiers worshipped their brave general, and were ready to follow where he chose to lead.

But the pleasure-loving officers grumbled. Cæsar had no need of such men in his army, and he determined to teach them a lesson.

So, first assembling the army, he sent for the discontented nobles, and when they came, he bade them, before all the soldiers, to go back to Rome, if they were afraid of difficult marches and battles with barbarians.

"As for me," he added, "I will take only the Tenth Legion with me, and with it I will conquer the barbarians, for I do not expect to find them more terrible than the Cimbri whom Marius conquered, nor am I a general inferior to him."

The Tenth Legion was proud indeed as it listened to these words. It never forgot how Cæsar had boasted of its courage and had trusted its devotion. Some of the members of the Legion were sent to thank him for the words he had spoken. And from that day, as you will easily understand, it fought with unfaltering zeal and such fierce determination that the enemy could seldom withstand its fury.

After the foolish young officers had listened to Cæsar's rebuke they were ashamed, and begged him to allow them to march with him against Ariovistus, that they might redeem their honour in the eyes of the army.

As for the other legions they had not waited for orders from their officers, but had already begun to prepare for the march. For the soldiers had never wished to desert Cæsar, and now after listening to his praise of the Tenth Legion, they were more than ever anxious to win his approval. So it was a united army that set out on the long and perilous march to the camp of Ariovistus.

CHAPTER CVIII

CÆSAR WINS A GREAT VICTORY OVER THE NERVII

Ariovistus was a great warrior and he was not afraid of the Roman army, but he was startled by the speed with which it reached his camp. He had thought that the marshlands through which it must go, and the forests through which it must penetrate, would have delayed it long on its way.

But if Ariovistus was unafraid, it was easy to see that his soldiers were not over glad to see the Roman army. If they might have attacked the enemy at once, they would have felt less gloomy. But there were soothsayers in the camp, and these went from tent to tent, bidding the soldiers wait until the new moon appeared before they fought.

Cæsar may have known what the soothsayers had said, but in any case, he saw that the Germans were not ready to fight, so he determined to attack their camp.

When the Romans began to advance, the Germans were roused to Fury. They forgot the words of the soothsayers, or, if they remembered, they paid no heed to them, for they dashed furiously upon the enemy and tried to break its ranks.

Again and again they hurled themselves upon the foe, but Cæsar's legions stood firm, and at length they, in their turn, attacked the Germans with irresistible force. The Germans could not stand the onslaught; they broke their ranks and fled.

If they could but reach the river Rhine and cross it they would be safe, but the river was about thirty-five miles away.

Still that was the direction in which they fled, followed and cut down not only by the Romans but by the Gauls, whose enemies they had always been.

Ariovistus himself was almost captured, but he at length succeeded in crossing the river with a few troops, and was then soon beyond the reach of the Roman legions. This was Cæsar's second great victory in Gaul.

The Nervii, with whom he fought his next battle, were perhaps the most terrible foes he encountered during the many years he spent among the barbarians.

So determined were the Nervii to fight, that they did not even wait to see if the Romans meant to attack them, but assembled in great numbers on the left bank of the river Sambre, a tributary of the Meuse.

The home of this fierce tribe was in the thick forests of their country, and here they had hidden their wives, their children, and their property, when they set out to seek for the Romans.

Cæsar soon reached the right bank of the Sambre, opposite the enemy, and ordered his men to encamp on a hill which sloped toward the river.

The Romans had put up their tents and were preparing to fortify the camp, when suddenly a party of the Nervii, that had been in ambush, dashed upon them. Almost at once they were followed by overwhelming numbers, who had crossed the river and now swarmed up the hill and passed into the camp.

Amid the wild confusion Cæsar was calm and undismayed. He ordered the bugle to be sounded to recall those who had gone in search of wood, then speedily gathering his men together he gave the signal to advance.

Bravely the Tenth Legion fought that day. Once, when it was posted on the hill, it saw that its beloved general was in danger, and swift as an arrow it sped to his side.

When it seemed as though the battle must indeed be lost, Cæsar snatched a buckler from one of his men and himself led them on to victory. For seeing their general before them the soldiers fought with new and grim determination.

They could not indeed force the Nervii to flee, for the barbarians scorned to turn their back to an enemy, but they could cut them down as they stood at bay. Out of 60,000, only 500, it is said, were left alive after the terrible slaughter on the banks of the Sambre.

Belgium and the whole of the north-west of France was now in the hands of the Romans, for one of Cæsar's officers had conquered Normandy and Brittany.

Rome was jubilant with delight when she heard of Cæsar's great victory over the Nervii. The Senate resolved to celebrate it with unusual festivities. For fifteen days the city was ordered to give itself up to rejoicing, and the people, who adored Cæsar, were able to show their pleasure in his success. Feasts and games followed each other day after day, while bounteous sacrifices were offered to the gods.

Winter had now come and Cæsar resolved to go to Lucca, a town near to the river Po. Here he was near enough to Rome to find out all that had been going on in the city during his absence.

Many Romans too went to Lucca to visit the victorious general, and at one time he entertained 200 senators.

Among the visitors in 56 B.C. came Pompey and Crassus, to renew the Triumvirate.

It was agreed that Pompey and Crassus should be Consuls the following year, while Cæsar should hold Gaul as his province for five years longer, from 53 B.C. to 48 B.C.

CÆSAR WINS A GREAT VICTORY OVER THE NERVII

Toward the end of that time he was to stand for the consulship and be permitted to do so, without, in the usual way, first entering the city.

CHAPTER CIX

CÆSAR INVADES BRITAIN

IN 55 B.C. Cæsar resolved to invade our own island home. He knew little about Britain, save that she was on good terms with the Gauls, and carried on trade with them.

When he questioned the traders, they told him that he would find tin and lead in the ground, as well as precious stones scattered over the land.

Curiosity, the desire for booty, as well as the wish to punish all who aided the Gauls, drove Cæsar to the adventure, and he ordered a fleet to be prepared for the great enterprise.

It was autumn when he set sail for Britain, with eighty vessels and an army of 12,000 men. He had not taken a larger fleet, as he thought that he would have little trouble in conquering the barbarians of the island.

Rumours had reached Britain of the coming of the great Roman general with a fleet, and the natives crowded to the shore, eager to keep the strangers from landing in their country.

CÆSAR INVADES BRITAIN

As he drew near to Deal, where he hoped to land, Cæsar saw that his ships were too big to sail close in to shore, so he ordered his soldiers to jump into the sea and make their way to land as well as they could.

The Romans looked at the sea and their hearts misgave them, brave soldiers as they were, for they were not used to the sea, nor did they love it as the Britons seemed to do.

They were already in the water, some on foot, some on horses, and they seemed to the astonished Romans as undisturbed as though they were on land.

And Cæsar had bidden them jump into the sea. Still they hesitated.

Then the officer who carried the eagle of the tenth legion jumped into the water, crying, "Leap, soldiers, unless you wish to betray your eagle to the enemy."

The soldiers could not risk their standard being captured by the barbarians, so now they hastily leaped into the water and followed their officer.

Then a fierce struggle began, many of the Romans falling before the battle axes of the Britains, many others slipping on the treacherous sand and being drowned.

But at length the Romans reached the shore, and the Briton chiefs were soon forced to submit to Cæsar.

The Roman general was disappointed to find little booty on the island which he had taken so

THE STORY OF ROME

much trouble to invade, and to see nothing of the precious stones which he had been told were strewn in plenty on the ground. And so he soon sailed back to Gaul.

In the following spring, however, Cæsar again returned to Britain. This time, instead of eighty vessels his fleet consisted of eight hundred, while his army numbered many thousands.

The Britons had again gathered in great strength to repel the invaders, but when they saw so many ships they grew afraid and fled to their forests. So Cæsar landed without difficulty at Romney marsh.

At length, led by a brave chief, called Cassivellaunus, the tribes determined to try to drive the Romans from their shore.

Cassivellaunus did not conquer the Romans, but he proved a brave and skilful commander, and constantly harassed them. At last, however, his capital was taken, and he then sent messengers to treat with Cæsar.

Cæsar received the envoys and demanded from them hostages, and the promise that their tribes would pay a yearly tribute to Rome.

Then in September 54 B.C., when his fleet, which had been damaged by a storm, was repaired, he again went back to Gaul.

Here he was greeted with the sad news that his daughter Julia was dead.

Julia had often smoothed away the jealousies of her husband, the irritations of her father, and both Pompey and Cæsar mourned for her loss.

Their friends also were troubled. They foresaw that now the beautiful Julia was no longer alive, it would not be long before the two great generals quarrelled. And that was a grave thought. For the peace of Rome depended on the friendship of Pompey and Cæsar.

Cæsar's work in Gaul was not yet finished. In 52 B.C. the tribes in the south made one more desperate stand against the power of Rome, which seemed to be pressing more and more heavily upon them.

The rebellion was led by a young chief named Vercingetorix, who had seized the town of Gergovia, the capital of his tribe and his own birthplace.

Cæsar, when he heard that Gergovia was in the hands of the barbarians, hastened to the town and at once laid siege to it. But to his surprise the town withstood every effort he made to take it. For the first time Cæsar was unable to capture a Gallic town, and not only so, but he was forced to raise the siege.

When Vercingetorix saw the Romans retreating, he believed that now was the time to attack them, and he led his followers against the foe.

But on the battlefield the Gauls were no match for the legions of Rome, and Vercingetorix was forced to flee from the field with only a remnant of his army.

The young Gaul succeeded in reaching the town of Alesia, which he at once began to fortify.

Cæsar speedily followed the enemy to Alesia, and when he saw the Gauls within the walls of the town, he determined to keep them there. He at once ordered his men to set to work to dig trenches, and to build forts round the walls, that no one might escape.

But one night, when it was dark, the young Gaul sent messengers to summon the neighbouring tribes to come to his aid.

The messengers passed the enemy's lines in safety, and galloped swiftly away to rouse their people. In a short time a large army of 300,000 of the bravest men in Gaul were marching to the aid of Vercingetorix.

Thus it was that one day, as the Romans worked at the trenches and the forts, they were unexpectedly attacked by a new Gallic army.

Vercingetorix seized the same moment to sally out of Alesia with his men, and the Romans were caught between two foes. For four days a terrible struggle raged, and then, as was almost always the way, Cæsar and his legions proved victorious.

To save his army, Vercingetorix gave himself up to the Romans, flinging first his arms and then himself at the feet of the conqueror. But Cæsar had no pity for the foe he had vanquished, and carried off the brave young Gaul to Rome to adorn his triumph.

For two years longer Cæsar stayed in Gaul, and although he fought some battles and put down some rebellions, his chief work was to pass laws that would make the Gauls content to live under the protection of Rome.

By the end of the two years Cæsar had shown that he was not only a great general, but that he was also a great ruler of men.

CHAPTER CX

CÆSAR CROSSES THE RUBICON

WHILE Cæsar was winning glory for himself and for his country in Gaul, Crassus was also fighting against a foreign foe, and in 53 B.C. he was tricked into leading his men into an ambush and was slain. Pompey was the only member of the Triumvirate in Rome.

The more the Senate approved of Pompey's rule, the more he wished that there was no Cæsar to come home to share his power. And however the Senate might receive the victorious general, Pompey knew that Cæsar was still remembered and adored by the people.

He himself had gradually withdrawn his sympathy from the popular party, and he now threw his influence wholly on the side of the Optimates, who disliked Cæsar, and like Pompey himself, dreaded his return.

Meanwhile Rome was in need of a strong ruler, for disorder and lawlessness was rife within the city, and the Senate seemed unable to restore order.

CÆSAR CROSSES THE RUBICON

In the streets riots took place, which often ended in bloodshed. And while there was violence among the people, among the nobles there was bribery.

The Senate in despair determined to appoint only one Consul for the year 52 B.C. If only one person was responsible for law and justice, it thought that order might be restored. The choice of the Senate naturally fell upon Pompey, and through its influence he was appointed sole Consul. But the people were not pleased, and muttered that Cæsar should have been elected as the colleague of Pompey.

To avoid this, for he was determined not to share his power with Cæsar, Pompey, after ruling alone for six months, arranged that Metellus Scipio should be chosen as second Consul.

There was no beautiful Julia now at hand to persuade Pompey to be true to Cæsar, and from this time the Consul showed plainly that he meant to separate his fortunes from those of his father-in-law. And what was worse was that he used his power to undermine the influence of the absent general to whom his faith was pledged.

Cæsar, who was always in touch with Rome knew what was being done. His friends, too, warned him that Pompey would soon be too strong for him unless he speedily returned to the city. But Cæsar was not yet ready to leave Gaul.

The Senate soon showed how it meant to treat the absent general. It proposed, more than once, that Cæsar should dismiss his army before being elected Consul for the year 48 B.C.

Pompey heard these proposals and at first said nothing, although he must have remembered the arrangement he and Crassus had made with Cæsar at Lucca.

When the Senate repeated its wish more decidedly, he said only, that what the Senate ordered Cæsar would doubtless do. But this he could scarcely have found it easy to believe.

While the Senate still hesitated to order Cæsar to lay down his command, Pompey fell ill. It was believed that his life was in danger, and throughout Italy prayers were offered for his recovery. In time Pompey grew better, but he was deceived by the anxiety the people had shown, and believed their affection for him was greater than it really was. He found it pleasant to think that they had forgotten Cæsar and were devoted to him alone.

Some foolish person told him that even his soldiers were ready to desert Cæsar. Pompey seemed to believe this also, and remarked complacently that he, if he but stamped his foot, would find soldiers ready to follow him from every town and village in Italy.

At length, in the autumn of 50 B.C., the Senate determined to act, and accordingly it sent a message to Cæsar, bidding him lay down his command and dismiss his army.

CÆSAR CROSSES THE RUBICON

Cæsar answered without the least hesitation, "If Pompey will give up his command and dismiss his army, I will do the same." But this, as you know, Pompey had not the least intention to do. The people of Rome began to tremble at the thought that civil war was drawing near. For if neither of the two great generals would yield, it seemed inevitable.

"There is no hope of peace beyond the year's end," wrote a friend to Cicero. "Pompey is determined Cæsar shall not be chosen Consul till he has given up his province and army. Cæsar is convinced that he cannot leave his army safely."

In Rome, the strife between Pompey's friends and those of Cæsar grew daily more bitter. At length the Senate boldly proposed that Cæsar should be told to give up his province on a certain day, otherwise he would be denounced as a traitor.

Mark Antony and another tribune, both of whom were friends of Cæsar, rose to their feet to protest against such a decree. But the Senate was in no mood to listen to them, and the tribunes were expelled from the house.

In the city, they soon found that their lives were not safe. So they disguised themselves, dressing in old clothes that had belonged to slaves. Then hiring carts they lay in the foot of them, covered with sacking, and thus passed safely through the city gates. Still in this strange garb they at length reached Cæsar's camp at Ravenna.

It was at Ravenna, in January 49 B.C., that the great general was told of the decree of the Senate.

Looking down upon the stream, he stood awhile deep in thought.

CÆSAR CROSSES THE RUBICON

He had only one legion with him, but leaving orders for the others to follow, he at once began to march toward the Rubicon. The Rubicon was the stream which divided his province from Italy.

Should he cross the stream with his army, it would be a declaration that he had determined on war.

So momentous was the decision, that as Cæsar drew near to the Rubicon he hesitated. Looking down upon the stream, he stood for a time deep in thought, while his soldiers watched him anxiously from the distance.

Turning at length to his officers, he said, "Even now we may draw back."

At that moment, so it is said, a shepherd on the other side of the stream, began to pipe carelessly upon his flute.

Over the stream dashed some of the soldiers, perhaps to dance to the shepherd's lilting measure.

It was an omen! Cæsar at once made up his mind. "Let us go where the omen of the gods and the iniquity of our enemies call us," he cried. "The die is cast."

Then at the head of his army, on the 16th January 49 B.C., Cæsar crossed the Rubicon.

So important was the decision, that the words, "to cross the Rubicon," grew into a proverb. And still to-day, when one takes the first step towards a great undertaking, one is said to have "crossed the Rubicon."

CHAPTER CXI

CÆSAR AND THE PILOT

As Cæsar marched through Italy, town after town threw open its gates to welcome the general who had at last returned from Gaul, where his victories had covered him with glory.

What Pompey thought as he heard of the triumphal progress of his rival we do not know. But he could not fail to see how he had been deceived when he believed that the affection of the people had been centered on himself alone.

Not a single battle did Cæsar have to fight before he reached the gates of Rome. Even here he was free to enter the city, for Pompey, although his army was as large as that of his rival, had fled.

The defence of the city had been left in the hands of the Consuls. But they felt unable to face the general, who came with his army behind him, so they also escaped from the city and joined Pompey. In their fear they did not even stay to open the treasury to take from it the money that would be needed to help Pompey to carry on the war.

CÆSAR AND THE PILOT

Pompey meanwhile crossed the Adriatic Sea and reached Epirus. He knew that in the East his name was still powerful, and would draw many brave warriors to fight for him.

And so it proved, for ere long the numbers of his army were nearly doubled. But the warriors of the East, even when they were brave, had neither the discipline nor the experience of Cæsar's faithful legions.

Cæsar did not stay long in Rome, but after adding to his army many strong soldiers from Gaul and from Germany, he went to Spain. Here he found that Pompey had left officers to guard the Roman provinces, but he forced them to withdraw and soon won over their troops.

Yet, although he was successful in this, the time he spent in Spain was beset with difficulties. Often he had not food enough for his army, while he himself was in danger from ambushes and from plots that were made by his enemies, to take his life.

After securing Spain, Cæsar went back to Rome, where he was at once made Dictator. He only held the position for eleven days, but during that time he used his power to recall the exiles whom Sulla's cruelty had driven away, and to restore to them, or to their children, their privileges as citizens of Rome. He also passed a law for the relief of debtors, which was sure to please the people.

Then having resigned his Dictatorship and been elected Consul, Cæsar hastened to Brundisium, where he had commanded his troops to assemble.

Here he found that there were not nearly enough ships to take his army across to Epirus. But no obstacle could turn him from his purpose, which just then was to pursue Pompey. So he determined to sail at once with seven legions, leaving the others, under Mark Antony, to follow as soon as a sufficient number of ships could be found.

It was only with great difficulty that Cæsar, with his seven legions, was able to land, for the coast of Epirus was being closely watched by Pompey's fleet.

But by sailing to the south he eluded its vigilance, and succeeded in landing at a town called Oricum. Here, day after day, he watched for Mark Antony, with the legions he had left behind. Months passed and still he did not come. For after Cæsar had landed, Pompey bade his fleet guard the coasts still more closely, and Antony was afraid to set sail.

Cæsar, at length, determined that he would wait no longer. He would himself go back and bring his army to Oricum. So he disguised himself as a slave, and hiring a small boat was rowed away, although the sea was covered with the ships of the enemy.

Not only his enemies, but Nature herself, threatened to endanger the life of the great commander. For a storm arose, and the wind blew more and more violently. The current too was strong against the boat, and at length the pilot, thinking that it was impossible to proceed, ordered the rowers to return.

CÆSAR AND THE PILOT

Then Cæsar went to the pilot, and taking his hand he said, "Go on, my friend, and fear nothing. You carry Cæsar and his fortune on your boat."

Cæsar! The name was as magic, and the sailors forgot their fears, and once again they pulled their hardest against waves and wind. But their efforts were vain, while each moment the danger became greater.

When the boat began to fill with water, even Cæsar had to yield, and bade the sailors pull for the shore.

As he reached the land, his soldiers, who had missed him, eagerly helped him from the boat, and chid him for risking his life so heedlessly.

Moreover, it seemed that their pride was hurt, for why, they said, should he go into danger for the legions who were at Brundisium? Could he not trust them to gain the victories he desired?

With the spring, Antony and the legions at length arrived, and Cæsar determined to force Pompey to fight without delay.

CHAPTER CXII

THE FLIGHT OF POMPEY

In the camps of both Pompey and Cæsar there was great suffering. The chief strength of Pompey's army was its cavalry, which was 7000 strong, and the horses had begun to die for want of food.

Pompey had many officers of noble rank in his camp, and they urged him to fight at once, or there would be no horses left for the soldiers to ride.

But Pompey knew that his large army was undisciplined, that many of the soldiers were rebellious, and he wished to avoid a battle. He hoped that the difficulty of providing food for his army would force Cæsar to retreat.

It was indeed true that Cæsar's legions were suffering from hunger, but they would have died rather than let the enemy know that this was so. They tried their utmost to mislead them. To stay their hunger they gathered a root which they found in the fields, and made it as palatable as they could by adding milk to it.

Sometimes they made the root into loaves of a kind, and some of these they threw into the

THE FLIGHT OF POMPEY

enemy's camp, as though to say, "Whatever you may think, we have food enough and to spare."

Not a murmur was heard in Cæsar's camp. Every man remained loyal to his general, and cheerful, even when suffering intensely from the pangs of hunger.

It had been spring when Mark Antony joined Cæsar. It was now nearly the end of summer, and still the two armies were encamped near to each other, but no battle had been fought.

Then, at length, it happened, that Pompey discovered a weak point in Cæsar's lines, which he believed he could attack with success.

His army, pleased to be at last in action, advanced with alacrity as soon as the order was given.

As Pompey had hoped, Cæsar's troops were soon driven back toward their camp in utter confusion, while the camp itself was in danger of being taken.

In vain did Cæsar try to rally his forces, heedless of his own danger, if he could but stem the flight of his men. As one strong active soldier ran past, Cæsar caught hold of him, to make him turn to face the foe.

Mad with terror, and scarce knowing what he did, the fugitive raised his sword. He was going to strike his general.

But, quick as lightning, Cæsar's armour-bearer struck off the soldier's arm, and his sword fell harmlessly to the ground. Cæsar had narrowly escaped with his life.

Had Pompey followed up his attack, he might have captured the camp and won a decisive victory, as Cæsar himself was aware. But Pompey sounded a retreat, and the decisive battle had still to be fought.

Cæsar wasted no time in bemoaning the losses of the day, although he must have felt that evening that his fortunes were at their lowest ebb.

He determined to march without delay into Thessaly, and so to entice Pompey away from the sea. For then he would not be able to get provisions for his army and would be forced to fight. And Cæsar was eager to meet his enemy fairly on the battlefield.

When Pompey's officers saw that Cæsar was retreating, they could scarcely believe their eyes, but their confidence in their own prowess was confirmed.

They begged Pompey to follow, and he reluctantly yielded, but for that day alone. Knowing well the strength of Cæsar's veterans, he had no wish to fight a regular battle, and so he ordered his soldiers to set up their camp again.

The patrician officers were exasperated with the indecision of their general. They did not cease to taunt him for not fighting, or to urge him still to follow Cæsar, until at length Pompey made up his mind that they should have their way and pit themselves against Cæsar's well-disciplined officers and troops.

THE FLIGHT OF POMPEY

Both armies accordingly reached Thessaly, although by different routes, and soon they were encamped on the plain of Pharsalia, where, in August 48 B.C., a great and decisive battle was fought.

Pompey's confidence was placed chiefly on his splendid cavalry, and he believed that his 7000 horsemen would speedily scatter the 1000 which was all that Cæsar had to oppose to his great force.

But if his body of cavalry was small, Cæsar had supported it well by his infantry and archers.

His horsemen were, it is true, driven back before the brilliant charge of the enemy, but the infantry and archers attacked Pompey's cavalry so furiously, that soon it was forced from the field in utter confusion.

Cæsar's infantry then advanced against the main body of Pompey's army. The soldiers first hurled their javelins at the enemy and then closed in upon them, doing deadly havoc with their swords.

Before long Cæsar sent a reserve troop of soldiers to their aid, and soon the army of Pompey was put to flight. For the patrician officers had not proved skilful on the battlefield, nor had they now any control over their undisciplined followers.

When Pompey saw that his cavalry was scattered at the beginning of the day, he lost hope and hastened to his tent, where he sat, amid the confused noise of battle, bewildered and dismayed.

Only when the victorious army began to attack the camp did he seem to realise that he must bestir himself, unless he would be captured by the enemy.

"What, into my camp too," he is said to have cried indignantly as he heard the clash of arms and shouts of victory drawing nearer and nearer. Then swiftly laying aside his military dress, the defeated general slipped into a simple garment, and hurrying from the tent, mounted a horse, and with a few followers fled toward the coast. It was useless for him to think of meeting Cæsar again, for his army was slain or scattered. So he resolved to seek shelter in Egypt.

It was a sad voyage on which Pompey embarked, for he had been overthrown, and that by his rival, who would reign supreme.

As the ship drew near to land, Pompey sent a messenger to Alexandria to beg for shelter.

The king, Ptolemy XII., was only a boy of thirteen, but the royal council, when it heard Pompey's request, proved cruel. It neither welcomed him nor sent him elsewhere to seek for safety. At first some of the members spoke on his behalf, but in the end they all agreed that he must die.

But they did not tell him their decision, they merely sent a boat to bring him to shore. In the boat was Septimius, a military tribune of Rome, who had once served in Pompey's army.

THE FLIGHT OF POMPEY

As Pompey prepared to step into the boat his wife clung to him, and filled with foreboding would hardly let him go. But he bade her and his followers farewell, and seated himself in the stern of the boat. As he did so he noticed Septimius and spoke kindly to him.

But Septimius had no answer to give to his former general. He had been unjustly degraded by him in former days as he believed, and he still owed him a grudge.

In response to Pompey's words, he only nodded sullenly and with averted face.

Did a swift dread of what lay before him flash across Pompey's mind as he heard the Roman's gruff response to his greeting.

He had at least no time to brood over the future, for, now they had reached the shore, and as Pompey stepped out of the boat, Septimius, who was behind him, drew his sword.

As Pompey felt the touch of the steel he swiftly drew his toga across his face, and then, without a cry for help, he fell to the ground.

When Cæsar reached Egypt ten days later, he was shown the head of his rival and his signet ring. From the first sight he turned away in horror, while, when he saw the ring, he wept.

CHAPTER CXIII

CATO DIES RATHER THAN YIELD TO CÆSAR

CAESAR found that a civil war was raging in Egypt, between the followers of the boy king and his sister Cleopatra. So the Roman general sent for the brother and sister, and said that he would settle their dispute.

Cleopatra was beautiful and charming, and this may have helped Cæsar to decide that she should reign along with her brother, Ptolemy.

The brother and sister might have been content with this arrangement, but the king's minister was dissatisfied, and he persuaded the army to side with him, and to besiege Cæsar in Alexandria.

But Cæsar had not enough troops to defend the city, so he sent to Asia for reinforcements. While he awaited them he withdrew from Alexandria to Pharos, which was quite close to the city, and connected with it by a drawbridge.

King Ptolemy, who was with Cæsar, begged one day to be allowed to go to Alexandria, where

CATO DIES RATHER THAN YIELD TO CÆSAR

Cleopatra's sister had now been established as queen.

Cæsar granted the boy's request, and he went off gleefully as if for a holiday. But he did not go to the city. Instead he joined the army which was fighting against Cæsar, and tried his boyish best to prevent provisions reaching the Romans by sea.

But in March 47 B.C., the reinforcements for which Cæsar had sent arrived in Egypt.

Ptolemy did not hesitate to march with his troops against this new army before it had joined Cæsar, whereupon the Roman general hurried swiftly after him. He speedily took Ptolemy's camp, and the young king was forced to flee. In his attempt to escape from the enemy he was drowned.

Soon after this Cleopatra's sister abdicated, and Cleopatra became queen.

Cæsar's troubles in Egypt were now over and he was able to return to Rome, where he had already been appointed Dictator for a year, and Consul for five years.

But although the Dictator's presence was needed in Rome, he could only stay three months in the city, for he was still more needed in Africa. For the leaders of the Pompeian Party had gathered together a new army and were ready to war against Cæsar.

After Julia's death, Pompey had married again, and his father-in-law, Scipio, was at the head of the army. Pompey's two sons too, Gnæus and Sextus, were eager to avenge their father's death. Cato was in possession of Utica. It was a formidable army, and Cæsar had not as large a number of men as the Pompeians. Moreover, he was hampered by having his supplies intercepted by the fleet of his enemy.

Until reinforcements arrived, Cæsar therefore contented himself with taking towns that did not make any serious defence. But in January 46 B.C. his army was reinforced, and he was eager to draw Scipio into battle.

One day, early in February, Cæsar began to march toward the town of Thapsus, meaning to attack it. Scipio followed him, and soon found himself in such a position that he was forced to fight.

The battle was fierce, but Cæsar in the end defeated Scipio with great loss. Leaving an officer to carry out the assault he had planned upon Thapsus, Cæsar himself then marched towards Utica, which town was held by Cato.

Now Cato might be a philosopher, and indeed such he was, but he had not the qualities of a soldier.

No sooner did he hear that Cæsar was on his way to Utica, than he decided that any attempt to hold the town would be useless, and he made none.

But the philosopher was not afraid of death, and he determined to die rather than to yield to the conqueror. So he withdrew quietly to his own room and threw himself upon his sword. His friends, hearing him fall, rushed to his aid; as the wound was not fatal, it was dressed and bandaged.

CATO DIES RATHER THAN YIELD TO CÆSAR

No sooner was Cato again alone, than he dragged off the bandages and let himself bleed to death.

Gnæus and Sextus Pompeius had gone to Spain, and Scipio escaped to a ship and sailed away, hoping to join the lads.

But Cæsar sent a vessel in pursuit of the defeated general, and Scipio, seeing that he must be captured, threw himself overboard and was drowned.

Numidia was now made a Roman province, and Cæsar's work in Africa was ended. He returned to Rome in July 46 B.C. as ruler of the great Roman Empire.

CHAPTER CXIV

CÆSAR IS LOADED WITH HONOURS

WHEN Caesar reached Rome in July 46 B.C., he found that he had already been appointed Dictator for ten years.

In the Senate there was now not a member who was not eager to agree to his slightest wish. Yet it was but a year or two since many of them had been ready to brand him as a traitor. But Cæsar had crossed the Rubicon now, and was king in all but name.

The conqueror had, however, no wish to remind those who had been his enemies of their unkindnesses. His return to Rome was made a joyous season, and was not spoiled by the punishment of those who had been opposed to him, much less by their murder.

Indeed, Cæsar not only pardoned those who had been the friends of Pompey, but he gave them positions of trust in the State.

If they were still half afraid of his true feelings, suspicion vanished when the Dictator ordered

CÆSAR IS LOADED WITH HONOURS

the statues of Pompey, which after his defeat had been thrown down, to be again erected.

His faithful soldiers Cæsar rewarded with gold, and to the citizens he gave feasts and gifts of corn as well. Games and shows also celebrated his return.

From this time his birthday was kept each year as a holiday, and to the month in which it fell was given his name, Julius, or as we say now, July.

His triumphs were the wonder of the citizens for many long days to come, for he celebrated his victories over Gaul, Egypt, Pontus, and Numidia. Many were the strange and marvellous treasures that adorned the processions.

Of his war with Pompey, as it was against a Roman, nothing was said, nor was it celebrated in a triumph.

For six or seven months Cæsar now stayed in Rome, making many good laws. As of old he was loved by the people, for he proved himself still their friend, taking from the Optimates the power they often used harshly or carelessly and giving it to them.

His friends often begged him to have a bodyguard, for although he was so beloved, he still had enemies. But Cæsar would take no precautions, saying in answer to the fears of his friends, "It is better to suffer death once, than always to live in fear of it."

About this time the Dictator ordered Carthage and Corinth, which had been destroyed at the same time, to be rebuilt. When the cities were ready, he sent many of his soldiers to settle in them, as well as many Italian citizens.

Thus many of those who had lived in poverty had a new chance given to them, while the overcrowded towns in Italy became healthier and less full of poverty. Wise men, too, came from Egypt at Cæsar's command, and among other reforms they altered and improved the Roman Calendar.

In December 45 B.C., Cæsar was again forced to leave Rome to put down a rebellion in the south of Spain, raised by Pompey's two sons, Gnæus and Sextus.

Now it chanced that popular as Cæsar was in most countries, he was not so in the south of Spain. This was because he had sent to the province a governor who, unfortunately, had treated the people badly, and for this Cæsar was held responsible.

So Pompey's sons had found it easy to stir up rebellion, and they had soon gathered together a large army, while the Pompeian leaders who had escaped from Africa had joined the lads.

When Cæsar reached Spain, he found Gnæus encamped in a plain near to the town of Munda.

Here a great battle was fought, Roman fighting against Roman, for the soldier in Gnæus's army were nearly all veterans who had been trained in the legions of Rome.

At one time it seemed as though Cæsar's troops were giving way. Then he himself ran from

CÆSAR IS LOADED WITH HONOURS

rank to rank of his men, asking if they were not ashamed to let their general be beaten by boys.

Urged by Cæsar's words to fresh efforts, his brave veterans fought desperately until the day was theirs.

Gnæus fled, but a few weeks later was captured and put to death. Sextus, however, escaped, and for many years was at the head of a fleet that caused great trouble along the coast of Italy.

When the hard-fought battle of Munda was won, Cæsar said to his friends, "I have often fought for victory, but this is the first time I have ever fought for life."

At Rome the tidings of the victory was received with an outburst of enthusiasm. No honour was too great for the victor. He had already been made Dictator for ten years; he was now appointed Dictator for life.

The Romans could not do enough to show their affection and pride. Honour after honour was heaped upon the victorious general. He was made Consul for ten years, was given entire control of the treasury. And to crown all, the title of Imperator, which carried with it the entire control of the army, was also bestowed upon him.

Rome had no honour left to give now, unless she gave to her Imperator the title of King.

There were already some among his friends who said that it would be well that he should wear the supreme title in the provinces, if not in Rome.

CHAPTER CXV

THE NOBLES PLOT AGAINST CAESAR

Since the days of Tarquin the Proud, the people of Rome had hated the very name of king. In some strange and subtle way, their love for Cæsar and their pride in his achievements began, from this time, to be touched with the suspicion that he wished to bear the title Rex, rex being the Latin word for king.

Slowly but surely the thought grew. Suppose Cæsar should claim the supreme title and then forget his gracious ways, and become like Tarquin of old, proud and cruel!

Cæsar's enemies were not slow to take advantage of the mood of the people, and they did all that they could to encourage their suspicion and dread.

His friends, too, foolishly played into the hands of his enemies, some of them one day saluting him as Rex.

Cæsar, whether he was pleased or not, was quick to see that the people standing near were angry. So he replied, as though to reprove his friends, that his name, as they knew, was not Rex but Cæsar.

Rex, as well as meaning king, was also the surname of a well-known Roman family.

It was all very well for Cæsar to pretend that his friends had mistaken who he was, but rumours were soon rife in the city—that Cæsar really wished the title, and had not been well pleased at the evident dislike of the people to hear him saluted as Rex.

And so gradually his words and movements came to be watched by his enemies and by the people too, always with this thought of kingship in their minds.

When, on his return from Spain, the consuls and senators went to tell Cæsar of the new honours that had been heaped upon him, he did not, as was his custom, rise to receive them, but remained sitting.

Not only the Senate, but the people, were indignant at such haughty behaviour, and Cæsar himself was quick to see that he had made a mistake.

He tried to excuse himself, saying that his health was not good, but few believed that that accounted for his action.

It is said that he really was going to rise as usual, had not one of his flatterers pulled him to his seat, saying, "Will you not remember you are Cæsar, and claim the honour which is your due?"

Soon after this, in February 45 B.C., an ancient festival called the Lupercalia was celebrated on the Palatine.

Cæsar sat, clad in a triumphal robe, in a golden chair to watch the games.

Mark Antony was taking part in the festival, and as he ran hither and thither amid the merrymakers, he reached the Forum and saw Cæsar seated on the chair of gold as on a throne. He stepped before him and held out a crown wreathed with laurel.

A few persons had been placed near Cæsar, with orders to applaud when Antony proffered the crown to the Dictator, and so some feeble cheers rose on the air, while the crowd looked on coldly and in silence.

But when Cæsar moved the crown aside, loud cheers burst from the multitude. There was no doubt that the Dictator's action had pleased them.

Again Antony offered the crown, while a few persons clapped their hands, but when once more Cæsar put it aside, cheer after cheer rent the air.

A third time Antony tried to force the crown upon Cæsar, but the temper of the people had been shown too plainly, and the Dictator now bade the crown to be taken to the Capitol and dedicated to Jupiter, for he alone was king.

A few days later, those who passed the statues of Cæsar found them adorned with crowns.

This roused the anger of two tribunes, who pulled off the crowns and arrested those who, they

THE NOBLES PLOT AGAINST CÆSAR

believed, had first called Cæsar Rex, and sent them to prison.

Whether Cæsar really wished to be king or not, he was angry with the tribunes for their hasty conduct, and ordered them to be suspended from the tribuneship.

As I told you, Cæsar's every act was now watched with suspicion. He had no sons to follow him, so he began to bring his great-nephew Octavius, who was eighteen years of age, to the front, and treat him as a prince and his heir should be treated. It seemed to the nobles that Cæsar was acting as a king, who claimed for his heir the respect due to royalty.

In this, and many other ways, the Dictator incensed the patricians. Little by little their hatred grew, until some among them began to think that it would be well if Cæsar were dead. For as long as he was alive it was not possible for them to be as powerful as they had been before he ruled in Rome.

But others, like Decimus Brutus, who was loved by Cæsar and who loved him, did not wish the Dictator out of the way, in order to satisfy their own ambitions. They truly believed that it would be better for Rome not to be ruled by one man, but by the Senate and the people, as had been the way of old.

So while different nobles had different reasons for plotting against Cæsar, they all had agreed at length that Cæsar must be put to death.

The chief conspirator was Cassius, who like Brutus had fought for Pompey, and had been pardoned and even favoured by Cæsar.

Cassius was crafty and ambitious, and his dark lean face smiled as he thought how soon Cæsar's power would now be at an end. Brutus, too, was one of the most active conspirators.

Before long the plot was complete, and the conspirators determined that it should be carried out quickly, lest it should be discovered. For already more than sixty or seventy people had been told the terrible secret.

CHAPTER CXVI

THE ASSASSINATION OF CÆSAR

An important meeting was arranged to be held in the Senate house on the 15th March 44 B.C. The conspirators fixed this, the Ides of March, as the day on which they would assassinate the Dictator. They knew that he would come to the Senate unarmed and without guards, as was his custom.

On the evening of the 14th, as Cæsar sat at supper, the conversation, strangely enough, was about the kind of death that one would wish to die.

The Dictator glanced up from the letters he was reading and said abruptly, "A sudden one," and then went on with his reading.

Rumours of the plot may have got abroad, but whether that was so or not, Cæsar had for some days been told of evil omens, and had been warned to beware of danger.

Among other warnings, a soothsayer had told him that evil would befall him on the Ides of March. Now the Ides of March fell on the 15th of the month.

The night before the 15th, Cæsar's wife, Calpurnia, tossed in her sleep, breaking out at length into sobs as though in great sorrow. She was dreaming that she held in her arms the dead body of her husband.

In the morning she begged him with tears not to go to the Senate-house that day.

At length her tears and the warnings that had reached him, made him first hesitate and then yield to her entreaties.

Meanwhile the senators had assembled, among them the conspirators armed with daggers which were concealed in the cases of their writing stilus.

When Cæsar did not come they grew impatient. What had happened? Had he perchance discovered their treachery? The conspirators were uneasy, and they found it hard to conceal their uneasiness.

At length Decimus Brutus, one of their number, offered to go to see why Cæsar had not come, and if necessary to entice him to the Senate.

Decimus found Cæsar at home, cast down by evil omens and by the fears of Calpurnia.

Then Decimus pretended to laugh at the great Cæsar for being disturbed by such forebodings. He scoffed at the soothsayer and his prediction that evil would befall Cæsar on the Ides of March, he mocked at the story of evil omens. "Will Cæsar let it be told

THE ASSASSINATION OF CÆSAR

that because of such things he would not come to the Senate-house?" said the false friend.

Perhaps Cæsar was half ready to laugh at his own fears, but in any case the words of Decimus hurt his pride, and in spite of all that Calpurnia could urge, he determined to go back with Decimus to the Senate.

It was now about eleven o'clock. As Cæsar crossed the hall of his house, his bust fell and broke in pieces.

Afterwards it was said that perhaps this was done by some friend or servant to warn him what would befall him should he leave the house. At the time, the broken bust seemed but another of the omens of evil with which of late he had been surrounded.

But he left the house and stepped into the street. As he walked along he passed the soothsayer, and with an attempt at gaiety he called to him, "The Ides of March have come."

"Yes," answered the wise man, "they are come, but they are not past."

As was ever the way, the crowd pressed close to offer petitions to him as he passed along the street.

One man seemed more eager even than the others to hand a paper to the Dictator, and when at length he succeeded, he said hurriedly, "Read it without delay, Cæsar, for it concerns your safety."

But the paper was never read, for the Dictator handed it with others to his attendant.

No sooner had Cæsar reached the Senate-house and taken his seat than the conspirators crowded around him, one of them, named Cimber, offering him a petition.

It was one which the Dictator had already refused to grant, and he was annoyed at the persistence shown by Cimber.

Moreover, the other conspirators joined him in his entreaties, pressing ever closer and closer around the Dictator, until only those in the plot were near to him.

Cæsar was now really angry and turned away from Cimber, again refusing his request. As he did so, Cimber pulled Cæsar's toga down from his neck. It was the signal upon which the conspirators had agreed.

Casca, who was to give the first blow, thereupon drew his dagger and struck Cæsar on the shoulder. Either through fear or haste he did little harm by his stroke.

In a moment Cæsar had sprung to his feet, and seizing hold of Casca's weapon, he cried, "Vile Casca, what does this mean?"

But immediately daggers were drawn on every side of him, and blow after blow descended upon his body, while angry faces looked into his.

Unarmed as he was, Cæsar yet struggled desperately with the assassins, until he caught sight of

THE ASSASSINATION OF CÆSAR

Decimus Brutus, whom he loved, among his murderers, ready to strike.

Then crying, "Et tu, Brute?" "Thou, too, Brutus?" he covered his face with his toga and fell to the ground, his body covered with many wounds.

Cæsar was dead. And it is said that nature herself mourned for the great man stricken to death by those whom he had befriended. For, for a whole year the sun shone dull and faint, while grey clouds were stretched across the sky like a funeral pall. Cæsar was dead.

CHAPTER CXVII

BRUTUS SPEAKS TO THE CITIZENS

WHEN the terrible deed was done, Brutus wished to tell those senators, who had known nothing of the plot, why it had been necessary to murder the Dictator.

But they, horrified with the murder, and dismayed that they had been unable to aid Cæsar, were in no mood to listen to the conspirators. They fled indeed from the Senate-house, not knowing what fate awaited them, and too sad perhaps to greatly care.

Not far from the Senate-house they met Mark Antony, Cæsar's most faithful friend, who had been purposely kept away from the meeting. They told him what had befallen Cæsar, and he and many others of Cæsar's friends hid themselves, lest the conspirators should wish to murder them also. But they need not have feared, for it was Cæsar's life alone that had been doomed.

BRUTUS SPEAKS TO THE CITIZENS

As the senators had not stayed to listen to their explanations, the conspirators now determined to tell the people that Cæsar was dead.

So they marched through the streets crying that the tyrant had been killed, and bidding all those who loved the Republic to join them.

But the citizens turned away, with scarcely concealed horror, and hurrying into their shops and houses, shut the doors.

They had seen Cæsar that very morning. It could not be true that he was indeed dead, as Brutus said. In awed whispers they spoke of him to one another, and many wept, for now they forgot their suspicions, and remembered only that they had loved Cæsar, and that he had been their friend.

The next day, when the people assembled in the Forum, Brutus spoke to them. He told them, not of the dead Cæsar's faults, but of the Republic and its needs, and the people listened in silence.

But when Brutus sat down, another of the conspirators began to speak, accusing Cæsar of one crime after another. This was more than the people could bear. The interruptions grew louder and more threatening every moment, until at length the conspirators, fearing that a riot would take place, fled to the Capitol for safety.

On the following morning the Senate met, and Antony, caring no longer to hide, was seen walking through the streets toward the Senate-house. The people feared for his safety, because he had been the friend of Cæsar, and begged him to beware, lest he too was murdered. But he lifted his toga that they might see that he was clad in armour.

Even to meet the Senate, the conspirators did not venture to leave the Capitol, but they sent Cicero to be their spokesman.

Cicero's eloquence may have moved the senators. In any case, Mark Antony, who was one of the Consuls, agreed that the conspirators should be received in peace.

It was also arranged that Cæsar should be given a public funeral.

Antony was now content. As Consul, he would speak at Cæsar's funeral, and he did not doubt his power to rouse the passions of the people against the murderers of his friend. Cassius foresaw what Antony would do, and tried to stir the fears of Brutus. But in this he failed.

As the Senate had agreed to receive the conspirators, and as the people were in the meantime pacified, they now ventured to leave the Capitol, and even to enter the Forum.

When the funeral day arrived, before Antony brought the body of his friend into the Forum, Brutus spoke once again to the assembled citizens, seeking this time to tell them why he had had anything to do with the murder of Cæsar whom he had loved. Here are his words, as Shakespeare tells them to us:—

BRUTUS SPEAKS TO THE CITIZENS

"Romans, countrymen, and lovers! hear me for my cause, and be silent that you may hear. If there be any in this assembly, any dear friend of Cæsar's, to him I say, that Brutus' love to Cæsar was no less than his. If then that friend demand why Brutus rose against Cæsar, this is my answer:—Not that I love Cæsar less, but that I loved Rome more.

"As Cæsar loved me, I weep for him; as he was fortunate, I rejoice at it; as he was valiant, I honour him: but, as he was ambitious, I slew him. There is tears for his love; joy for his fortune; honour for his valour; and death for his ambition."

With these and many other words Brutus so pleased the people, that it did not seem likely that they would care to listen to what Antony had to say.

"Live Brutus, live Brutus!" shouted the crowds, well content for the moment with the defence which he had made.

CHAPTER CXVIII

MARK ANTONY SPEAKS TO THE CITIZENS

The people were still shouting "Live Brutus!" when Mark Antony entered the Forum with the dead body of Cæsar.

Brutus at once prepared to go, bidding the citizens listen to what Mark Antony had to say.

The body of Cæsar, covered with a purple cloth, had now been placed where all might see.

Close to Antony lay the toga which his friend had worn as he went to the Senate-house on the Ides of March. It was torn and stained, where the daggers had done their deadly work. It too could be seen by the crowds.

A wax figure of Cæsar, with each wound which he had received, plainly marked, was placed near the dead body.

Antony, clad in robes of mourning, then began to read Cæsar's will aloud. The people listened spellbound. Was it true that Cæsar had cared for them so much?

MARK ANTONY SPEAKS TO THE CITIZENS

What did Antony say? That to each Roman citizen Cæsar had left a sum of three pounds!

His garden too, his beautiful garden! It also was left to them and to their children, to walk in when it pleased them, to be there at all times a retreat from the heat and the dust of the streets.

To some of those who had slain him too, Cæsar had willed large sums of money. Already the people were muttering in a way to fulfil the forebodings of Cassius. It had certainly been unwise to leave the people alone with Mark Antony.

They had forgotten that they had applauded Brutus but a few moments before. Now they were declaring that the conspirators had killed, not a tyrant, but a friend of the people, one who had ever served his country well. The conspirators deserved to be punished for their cruel deed, and they would see to it that——

But hush! Antony was speaking, was trying to make himself heard. They must certainly listen to what he had to say. And here are his words, as Shakespeare tells them to us:—

> "Friends, Romans, countrymen, lend me your ears;
> I come to bury Cæsar, not to praise him.
> The evil that men do lives after them;
> The good is oft interrèd with their bones;
> So let it be with Cæsar. The noble Brutus
> Hath told you Cæsar was ambitious:
> If it were so, it was a grievous fault,
> And grievously hath Cæsar answer'd it.
> Here, under leave of Brutus and the rest—

For Brutus is an honourable man;
So are they all, all honourable men—
Come I to speak in Cæsar's funeral.
He was my friend, faithful and just to me:
But Brutus says he was ambitious;
And Brutus is an honourable man.
He hath brought many captives home to Rome.
Whose ransoms did the general coffers fill:
Did this in Cæsar seem ambitious?
When that the poor have cried, Cæsar hath wept:
Ambition should be made of sterner stuff:
Yet Brutus says he was ambitious;
And Brutus is an honourable man.
You all did see that on the Lupercal
I thrice presented him a kingly crown,
Which he did thrice refuse: was this ambition?
Yet Brutus says he was ambitious;
And, sure, he is an honourable man.
I speak not to disprove what Brutus spoke,
But here I am to speak what I do know.
You all did love him once, not without cause:
What cause withholds you then, to mourn for him?
O judgment! thou art fled to brutish beasts,
And men have lost their reason! Bear with me,
My heart is in the coffin there with Cæsar,
And I must pause till it come back to me."

As Antony finished speaking, he turned to pull away the cloth that covered Cæsar's body, so that the people could see his wounds.

Already as they listened to Antony's words and looked at the wax figure of Cæsar, with its painted wounds, the fierce anger of the people had been roused. But now, when they saw the real

MARK ANTONY SPEAKS TO THE CITIZENS

wounds in Cæsar's own body, their passion knew no bounds.

They shouted that they would be revenged on the murderers of Cæsar, that not one of the conspirators should live, that they would burn the houses of Brutus and Cassius.

But first they would themselves make Cæsar's funeral pyre. So they rushed into the houses and shops in the Forum, and pulled out chairs, tables, benches, anything on which they could lay their hands.

Then they placed these together in a great heap, and when all was ready, they laid the body of Cæsar reverently on the top. A moment more and they had set fire to the funeral pyre with torches.

As the fire blazed, the citizens armed themselves with faggots which they lighted at the flames. Then they hurried away to the houses of Brutus and Cassius, shouting and waving their fiery brands in a frenzy of rage.

But the houses they found guarded, the conspirators fled.

CHAPTER CXIX

THE SECOND TRIUMVIRATE

FOR a short time Brutus had seemed a hero to the citizens of Rome, but Antony's speech had speedily changed their feelings.

It was now Mark Antony whom they wished to rule, and with the help of the people he soon made himself master of Rome.

But he was not left long to enjoy his power undisputed. For Cæsar's heir Octavius came to Rome in the month of May, to claim his inheritance.

Octavius was only eighteen years of age, but he had a will resolute beyond his years. He had already made up his mind to punish the assassins of Cæsar, and to make himself as powerful as might be in the State.

At first he threw his influence on the side of the Optimates, who were doing all they could to curtail Antony's power.

To support his claim to the first place in the kingdom, Antony soon found it necessary to place himself at the head of an army. He determined to besiege Decimus Brutus, who had threatened to seize the province of Cisalpine Gaul, which Antony wished for himself.

Octavius also gathered together an army, with which to attack Antony.

The Senate now declared Antony a public enemy, for taking up arms. When Octavius attacked his camp and forced Antony to flee, the Senate was greatly pleased.

But it was soon disappointed to find that Octavius would not support the claim of Decimus Brutus to Cisalpine Gaul. It had forgotten, if it ever knew, that the young general had vowed to punish all who had betrayed Cæsar, and had not this man enticed the great Dictator to his fate?

Octavius even refused to pursue Antony, but demanded that the Senate should now see that he, Cæsar's heir, was elected Consul.

When the Senate hesitated, Octavius marched at the head of his army to Rome, first sending a message to Antony to suggest that they should meet and agree to lay aside their quarrel.

With his army to support him, Octavius had no difficulty in being made Consul, or in gaining from the Senate other powers. He then forced it to withdraw the decree which had made Antony a public enemy, before he set out to meet him and Lepidus, who was also at the head of an army.

The three commanders met on a small island in the river Po, and there they formed an alliance which was known as The Second Triumvirate. They then gravely divided among themselves the Roman Empire.

One of the agreements made by the three commanders was this terrible one, that each should be free to put to death those senators or Optimates who had displeased them.

The murderers of Cæsar were already doomed, but a list of seventeen names was drawn up, and in this list was the name of the great orator Cicero.

Cicero had befriended Octavius it is true, but that could not save him after The Second Triumvirate had been formed. For he had drawn upon himself the fierce anger of Antony, by many bitter speeches. So, one day, early in December 43 B.C., Cicero was seized by a band of soldiers and executed by the order of Antony.

When the Triumvirate returned to Rome a reign of terror began. As in the time of Sulla lists were again hung in the Forum, with the names of proscribed persons, until at length two or three thousand were either put to death or forced to flee from the city.

Many of these fugitives joined Brutus and Cassius, who had escaped to the East, and had each assembled a large army. Others fled to Sicily, where Sextus Pompeius was still at the head of a fleet, and threatening to stop the corn supply which reached Rome from Sicily, Africa and other countries.

CHAPTER CXX

THE BATTLE OF PHILIPPI

THE Triumvirs began to rule on the 1st January 42 B.C. But neither Antony nor Octavius was able to stay long in Rome, for Brutus and Cassius had still to be pursued and punished. So Antony with a large army set out for Greece to fight against the conspirators, while Octavius, also with an army, went to Sicily to attack Sextus.

Lepidus was left in Rome to watch over the welfare of the city.

Octavius did not conquer Sextus, but in August he left Sicily to join Antony in Greece. They found Brutus and Cassius, each with his army, encamped in a strong position at Philippi in the north of the country.

The rebels, for such Rome now called the two conspirators, were in no haste to fight, for they had a plentiful supply of food for their armies, which was constantly renewed by the fleet which they commanded.

Antony and Octavius had no fleet, and their supply of provisions was uncertain; for it was brought to them by the country folk, who were not able to give them easily all that was necessary.

Before the armies met, Brutus was one night sitting alone in his tent, after his soldiers had gone to their quarters.

It was late and the light was dim, for he was not working, but brooding, as he had begun to do since the death of Cæsar.

Suddenly he felt that he was no longer alone in the tent, and looking up, he saw that a strange figure was standing close beside him. In silence Brutus and his unknown guest gazed the one at the other, until at length Brutus spoke.

"What are you," he demanded, "of men or gods, and upon what business come to me?"

"I am your evil genius, Brutus," a sombre voice replied, "you shall see me at Philippi."

The words sounded almost as a threat, but Brutus answered steadily, "Then I shall see you."

As he spoke the figure vanished. Brutus at once called his servants and asked them if they had heard any one enter the camp, but none of them had either heard or seen the mysterious stranger.

Soon after this Brutus and Cassius resolved to put their fortune to the test. They hung out a scarlet coat in their camp as a signal of battle.

The soldiers of Antony were at the time busy digging trenches, which they hoped would stop provisions from the sea reaching the enemy.

THE BATTLE OF PHILIPPI

Cæsar, as Octavius was now called, was not with Antony, but being ill, was in his camp, a short distance away. His soldiers seem not to have seen the scarlet coat in the camp of the enemy, for they made no preparations for battle. Even when they heard shouts and the clash of arms coming from the direction of the trenches, they paid no attention to the confused noises. If they had bestirred themselves, the result of the battle might have been different.

Cassius had fallen upon Antony's men as they worked in their trenches, but he had been repulsed. Then, following up their advantage, the soldiers of Antony had captured his camp.

Meanwhile Cassius had drawn up his soldiers behind the camp, but when the enemy attacked his cavalry, it suddenly gave way and fled toward the sea.

When his infantry also began to waver, Cassius snatched an eagle from a standard-bearer who had turned to flee, and himself thrust it in the ground and tried to rally his men.

But his troops refused to be rallied, and in a short time Cassius found himself deserted, and was forced to ride off the field with only a few followers. He halted on a hill from which he could see the battlefield.

Brutus meanwhile had attacked Cæsar's army, and all but captured Cæsar himself. For he had been carried out of the camp only a few moments before the soldiers of Brutus dashed into it.

The first thing their eyes fell upon was the litter in which Cæsar had been resting. Supposing that he was still lying there, the soldiers hurled their darts at it, and a rumour at once arose that Cæsar was killed. But it was soon discovered that the general had fled, that his litter was empty.

And now a sad mistake took place. Brutus, eager to tell Cassius of his victory, sent off a body of cavalry to find him and tell him the good tidings.

Cassius saw the horsemen riding across the plain, and thinking that it might be the enemy in search of him, he sent one of his followers to reconnoitre.

When the messenger reached the horsemen he was greeted heartily. Some hastily dismounted to gather around him and tell the story of their triumph, others shouted or clashed their arms.

Cassius was watching anxiously from the distance, and he imagined that his follower had been captured by the enemy. Then he thought that Brutus must have been defeated, perhaps even had been slain, and he determined that he himself would live no longer. Without waiting to learn the truth, Cassius stole into an empty tent and stabbed himself.

When the sad news was told to Brutus, he was greatly grieved. "The last of the Romans has fallen," he cried in his sorrow, "for it is not possible that the city should ever produce another man of so great a spirit."

CHAPTER CXXI

THE DEATH OF BRUTUS

THE battle of Philippi had decided nothing, as one general on each side had been victorious.

Cæsar and Antony would willingly have fought again without delay, for they were finding it always more difficult to provide food for their armies.

But Brutus seemed loth to take the field, and for fourteen days his soldiers vainly begged him to lead them against the enemy. Their persistence at length forced him to yield, and he placed himself at their head and advanced against the foe.

A desperate struggle followed, and while the division led by Brutus was again victorious, the main body of the army was scattered and put to flight.

As Brutus himself fled with a few friends, a band of horsemen followed him, determined if possible to capture him and bring him alive to Antony.

With Brutus was his comrade Lucilius, and he, seeing what the horsemen wished, determined that he would save his friend although he himself should perish in the attempt.

As the enemy drew near, Lucilius, apparently unnoticed by Brutus, dropped behind, and when the horsemen seized him, he let them believe that they had indeed captured Brutus. So in great good temper the horsemen carried Lucilius to Antony. He, hearing that Brutus was a prisoner, was mightily pleased, and ordered him to be brought before him.

The prisoner no sooner saw Antony than he said without any trace of fear, "Be assured, Antony, that no enemy has taken or ever shall take Brutus alive. . . . As for me, I am come hither by a cheat that I put upon your soldiers, and am ready . . . to suffer any severities you will inflict."

But Antony turned to the crestfallen horsemen and said, "You have brought me better booty than you sought. For indeed I am uncertain how I should have used Brutus if you had brought him alive, but of this I am sure, it is better to have such men as Lucilius our friends than our enemies." From that day Antony and Lucilius were friends.

Brutus meanwhile had ridden on until he reached a little stream, and here, sheltered by steep cliffs he sat down to rest. His heart was sad, for many of his friends were slain. He murmured the long list of their names, sighing heavily as he did so.

Hour after hour passed, and his people grew anxious lest the enemy should overtake them, and they urged Brutus to fly.

THE DEATH OF BRUTUS

Here, sheltered by steep cliffs, he sat down to rest.

"Yes indeed we must fly," answered the stricken general, "but not with our feet, but with our hands." Then he went aside with only his friend Strato, and flinging himself upon the point of his sword, he died.

Antony, when he found the dead body of Brutus, ordered it to be covered with a beautiful purple mantle of his own.

A soldier, too full of greed to show reverence to the dead, dared to steal the mantle. Antony did not rest until the thief was discovered and put to death.

CHAPTER CXXII

ANTONY AND CLEOPATRA

Now that Brutus and Cassius were both dead, there was no one to dispute the division of the empire between Cæsar and Antony.

Lepidus, although one of the Triumvirs, was not consulted when the new arrangement was made, for he was suspected of having joined Sextus in a plot to overthrow Cæsar.

If it proved that he had been loyal, Antony agreed to give up Africa to him; if he were proved to have been disloyal he would have no share in the empire.

Six weeks later, in 36 B.C., Lepidus was accused again of plotting to slay Cæsar, and from that time he no longer belonged to the Triumvirate.

After the second battle of Philippi in 42 B.C., Cæsar took Spain and Numidia as his share of the empire, Antony Gaul and Africa. Italy was to belong to both, for it was the centre of the kingdom.

When this was settled, Antony went to Asia to put down rebellion in the different provinces, while Cæsar returned to Rome.

Now Cleopatra, Queen of Egypt, had sent generals and troops to help Cassius in his war against Cæsar and Antony. One of Antony's duties was to demand an explanation of this act. So when he was in Tarsus in the summer of 41 B.C., he summoned the queen to come and explain her defiance of Rome.

At first Cleopatra paid no attention to the letter Antony sent to summon her to come to Tarsus. Other letters came and apparently she heeded them not. But all the while she was making great preparations for her journey, and at length "as if in mockery of the orders she had received, she came sailing up the river Cydnus, in a barge with gilded stern and outspread sails of purple, while oars of silver beat time to the music of flutes and pipes and harps. She herself lay all along under a canopy of cloth of gold, dressed as Venus in a picture, and beautiful young boys, like painted Cupids, stood on each side to fan her. Her maids were dressed like sea nymphs and graces, some steering at the rudder, some working at the ropes."

Crowds ran along on either bank of the river to gaze at the magnificent barge. As it drew near to the city, the people left their work and play and ran to the harbour to see the marvellous beauty of the Queen of Egypt.

Antony did not run to the river. He stayed where he was, sitting on the tribunal in the deserted market-place, but when the queen had arrived, he sent a message asking her to supper. But Cleopatra refused, begging him rather to come to the barge to sup with her.

Then Antony, wishing to appear courteous, went to the barge, and Cleopatra began to weave the spell that was to be his undoing. Bewitched by her charm, he forgot Rome, his wife, his duties in the East, and when she went back to Alexandria he followed her.

In Egypt he became her most favoured courtier, while, to please her, he laid aside his Roman garb and dressed as did her people. For a year he lived thus in a mad whirl of gaiety.

And while Antony wasted his time in Egypt, Cæsar grew daily more trusted and more beloved in Rome.

Fulvia, the wife of Antony, saw how Cæsar was winning the hearts of the people, and she determined that she would alienate them from him, if that were possible. For then she thought that the people would turn to Antony again.

So she raised an army, and Cæsar was forced to send his general Agrippa against her.

Fulvia had hoped that Antony, when he heard of her efforts, would hasten to support her, as he would know that it was for his sake she had taken up arms.

THE STORY OF ROME

But her husband still lingered in Egypt. It was not until the autumn of the year 40 B.C., that he came to Greece. Even when he did come he showed no gratitude to Fulvia for what she had done; he even reproached her. Nevertheless he determined to carry on the quarrel that she had begun.

Rome was in despair, for it seemed that once again their land would be distracted by civil war.

But Fulvia, whose influence might have kept Antony to his purpose, died, while the soldiers themselves did not wish to fight against their own countrymen. So Antony agreed to make terms with Cæsar. In this way the Peace of Brundisium was arranged, and the empire was once again divided between the Triumvirs.

Antony, to show that he meant to be true to the new agreement, now married Octavia, the sister of Octavius. She was a beautiful woman, and as wise as she was beautiful. Her love for her husband and her brother caused her great suffering in the years to come. For a time, however, her influence helped to strengthen the bonds between the two men.

Soon after the Peace of Brundisium, peace was also made with Sextus, Cæsar and Antony going to meet him on one of his own vessels. On being granted certain privileges, Sextus promised no longer to interfere with the corn trade, and thus Rome was freed from a long-continued evil.

Antony and Octavia then went to Greece, where Antony stayed for two years. He gained little credit in his wars with the Parthians, who had invaded Syria, while he behaved so treacherously in his battles against Armenia, that the people at home said that he had disgraced the Roman name.

But he grew more and more disliked in Rome because of his unkindness to Octavia. For after two years he sent her back to Octavius, pretending that it was not safe for her to stay with him while he was engaged in the Parthian War.

But she had no sooner left him than he went to Alexandria, where he lived as he had done before with Queen Cleopatra.

The Romans were angry with Antony for making Alexandria his headquarters. They began to fear lest he should try to found a new empire in the East, of which this town would be the capital. And then in time to come the greatness of Alexandria might eclipse that of Rome.

Cæsar meanwhile was in Rome, doing all that he could for the welfare of the people. But Sextus had broken his promise, and was interfering again with the corn trade, and so making the price of bread ruinous. Thus, in spite of all Cæsar's efforts, the distress of the people was great.

At length Cæsar determined that Sextus should not be allowed to go on injuring the corn trade, and he sent an army against him. But it was not for three years that Sextus was at last defeated by Agrippa, the general on whom Cæsar relied for his victories. Sextus then fled to Asia, where he was at length captured and put to death.

For this and many other services rendered to the State, Cæsar was loaded with honours by the Senate. One of these honours was, that he was allowed to wear the triumphal robes when he pleased; another that a public residence was set aside for him on the Palatine, while his person was declared sacred.

When Antony heard of all that had been bestowed upon Cæsar, he thought that it was time to bestir himself, unless he wished to be entirely forgotten by Rome.

So he sent to the Senate an account of his Acta, that is, an account of what he had been doing in Egypt. There was indeed little to tell, save that he had been bestowing kingdoms on his and Cleopatra's children. He, however, asked the Senate to confirm his Acta. In his anger and jealousy against Cæsar, he added that when the Triumvirate came to an end in 33 B.C., he did not wish to renew it.

From this time the quarrel between Antony and Cæsar grew rapidly more acute, and at length it was plain that only war would determine whether Cæsar or Antony was to rule the empire.

Antony now began to gather together an army and a fleet, even preparing to attack the coasts of Italy. But this was more than the Senate would allow, and in 32 B.C., war was proclaimed against Cleopatra, who was supporting Antony in his preparations, while Antony was now treated as a public enemy.

CHAPTER CXXIII

THE BATTLE OF ACTIUM

THE great battle which was to decide who was to rule over the Roman Empire was fought at Actium, on the west coast of Greece, in 31 B.C.

Here Cæsar and Antony arrived, each with a great fleet and a great army. Antony was not accustomed to fight at sea, nor were his generals or soldiers. Yet to please Cleopatra he had decided that the first battle should be between the fleets.

The queen herself was at Actium, and had sent sixty of her own vessels to join Antony's fleet.

Several skirmishes took place, in which Cæsar was successful, and Cleopatra grew impatient and anxious. Then she tried to persuade Antony to withdraw without risking a battle.

In Alexandria, she said, they would be safe, for her towers were strong, and could be well garrisoned. If Cæsar followed and attacked them there they could easily defy him.

To withdraw should have been impossible to a soldier, yet so strong was the influence of Cleopatra that Antony at length promised to do as she wished. But for four days a gale blew so fiercely that it was not possible to leave Actium.

Early on the morning of the 2nd September, Cleopatra saw with delight that the weather was favourable. She knew no rest until the signal was given, and Antony's fleet began slowly to sail out of the bay.

Cæsar saw that the enemy's fleet was moving, and he at once ordered his vessels to follow, and if possible to surround it.

By yielding to Cleopatra, Antony had really only provoked battle, and he was now forced to give the signal to attack. Then as he knew that his soldiers were uneasy at having to fight at sea, he went in a small boat from one ship to another and urged them to think of their large decks as solid earth and to fight for victory.

Antony's ships were larger than those of Cæsar, and proved difficult to manage when the sea was heavy, as it was that day. The smaller vessels of Cæsar were able to move swiftly, and after hurling darts on to the enemy's deck, they could easily withdraw out of reach of Antony's missiles. Fiercely the battle raged, but when morning had passed, neither side had gained the victory.

Cleopatra was not used to the strain of battle, and her anxiety made her fretful and peevish. She determined to endure the miserable uncertainty no longer. It was intolerable. Away from the noise and

THE BATTLE OF ACTIUM

the confusion, she could forget that Antony was fighting for an empire.

With no thought save the desire to escape, she gave the signal for retreat. Her sixty vessels at once hoisted their sails, and struggling past the ships that were engaged in battle, they fled for safety and for home.

Antony saw the ships with their sails filled, speeding away, and he knew that Cleopatra had deserted him.

Perhaps he thought that this would seal the fate of the battle, that the sight of the flying vessels would soon spread a panic through the entire fleet, perhaps his one desire was to follow the queen. In any case, Antony sprang into a galley and set off in pursuit of Cleopatra.

But when he reached the vessel in which the queen was seated, happy now and at her ease, and was taken on board, the thought of his dishonour suddenly took hold of him. Without a word to Cleopatra or even a look in her direction, he walked to the prow of the ship, and there, covering his face with his hands he bemoaned his dastardly deed. He thought that in the eyes of his army he was disgraced even now, and he did not hide from himself that he had become unfit to be a leader of men.

But the soldiers could not believe that the general who had often led them to battle had fled, and they fought bravely on, thinking that at any moment he would be among them to lead them to victory.

And so firm was their faith in Antony, that when the fight was over, they refused, for seven days, to surrender to Cæsar, lest their own general should yet appear. The officers were less loyal than the men, or perhaps they knew Antony better. They did not hesitate to leave their troops and to submit to Cæsar. Only then did the soldiers believe that Antony had indeed gone, and they also went over to the conqueror.

When the battle of Actium ended, Cæsar had won a decisive victory. He did not, however, go to Egypt until winter was over.

Antony, who had resolved if it were possible to redeem his flight, at once began to gather together an army ready to oppose Cæsar. But at the same time, both he and Cleopatra were trying to pacify the victorious general.

The queen sent him a gift of a gold crown, and offered to abdicate if Cæsar would allow her sons to reign. Antony also sent a gift of money, and begged to be allowed to live in Athens as a private citizen. If Cæsar proved ungracious they both hoped to be able to flee beyond his reach.

To Antony's request Cæsar paid no heed. But he encouraged Cleopatra to believe that he would do all that she wished for herself and for her children, if she would put Antony to death, or send him away from Egypt.

But even if she proved faithless to Antony and betrayed him to his enemy, Cæsar still meant to take the queen to Rome to adorn his triumph.

CHAPTER CXXIV

ANTONY AND CLEOPATRA DIE

WHEN Cæsar at length came to Egypt with his army, he landed at Pelusium. Before the soldiers had rested after the fatigue of their journey, Antony fell upon them and won a slight victory, which encouraged him to face a general battle.

The night before the battle, he feasted with his friends, in gayer mood than since his flight from Actium, for now he hoped to conquer or to die honourably on the battlefield.

Early in the morning he led his infantry to a position from which he could see his fleet, for he believed that two battles would be fought that day, one on sea and one on land.

But to his dismay, as his fleet drew near to Cæsar's vessels, he saw that his men saluted the enemy and then joined it. A moment later his cavalry also went over to Cæsar's army, while his infantry was soon after utterly beaten.

Crushed and humiliated, Antony tried to escape on board a vessel, but finding that he was watched by the enemy he stabbed himself to death.

Such, say the history books, was the sad end of Mark Antony, but Plutarch, who writes his life, tells us of his last days in another way.

After his defeat, Plutarch says that Antony went back to Alexandria, complaining that he had been betrayed by Cleopatra into the hands of Cæsar.

His anger against the queen was so fierce that she was afraid and hastened to shut herself into the mausoleum or tomb which she had built in preparation for her death.

She then bade servants go tell Antony that she was dead. Such tidings would, she knew, speedily change his anger into sorrow.

But she had not stayed to think to what desperate step his grief might drive Antony. He no sooner believed that she was dead, than he determined that he too would die.

"I am not troubled, Cleopatra," he said, "to be at present bereaved of you, for I shall soon be with you, but it distresses me that so great a general should be found of a tardier courage than a woman." Then he called his servant Eros, who had sworn to put him to death when he should demand it, and bade him now fulfil his promise. Silently the faithful servant drew his sword, not to kill his master—that he found he could not do—but to slay himself.

When Antony saw that his servant was dead, he cried, "It is well done, Eros; you show your master how to do what you had not the heart to do yourself." He then threw himself upon his sword, but the wound did not at once cause his death.

As Antony lay dying upon his couch, a messenger came from Cleopatra to tell him that she was not dead, but alive and in the mausoleum.

The dying man begged to be taken to her, and his servants carried him to the door of the tomb.

Then the queen, looking out of her window, saw him lying below wounded and near to death.

She had only her two women Iras and Charmian with her, and so, instead of tarrying to open the heavy door with its numerous bolts, she let down cords from the window.

When these had been fastened round Antony, Cleopatra and her two women, slowly and painfully pulled up the wounded man and dragged him through the window into the mausoleum.

Gently the queen laid Antony on her bed and wept over him, calling him her Emperor and her Lord.

But Antony, after drinking a little wine, bade her not to mourn for him, for he had "fallen not ignobly, a Roman by a Roman overcome." With these words upon his lips he died.

When Cæsar heard of the death of Antony, he wept, for he thought of the many dangers that they had shared together, and of the friendship that Octavia had tried to foster between them.

Then he quickly sent one of his officers named Proculeius to Cleopatra, bidding him see that she was safe, for he still cherished the wish to take her alive to Rome, that she might adorn his triumph.

When he reached the door of the mausoleum Proculeius found that it was barred, so he took a ladder, fixed it on to the window and climbed up, and entered the room before the queen was aware.

"Miserable Cleopatra, you are taken prisoner," cried one of her women.

Then quick as lightning the queen drew a dagger which she had hidden in her dress, and would have stabbed herself had not Proculeius seized her hands, at the same time reproaching her for not trusting Cæsar to prove a generous foe.

He then took away the dagger, and shook her clothes lest she had hidden poison in them.

A few days later, Cæsar himself came to see the queen. She, grown wise since the visit of Proculeius, deceived him, making him believe that she had now no desire save to live. So artful was she that she told Cæsar that she had kept some of her treasures that she might have gifts to bestow on Livia his wife and on Octavia his sister, when she went to Rome. Then Cæsar left her, satisfied that she would yet adorn his triumph.

Now by the queen's desire, a basket of figs was brought to her from the country.

ANTONY AND CLEOPATRA DIE

The guards stopped the countryman who brought it to the gate of the mausoleum, asking to see the contents of his basket.

He, pushing aside the leaves that lay on the top, showed them the figs. The men admired their size, and bade him take them to the queen.

But at the foot of the basket, although the guards did not suspect it, there lay concealed under the fruit, an asp, whose bite was deadly poison.

When Cleopatra had the basket safe in her possession, she wrote to Cæsar to beg that she might be buried beside Antony. Then she bade her women array her in her royal robes and set her diadems upon her head.

And when this was done she lifted the asp from the basket and placed it upon her arm.

No sooner did the queen's letter reach Cæsar, than he sent in great haste to the mausoleum, for he feared that Cleopatra had found a way to die, although she had neither poison nor a dagger in her possession.

When Cæsar's messengers reached the guards, they asked if all was well. "All is well," answered the soldiers, but "when they had opened the door they found Cleopatra stark-dead, laid upon a bed of gold, attired and arrayed in her royal robes, and one of her women, called Iras, dead at her feet, but her other woman, called Charmian, half dead and trembling, trimming the diadem which Cleopatra wore upon her head.

One of the soldiers seeing her, angrily said unto her, "Is this well done, Charmian?"

"Very well," she said again, "meet for a princess descended from the race of so many noble kings." She said no more, but fell down dead, hard by the bed.

The queen's last request was granted, for she was buried with royal splendour by the side of Antony.

CHAPTER CXXV
THE EMPEROR AUGUSTUS

THE Roman Republic came to an end after the Battle of Actium.

Henceforth until his death Cæsar ruled over the great Roman Empire, and he was now known as the Emperor Augustus. His reign began in 30 B.C., and ended in 14 A.D.

If he did not add much to his great dominions, he saw to it that, during his long reign of forty-four years, those within his realm were able to live at peace with each other and with foreign peoples. Once again, and for the third time since Romulus built the city of Rome, the gates of the temple of Janus were closed.

The Emperor came to be adored by the people of Rome, because his rule was kind and just. His magistrates were not allowed to oppress or rob the poor, while his merchants' ships were able to ply their trade without fear of pirates.

At one time Augustus was away from Italy for three years. His people longed for his return. Here are the very words in which the poet Horace expressed their desire.

"O best guardian of the race of Romulus," he wrote, "return ... your country calls for you with vows and prayers ... for when you are here the ox plods up and down the fields in safety; Ceres and bounteous blessing cheers our farms; our sailors speed o'er seas infested by no pirate; credit is kept unspotted; crime is checked, family life purified, none fears the invasion of the Parthian or German ... each man closes a peaceful day on his native hills, trains his vines to the widowed trees, and home returning, light of heart, quaffs his wine and blesses you as his god."

When Augustus knew that the people really believed what the poet said in language more beautiful than they could frame, he must surely have felt rewarded for all the labours which he had undertaken for the sake of his country.

The Emperor died in 14 A.D. His wife Livia was with him to the end, and as he kissed her for the last time he said, "Good-bye, never forget our married life." Nor was she likely to do so, for Cæsar had ever loved her well, and treated her with respect. His adopted son, Tiberius, succeeded him.

Thus from the single city founded by Romulus in the Palatine Hill in 753 B.C. there grew up through struggle and victory, the mighty Empire, over which Augustus first ruled as Emperor. And this mighty Empire held within its bounds the whole of Europe south of Germany and the Danube, Asia

Minor, Syria, Egypt, as well as a large part of the northern district of Africa.

"Thine, Roman, be the task to rule the nations with thy sway. These shall be thine arts—to impose the laws of peace, to spare the humbled and to crush in war the proud."

www.ingramcontent.com/pod-product-compliance
Lightning Source LLC
Chambersburg PA
CBHW030236170426
43202CB00007B/25